Cold War
Combat Prototypes

Cold War
Combat Prototypes

Robert Jackson

The Crowood Press

First published in 2005 by
The Crowood Press Ltd
Ramsbury, Marlborough
Wiltshire SN8 2HR

www.crowood.com

© Robert Jackson 2005

All rights reserved. No part of this publication may be reproduced or transmitted in any form or by any means, electronic or mechanical, including photocopy, recording, or any information storage and retrieval system, without permission in writing from the publishers.

British Library Cataloguing-in-Publication Data
A catalogue record for this book is available from the British Library.

ISBN 1 86126 772 X

Frontispiece: The Convair XF-92A, the first jet-powered aircraft of delta-wing configuration to fly, was used in the development of the XF-92 mixed-power interceptor; but the XF-92 was cancelled before its construction was complete. (Convair)

Title page: The Douglas XA2D-1 Skyshark was intended to succeed the Douglas AD Skyraider, but continual problems with its power plant led to its cancellation. (McDonnell Douglas)

A note on measurements
Measurements originating in countries that, during the period covered by this book, usually used imperial measures (e.g. the USA and UK) are quoted in imperial first with metric in parenthesis. The reverse has been applied to measurements originating in countries, such as France and the former USSR, where metric measures are the norm.

Typeset by NBS Publications, Hampshire, RG21 5NH
Printed and bound in Great Britain by CPI Bath

Contents

List of Abbreviations	6
Introduction	7

Part I: The Quest for the Global Bomber, 1945–55
1	The United States	9
2	Soviet Heavy Bomber Development, 1945–55	20

Part II: Medium and Light Jet Bombers – the First Generation
3	The USAF's Medium and Tactical Bomber Force, 1945–55	25
4	The RAF's Early Jet Bombers	32
5	France's Post-War Recovery	36
6	The USSR's Tactical Bombers and Assault Aircraft	39

Part III: Fighter Development, 1945–55
7	The USAF: The Supersonic Challenge	44
8	United Kingdom: Transition to Transonic	54
9	France's Road to Success	64
10	The USSR's Early Interceptors	71
11	The Heavy Brigade: Long-Range Fighters	78

Part IV: Naval Aircraft Prototypes, 1945–55
12	US Naval Prototypes	86
13	Britain's Naval Experimentals, 1945–55	98
14	France's Naval Prototypes, 1945–55	104

Part V: Great Britain, 1955–65 – the Turbulent Years
15	Lost Opportunities	109
16	TSR2: The Assassination of an Aircraft	121

Part VI: Other Developments, 1955–90
17	Lightweight Fighters	128
18	Supersonic Bombers and Reconnaissance Aircraft	134
19	Vertical Take-Off	140

Appendix: Miscellaneous Other Prototypes	149
Index	158

List of Abbreviations

A&AEE	Aircraft & Armament Experimental Establishment	NEPA	Nuclear Energy for the Propulsion of Aircraft
AAM	Air to Air Missile	OR	Operational Requirement
AFB	Air Force Base	R&D	Research and Development
AI	Airborne Intercept (radar)	RAAF	Royal Australian Air Force
BuAer	Bureau of Aeronautics	RAE	Royal Aircraft Establishment
DA	*Dal'naya Aviatsiya* (Soviet Long-Range Aviation)	RAF	Royal Air Force
		RCAF	Royal Canadian Air Force
DME	Distance Measuring Equipment	RN	Royal Navy
ECM	Electronic Countermeasures	RPM	Revolutions Per Minute
ESD	Extra-Super Duralumin	SBAC	Society of British Aircraft Manufacturers
FA	*Frontovaia Aviatsiya* (Soviet Frontal Aviation)	SRS (F)	Strategic Reconnaissance Squadron (Fighter)
FICON	Fighter Conveyor	SRW (F)	Strategic Reconnaissance Wing (Fighter)
Http	High-Test Peroxide	s.t.	static thrust
HVAR	High Velocity Aircraft Rocket	SAC	Strategic Air Command
ICBM	Intercontinental Ballistic Missile	SLBM	Submarine-Launched Ballistic Missile
IFF	Identification Friend or Foe	SST	Supersonic Transport
ILS	Instrument Landing System	TAF	Tactical Air Force
IOC	Initial Operational Capability	TFR	Terrain-Following Radar
IRBM	Intermediate Range Ballistic Missile	UHF	Ultra-High Frequency
LAL	*Letayushaya Atomniaya Laboratoria* (Soviet Flying Atomic Laboratory)	USAAC	United States Army Air Corps
		USAAF	United States Army Air Force
LP	Low Pressure	USAF	United States Air Force
MoS	Ministry of Supply	VG	Variable Geometry
MRBM	Medium Range Ballistic Missile	V/STOL	Vertical/Short Take-Off and Landing
NACA	National Advisory Committee on Aeronautics	VTOL	Vertical Take-Off and Landing
NBMR	NATO Basic Military Requirement		

Introduction

This is the story of those combat aircraft that might have been a familiar sight in the skies during the Cold War, but which never made it into service. Sometimes the reason for their demise was technical; sometimes it was political.

In 1940, military aviation was dominated by two distinct and uncomplicated types of aircraft, the fighter and the bomber. Their roles were uncomplicated, too. The fighter's primary task was to destroy bombers, the majority of which were reserved for the tactical support of ground forces. Of the belligerent nations, only Britain and Japan, which was then at war in China, had formed strategic bombing forces.

The evolution of combat aircraft under the pressures of war during the next five years brought about profound changes. Existing fighter types were converted into fighter-bombers to provide battlefield support on a massive scale, while the strategic bomber was forged into the mightiest and most devastating weapon in the history of warfare up to that time.

Only at the end of the war in Europe did the Allies begin to realise what enormous strides in aviation technology had been made by Germany's scientists. The Germans already had operational jet fighters and bombers, and other futuristic jet aircraft projects, some of them close to completion, were found amid the ruins of Germany's aircraft industry. These projects, and the new aerodynamic technology that was built into them, formed the basis of much experimentation in the post-war years, as brave men probed into the unknown regions beyond the speed of sound.

In the years immediately after the Second World War, the power and the menace of the strategic bomber led to the re-awakening of old concepts. By the end of the war almost all fighter aircraft were in fact used as fighter-bombers, but the jet age saw the rebirth of the pure interceptor, aircraft such as America's F-86 Sabre, Russia's MiG-15 and Britain's Hawker Hunter: high-speed gun platforms whose sole purpose, originally, was to climb fast enough and high enough to destroy the strategic bomber. But such a task had to be undertaken by day and night, in all weathers, and this in turn led to the evolution of the 'weapon system', a fully integrated combination of airframe, engine, weapons, fire-control systems and avionics. Early examples of the weapon system concept were the Northrop F-89 Scorpion, the Lockheed F-94 Starfire and the Gloster Javelin.

In the mid-1950s yet another concept of air warfare evolved, partly as a result of the lessons learned during the Korean War and partly because of the wildly escalating cost of developing new combat types. This reached fruition in such highly successful types as the McDonnell F-4 Phantom and the Dassault Mirage family, whose basic airframe/engine combination was designed from the outset to support long-term development compatible with a wide variety of operational requirements. The high cost of developing new and complex airborne weapon systems also brought about international co-operation on an unprecedented scale, with a highly beneficial pooling of brains, expertise and financial resources that was to result in the production of advanced and versatile military aircraft such as the Panavia Tornado and Eurofighter Typhoon.

The list of success stories in the field of military jet aircraft production since 1945 is a long one. In terms of longevity Britain's Canberra and America's B-52 are unmatched, both remaining in first-line service more than half a century after their prototypes first flew, while for sheer proliferation Russia's MiG-15 remains unsurpassed, having been produced in far greater quantities than any other combat type of the post-war era. Then there have been the post-war export successes of France's military aircraft industry, whose products have admirably upheld the French tradition for building machines that combine a high degree of potency with aesthetic appeal.

Against the successes must be measured the many failures, some resulting from changing policies, others from prohibitive costs, and still others from political misconceptions — or a combination of all three. Some of the greatest political misconceptions of all time were contained in the British Defence White Paper of 1957, which announced the phasing out of manned aircraft in favour of missiles and which sounded the death-knell of several promising projects that might have become Britain's military best-sellers in the 1960s. None of them, however, had such a profound and damaging effect on the British aerospace industry as the later cancellation of the British Aircraft Corporation's superb TSR2. In 1965, amid much fury in the RAF and the British aerospace industry, the TSR2 – which has been described as one of the most potent and advanced weapon systems in the world – was cancelled by the British government, leaving the Hawker Siddeley Buccaneer to fill the gap as an interim aircraft until the Panavia Tornado entered service fifteen years later. But the TSR2 was by no means unique in falling victim to the political axe. In 1946, an amazing aircraft called the Miles M.52, which might have become the first in the world to exceed the speed of sound and so placed Britain at the very forefront of aviation technology, was also cancelled on very dubious political grounds.

The Americans had their troubles too, as did the Russians, but the budgets of both these superpowers were far better placed to support the cancellation of advanced aircraft projects than those of economically weaker nations. The Americans almost fell into the 'all-missile' trap when they cancelled the variable-geometry Rockwell B-1 in favour of cruise missiles; fortunately a later government saw folly in this and resurrected the project as the B-1B. In many respects the Russians seem to have had a shrewder appreciation of defence requirements, adhering to well-tried formulae. For example, lacking aircraft carriers, they developed the Tupolev Tu-22M 'Backfire' supersonic variable-geometry bomber, which with in-flight refuelling placed targets thousand of miles from the Russian homeland, on land or at sea, within their offensive reach.

This book is concerned with the many combat aircraft prototypes that failed to come to operational fruition during the years of the Cold War, from 1945 to 1990. It is a story of hope and endeavour; of frustration and bitter disappointment; of brilliant technical innovation and also appalling accidents that cost the lives of some of the world's most experienced test pilots.

Part I
The Quest for the Global Bomber, 1945–55

Chapter 1
The United States

At the outset of the Second World War in 1939, Great Britain was alone among the belligerent powers in possessing a bomber force that could truly be described as strategic. Such a force had in fact been in existence since the summer of 1918, when a strategic bombing element – known as the Independent Force, RAF – had been formed under the command of Major-General Sir Hugh Trenchard to carry out attacks by day and night against industrial targets in Germany, and against railway centres and aerodromes. This was the first time that an air force had been formed for the express purpose of conducting a war without reference or subordination to either army or navy.

Small though RAF Bomber Command's strategic force was in 1939, it nevertheless provided the anvil on which a mighty sword was hammered out: the striking force of four-engined heavy bombers which, from the summer of 1942, began to attack Germany's industrial heartland with growing power. In that year, too, the United States entered the strategic bombing war with the arrival in Britain of the first units of the US Eighth Army Air Force. For the Americans, however, the strategic bomber was a relatively new concept, their land-based air power having been assigned to the role of army support. The same was true of the air arms of both Germany and the USSR, neither of which succeeded in creating a significant strategic bombing force during the war. The Japanese, on the other hand, followed Britain's lead by creating a formidable strategic bombing arm, which mostly came under the umbrella of the Imperial Japanese Navy and which was used to good effect in the Sino-Japanese Manchurian campaign and, later, in Japan's offensives in South-East Asia.

By the war's end, the United States had taken over the lead in strategic-bomber design. Whereas the RAF's requirements had called for a bomber capable of delivering a heavy bomb load over medium ranges, resulting in the Short Stirling, Avro Lancaster and Handley Page Halifax, the United States Army Air Force's requirement had been different, mainly because of geographical considerations. In the late 1930s, with Imperial Japan posing an increasing threat to American interests in the Pacific, several US aircraft companies were asked to submit design studies for a new and advanced bomber capable of carrying a substantial bomb load over great distances, one which would be able to strike at Japan from forward US bases in the Pacific. The result was the Boeing B-29 Superfortress, the strategic bomber that would ultimately project US air power into the atomic age.

The Boeing B-29 and B-50

At the end of the Second World War, the B-29 was the most powerful and effective bomber aircraft in the world. Yet even the B-29 was limited in its effectiveness by lack of range: during its early operations against Japan in 1944, operating from bases on mainland China, it had to lift so much fuel to reach Japan that it could only carry a relatively small bomb load. It was not until the Americans captured the Marianas Islands and built airfields on them that the B-29's full potential as a strategic weapon against Japan was realised.

Soon after the war America's new Strategic Air Command had began to replace its B-29s with a straightforward but more advanced development

The Boeing B-29 Superfortress gave the Americans a commanding lead in strategic-bomber design at the end of the Second World War, and its attacks brought Japanese industry to its knees. (USAF)

of that aircraft, the Boeing B-50. Improvements included more powerful engines and a taller fin and rudder. It originated as the B-29D, though it was in fact 75 per cent a new aircraft, with a new aluminium wing structure some 16 per cent stronger and 26 per cent more efficient than that of the B-29 yet weighing 650lb (290kg) less. The vertical tail surfaces were 5ft (1.5m) higher than those of the B-29 and were hinged to fold horizontally over the starboard tailplane, enabling the B-50 to be housed in existing hangars. The wings, tail unit, landing gear and other items of equipment of the B-50 were interchangeable with those of the Boeing C-97A transport aircraft. The first B-50A (serial 46-017) was delivered to the 43rd Bomb Group at Davis-Monthan AFB, Arizona, on 20 February 1948, and further examples were delivered to the 509th Bomb Group at the same location soon afterwards. The 43rd and 509th Bomb Groups were the Strategic Air Command's nuclear strike force, and the advent of the B-50 gave a considerable boost to their operational efficiency. Powered by four Pratt & Whitney R-436055 Wasp Major engines, the B-50 had a range of 6,000 miles (10,000km) carrying a 10,000lb (4,500kg) nuclear store; maximum speed was 400mph (640km/h) at 25,000ft (7,600m), and operational ceiling was 40,000ft (14,000m). The aircraft could also lift up to 28,000lb (13,000kg) of conventional bombs. All B-50s were equipped for flight refuelling and in July 1948 the 43rd and 509th Air Refueling Squadrons were activated at Davis-Monthan and assigned to the 43rd and 509th Bomb Groups. These two squadrons were the first flight-refuelling units in the USAF, and began to receive their KB-29M tanker aircraft later in the year. The combination of B-50 and KB-29M enabled SAC to extend its operational range enormously, but an even more important step in this direction came on 26 June 1948 with the delivery of the first Convair B-36 bomber to the 7th Bomb Group at Carswell AFB, Texas.

The Convair B-36

As early as April 1941 the United States Army Air Corps (USAAC), as it then was, had issued a specification calling for an advanced bomber aircraft capable of carrying a 10,000lb (4,500kg) bomb load over 5,000 miles (8,000km), or a 72,000lb (33,000kg) load over shorter ranges; it was to have a top speed of 300–400mph (480–640km/h) at an operational ceiling of 35,000ft (11,000m), and to be able to operate from runways 5,000ft (1,500m) long. Among the companies that produced designs to meet this specification was Convair, whose project envisaged a massive, heavily armed bomber with a 230ft (70m) wingspan and powered by six 'pusher' piston engines. It was designated XB-36, and on 15 November 1941 the USAAF signed a contract for two prototypes. Early development was slowed down by the war, but the XB-36 programme was stepped up when, in 1943, the only way of striking hard at Japan seemed to be heavy bombing attacks on her home islands: on 23 July that year 190 production aircraft were ordered. The prototype XB-36 first flew on 8 August 1946.

The first XB-36 was followed by two more prototypes, the YB-36 and the YB-36A, both of which flew in 1947. Unlike the two earlier aircraft, which had conventional undercarriages, the YB-36A had a bogie-type assembly and a modified cockpit, the canopy being raised above the line of the fuselage to improve visibility. The B-36 carried a crew of sixteen. Maximum speed over the target was 435mph (670km/h), service ceiling was 42,000ft (13,000m) and range 8,000 miles (13,000km). The aircraft carried a heavy defensive armament,

THE UNITED STATES

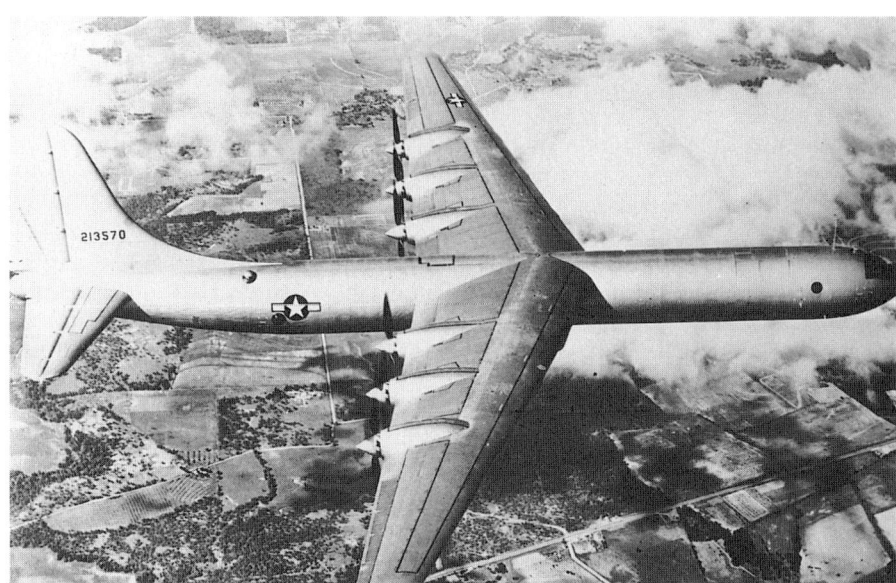

The Convair XB-36 prototype in flight. This massive aircraft was the most complex project undertaken by the US industry at that time. (Convair)

being equipped with six retractable remotely controlled turrets each housing twin 20mm cannon, plus two 20mm cannon in the nose and two in the tail. Normal bomb load was a single 10,000lb (4,500kg) nuclear store, but the aircraft could lift a maximum conventional bomb load of 84,000lb (38,000kg) over short ranges. An initial production batch of twenty-two B-36As was built, the first being delivered to Strategic Air Command in the summer of 1947. These aircraft were unarmed, and were used for crew training. The second production model, the B-36B, was powered by six Pratt & Whitney R-4630-41 engines with water injection, and was fully combat-equipped with twelve 20mm KM24A1 cannon in the six remotely controlled turrets, together with nose and tail armament. Seventy-three were built, the first flying on 8 July 1948. Thirty-five B-36A/B models had been delivered to SAC by the end of 1948.

The Northrop Flying Wings

The B-36 was selected in preference to a design submitted by the other principal contender for the wartime USAAC heavy-bomber contract, Northrop Aircraft Inc. This was based on a concept that was to have a profound effect on American strategic bombing policy half a century later, the concept of the flying wing.

Jack Northrop's experience in all-wing aircraft development stretched as far back as 1927 and the

An early production Convair B-36. The bomber gave Strategic Air Command a true global capability. Later variants were fitted with podded auxiliary turbojets. (Convair)

first aircraft to use this formula, the N1M, had been delivered to Muroc Army Air Base for evaluation by the USAAC in July 1940. This machine, powered by two Franklin pusher engines, had made more than 200 test flights by September 1941, and the results encouraged Northrop to submit a design for a four-engined, long-range bomber to the USAAC in a bid to meet the new heavy-bomber specification.

In November 1941 a prototype was ordered under the designation XB-35, a week after Convair received the order for their prototype XB-36. Both designs benefited from the experience gained with an earlier design, the Douglas B-19, which in effect became a flying laboratory for the new generation of heavy bombers. Detail design work on the XB-35 started at the beginning of 1942, with the help and co-operation of the USAF's Wright Field Engineering Division, and construction of a prototype was approved on 5 July. As Northrop were heavily involved in the development of the P-61 Black Widow night fighter, the final design of the XB-35's wing and the installation of the engines was allocated to the Glenn L. Martin Company of Baltimore, Northrop undertaking the aerodynamic research as well as the building of the undercarriage, the control systems and surfaces, and the ancillary equipment. In a bid to accelerate the programme, personnel from the design department of the Otis Elevator Company of New York were also drafted in to help with the design of the wing structure.

While design work on the prototype continued, four scale models were built to test the flight characteristics of the all-wing formula, continuing the programme where the N1M had left off. They were also to serve as training aircraft for the pilots who were destined to fly the full-scale machines. The first two models, designated N-9M, were powered by two 275hp Menasco engines while the third and fourth, the N-9M-A and N-9M-B, were fitted with 300hp Franklin motors and had a greater wingspan, at 60ft (18.3m).

Construction of the XB-35 began in January 1943, the aircraft bearing the serial 42-13603, and at the same time a second prototype (42-38323) was ordered. Before the end of the fiscal year this was followed by an order for thirteen pre-series YB-35s, which were allocated serial numbers from 42-102366 to -102378. Finally, the Glenn Martin Company received an order for the construction of 200 series-production B-35As.

The advent of the jet engine in operational service towards the end of the war, however, changed everything: the order for the 200 production aircraft was cancelled and on 1 June 1945 it was decided to convert the second and third YB-35s (42-102367 and -102368) to YB-35Bs, the four piston engines being replaced by eight Allison J35-A-5 turbojets.

The piston-engined XB-35 prototype flew for the first time on 25 June 1946, test pilot Max Stanley flying it from Hawthorne to the test centre at Muroc. It was an impressive machine, its huge all-metal wing spanning 172ft (52.5m) and having a root chord of 36ft 6in (11.44m). The leading edge was swept at an angle of 28 degrees and had a lower surface dihedral of 1 degree. Directional control surfaces were fitted at the wingtips, with elevons installed between these and the outboard engine nacelles; large flaps extended along the trailing edge from the outboard engines to the central fuselage nacelle. All control surfaces were hydraulically assisted, and leading-edge slats, which opened automatically when the aircraft approached stalling speed, were fitted near the wingtips.

The fuselage nacelle, which was fully pressurized and of monocoque construction, normally housed a nine-man crew consisting of pilot, co-pilot, bombardier, navigator, flight engineer, radio operator and three air gunners. The aircraft was also equipped to carry a reserve crew, and six folding bunks were fitted for this purpose. The pilot's cockpit was situated slightly to the left of the centreline under a bubble canopy; the bombardier's station was buried in the wing on the right, with forward vision through windows built into the leading edge. Because of the B-35's relatively modest speed it carried heavy defences, the gunners – housed in blisters above and below the wings – controlling six turrets armed with 0.5in machine guns. One four-gun turret was positioned above and one below the fuselage nacelle; the other four were fitted above and below the wing, outboard of the engines. In addition to these sixteen machine guns, four more could be fitted in the tail cone of the fuselage nacelle, depending on operational requirements. On the XB-35 prototype, these weapons were represented by metal blisters.

The XB-35 was powered by four 18-cylinder Pratt & Whitney Wasp Major air-cooled engines, three of which drove eight-bladed Hamilton Standard co-axial propellers. The No. 4 (port outer) engine was fitted with a six-bladed propeller, and retained this throughout testing. Large air intakes were fitted in the wing leading edge,

The Northrop XB-35 'flying wing' first flew on 25 June 1946. (Philip Jarrett)

and the wing fuel tanks had provision for up to 18,000 US gallons (68,200ltr). The aircraft had a tricycle undercarriage, the main units retracting forwards and the nosewheel laterally, and the landing gear was electrically operated.

Empty weight of the XB-35 was 90,500lb (41,000kg), rising to a fully laden take-off weight of 164,700lb (74,600kg). However, the maximum permissible overload weight of the aircraft was 212,544lb (96,280kg), a figure that reveals the astonishing potential of the flying-wing formula. Estimated maximum speed of the XB-35 was 393mph (632km/h) at 34,650ft (10,570m), and economical cruising speed was 183mph (294km/h); this gave the aircraft a range of 8,125 miles (13,073km) – equivalent to a non-stop flight from New York to Paris and back – with a 16,500lb (7,500kg) bomb load. When the range was reduced to 725 miles (1,170km), the aircraft could carry a bomb load of 51,500lb (23,300kg). The XB-35 was able to reach a cruising altitude of 35,000ft (11,000m) in fifty-seven minutes, and had an operational ceiling of 40,000ft (12,000m).

Right from the beginning, however, difficulties were experienced with the aircraft's propeller-governing mechanisms and engine-reduction gears, and after only a few flights had been made testing was suspended until the problems were resolved. It was eventually decided to fit simplified four-bladed propellers of a type specially adapted for the B-35, but so that flight testing might continue while Hamilton Standard were working on these, the XB-35 was temporarily equipped with Curtiss Electric propellers of the type destined for Convair's B-36.

In 1947 the second XB-35 was delivered to Muroc together with the first pre-series YB-35 (42-102366) – shortly afterwards the latter was 'winterized' for Arctic trials, being re-designated YB-35A. The second pre-series YB-35 (42-102367) flew on 21 October that year, and it was this machine that was converted to take eight Allison turbojets. Initially known as the YB-35B, its designation was changed soon after to YB-49. The jet engines were closely mounted in two groups of four at about one-third span; each group was flanked by vertical

The Northrop YRB-49 jet bomber suffered from stability problems. It nevertheless proved the concept of the flying wing. (Northrop)

fins that extended well clear of both the upper and lower trailing edges and that were intended to improve directional stability. The crew was reduced to seven men, there now being only one gunner in command of a twin-gun turret positioned at the rear of the central fuselage cone. Empty and loaded weights of the YB-49 were 89,600lb (40,600kg) and 216,600lb (98,200kg), respectively, and there was provision for a bomb load of 37,400lb (17,000kg). More usually, a bomb load of 10,000lb (4,500kg) would have been carried over a range of 2,800 miles (4,500km).

Although the jet-powered YB-49 showed a considerable speed increase over the B-35 (520mph/840km/h against 393mph/632km/h), its reduced range was a considerable drawback, being only about half that of its piston-engined predecessor. Moreover, the YB-49 proved to be a poor weapons-release platform because of an instability problem that proved seemingly impossible to correct. Two YB-49s were built and flown, the second aircraft (42-102368) being handed over to the USAF on 28 May 1948. Only a few days later, tragedy struck: on the morning of 5 June 42-102368 crashed just north of Muroc Dry Lake. The pilot, US Air Force Captain Glenn Edwards, and the four other crew were killed. What caused the crash is not known, but it was suspected that Captain Edwards managed to surpass the never-exceed speed of the aircraft while descending from 40,000ft (12,000m), causing the outer wing panels to detach and the aircraft to disintegrate in mid-air. Muroc AFB was renamed Edwards AFB on 5 December 1949 in honour of the late Captain Edwards.

Flight testing with the surviving YB-49 quickly revealed the type's inherent unsuitability as a strategic bomber. Apart from its aerodynamic problems, its bomb-bay cells were too small to accommodate the bulky Mk 3 and Mk 4 nuclear bombs, which could easily be carried by the B-36. However, during an endurance test the aircraft remained airborne for 9 hours 30 minutes, covering a distance of 3,458 miles (5,564km) at an average speed of 382mph (615km/h) and an altitude of 35,000–40,000ft (11,000–12,000m), and this seemed to lend weight to the idea that the aircraft might find an application in the strategic-reconnaissance role. In fact, in February 1948 it had already been decided to produce thirty examples of a strategic-reconnaissance variant, the RB-49A; nine of the pre-series YB-35s were to be converted to YRB-49A standard for evaluation, this work being carried out under sub-contract by Convair. To save weight and increase the range, the reconnaissance version was to have six turbojets instead of eight.

The Northrop X-4 Bantam yielded much valuable data on the aerodynamic characteristics of tailless aircraft. (Northrop)

In April 1949, however, the RB-49A order was cancelled and conversion work was stopped, although one YRB-49A (the eleventh YB-35, 012376) was completed and made its first flight from Hawthorne to Edwards AFB on 4 May 1950. This aircraft had six Allison J35-A-19 turbojets, four of which were buried in the wing and the other two suspended in pods beneath it. The YRB-49A carried a six-man crew and its equipment included the latest high-altitude cameras, situated in a compartment at the rear of the fuselage nacelle and protected from icing by a special hot-air circulation system.

On 15 March 1950 the entire YB/YRB-49 programme was cancelled. On that same day, the first YB-49, 102-367, was totally destroyed by fire following a taxiing accident at Edwards. It left behind it a small taste of stardom: an appearance in the film version of H.G. Wells' classic *The War of the Worlds*, in which it dropped an atomic bomb on the invading Martians (without, it must be said, much result!).

Another interesting project in the Northrop flying-wing programme was the EB-35B, which was to have been fitted with Turbodyne XT-37 turboprops. The XT-37 was a Northrop design and the company received a contract to build two prototype engines on 1 July 1943; the first was bench-tested in December 1944 and was the first American turboprop to be run with a propeller fitted. The Turbodyne had an eighteen-stage compressor and a four-stage turbine, and its development was undertaken by a joint company formed between Northrop and the Joshua Hendy Iron Works. The XT-37 had originally been intended as a potential power plant for naval aircraft, but when the US Navy lost interest in the project in 1945 development continued under a USAAF contract.

In 1948 Northrop acquired Hendy's shares and formed a new company, the Turbodyne Corporation. Work on the new turboprop went on, and in 1950 the engine, now rated at 10,000shp, passed a 50-hour bench test without failing. At the end of that year, all assets of the Turbodyne Corporation were absorbed by the General Electric Company, who continued with the work of advanced engine testing for a time, but then the whole project was abandoned following a spate of teething troubles and the EB-35B never flew.

By the end of 1950, the YRB-49A was the only one of Northrop's huge flying wings still in existence, the two YB-49s having been accidentally destroyed and the others scrapped; the YRB-49A was scrapped in its turn in October 1951. By that time the Convair B-36, which was far more suited to the global strategic-bombing role, had already been in service with Strategic Air Command for four years.

The demise of the B-35/49, however, was not quite the end of the Northrop flying-wing story. In 1948 the company built a small tailless swept-wing jet research aircraft, the X-4 Bantam, which flew in December and was powered by two Westinghouse

J30-WE-1 turbojets. It was followed by a second aircraft, and both machines were used in an extensive high-speed research programme by the NACA. The X-4 could reach Mach 0.95 in a shallow dive. Although not strictly a military prototype, the information gathered by the X-4 on the flight characteristics of swept-wing tailless aircraft at high subsonic speeds was put to good use in the design of operational types such as the Chance Vought F7U Cutlass and the Douglas F4D Skyray

Northrop and the Horten Flying Wings

Returning to the strategic-bomber issue, the failure of the YB-49 effectively removed Northrop from the running in the race to provide the USAF with a heavy jet bomber capable of delivering nuclear weapons into the heartland of the West's potential enemy, the Soviet Union. One of the main problems with Northrop's design, perhaps, was that it had been ahead of its time; two other contending companies, Boeing and Convair, starting virtually from scratch with jet-bomber studies at the end of the war, were able to benefit from the wealth of advanced aerodynamic research material that had come out of defeated Germany.

Despite determined efforts by the Germans to destroy it, such material still remained intact in large quantities at locations all over Germany in May 1945, and became the object of an intelligence-gathering race between the Allies. It was a race won by the Americans, mainly for geographical reasons: in the closing months of the war most secret German research facilities had been removed from the north to the more secure mountainous regions of central and southern Germany, which placed them precisely in the path of the main American advance. It was therefore hardly surprising that the bulk of the material should fall into American hands.

It was only now that Northrop became fully aware of the extent of the research carried out by German industry – and in particular by the Horten brothers, Reimar and Walter – into tailless-aircraft design. The story of the flying wings designed by the Hortens begins with a series of models, followed by the Horten Ho I sailplane of 1934, in which the pilot occupied a prone position in the wing centre-section. As with all Horten aircraft, the Ho I had no vertical flying surfaces, elevons being used for pitch and roll control, and yaw control being effected by brake flaps above and below the leading edges near the wingtips. Although it was quite a successful design, the Hortens were not satisfied with the Ho I so they destroyed it and replaced it with the Ho II.

The main feature of the new aircraft was that it had sweepback on the wing's trailing edges, as well as the leading edges. Four Ho IIs were built, one of which was fitted with an 80hp Hirth engine in 1935. This was tested in 1938 by Hanna Reitsch and attracted the attention of Ernst Udet, Director of the Technical Department of the German Air Ministry, who made funds available for further development. In 1938, with this official backing, the Hortens set up a facility at Berlin's Tempelhof Airport where they constructed the Ho III sailplane. This was in effect a scaled-up Ho II and was fitted with a retractable tandem-wheel undercarriage. Four Ho IIIs were built, one of which was fitted with an engine, the propeller blades folding in flight to reduce drag.

The next Horten flying wing design, the Ho IV, was built primarily to investigate the effects of high aspect ratio. Two Ho IVs were built, one of which crashed after entering a spin. The Ho V, built between 1936 and 1938, was constructed as a two-seater sailplane, but in 1942 it was converted to single-seat configuration. A second Ho V made much use of plastic in its construction. From the outset, the Ho V was designed as a powered research aircraft. Its wing had pronounced sweepback on the outer panels, but the centre-section had greatly reduced sweep on the leading edge and a straight, unswept trailing edge. The centre-section had a welded steel-tube structure to support two 80hp Hirth engines, driving pusher propellers through extension shafts. In a bid to acquire more funds, the Hortens proposed a glider-tug version of the Ho V, but this was not taken up.

The Horten Ho VI, only one prototype of which was built, had a wing with the very high aspect ratio of 32.4:1, which proved to be structurally weak and too flexible for practical ground handling. The next design, the Ho VII, was similar to the Ho V, but was fitted with more powerful 240hp Argus As 10C engines. The sole Ho VII is thought to have been tested at Oranienburg, where it was located in March 1945.

The Ho VIII was by far the largest of the Horten flying wings, and was designed as a com-

The Gotha Go 229V-3, developed from the Horten Ho IX, under construction at the end of the war in Europe. (US Army)

mercial aircraft with accommodation for about sixty passengers. It was originally to have had a span of 80m (260ft) and was to have been powered by six 600hp BMW pusher engines; range was estimated to be 6,000km (3,700 miles) at a cruising speed of 300–350km/h (190–220mph). A prototype was expected to fly in November 1945, but the defeat of Germany prevented its development. The concept was resurrected after the war by Reimar Horten, who went to Argentina and incorporated the idea into the unsuccessful I.A.38 tailless cargo aircraft, which flew in prototype form in 1958.

The Horten Ho IX was the Horten brothers' only combat aircraft design. It was intended to power the prototype with two BMW 003A-1 turbojets, but as these were not available for installation the first Ho IXV-1 was completed as a glider and tested at Oranienburg in 1944. The second prototype was completed with two Junkers Jumo 004B turbojets and flew for the first time in January 1945. The initial success of the flight tests resulted in the placing of an order for thirty aircraft with the Gothaer Waggonfabrik at Friedrichshafen. The production model was to have been designated Gotha Go 229, but the production prototype, the Go 229V-3, had not been completed when development ceased. The second aircraft, the Ho IXV-2, was destroyed on the ground after two hours of flight testing.

What was of particular interest to Northrop, however, was a long-range jet bomber project, the Horten Ho VIIIB, known as the *Amerika Bomber*. The design was of all-wing configuration with very high aspect ratio and a kinked trailing edge where the swept-forward trailing edge of the centre-section met the swept-back outer wing panels. The design featured a large delta-shaped vertical fin and rudder, the three-man crew being accommodated in the glazed and pressurized forward section of

The Boeing YB-52 prototype taxies past a Convair B-36 prior to its maiden flight in April 1952. (Boeing)

this fin. The rear section of the fin housed a barbette with four 20mm cannon, this section extending beyond the wing trailing edge. The aircraft was powered by six Junkers Jumo 109-004D turbojets, grouped under the wing centre-section. A bomb load of 4,000kg (8,800lb) was to be carried. The wing had a span of 42m (137ft 9in). Estimated performance included a maximum speed of 900km/h (560mph) at 6,000m (20,000ft) and a range of 9,000km (5,600 miles). A prototype was ordered to be built in March 1945, far too late to be practical.

The German research seemed to vindicate Northrop's belief that the all-wing approach to strategic-bomber design was the right one, the argument being that a flying wing will carry the same payload as a conventional aircraft while weighing less and using less fuel. The weight and drag of the tail surfaces are absent, as is the weight of the structure that supports them. The wing structure itself is far more efficient because the weight of the aircraft is spread across the wing rather than concentrated in the centre.

This was the formula to which Northrop returned in 1978 when the company began development of the Advanced Technology Bomber, which was to emerge as the B-2 Spirit. The all-wing approach was selected because it promised to result in an exceptionally clean configuration for minimizing radar cross-section, including the elimination of vertical tail surfaces, with added benefits such as span-loading structural efficiency and high lift/drag ratio for efficient cruise. Outboard wing panels were added for longitudinal balance, to increase lift/drag ratio and to provide sufficient span for pitch, roll and yaw control. Leading-edge sweep was selected for balance and transonic aerodynamics, while the overall planform was designed to have neutral longitudinal (pitch) static stability. Because of its short length, the aircraft had to produce stabilizing pitch-down moments beyond the stall for positive recovery. The original ATB design had elevons on the outboard wing panels only, but as the design progressed additional elevons were added inboard, giving the B-2 its distinctive 'double-W' trailing edge.

The Convair YB-60, based on the design of the B-36, was an elegant aircraft, but was inferior in almost every respect to the YB-52. (Convair)

The Boeing B-52 and Convair B-60

In April 1945 the USAAF issued a requirement for a new jet-powered heavy bomber as the eventual replacement for the Convair B-36, which was by then in the advanced development stage. Boeing, with a vast amount of bomber experience through the B-17/B-29 line, originally proposed a swept-wing, turboprop-powered design, and this still remained a possibility when two prototypes were ordered in September 1947. Design and performance problems, however, resulted in a considerable revision, and the decision was taken to power the new aircraft with eight turbojets. The first prototype, the XB-52, began ground testing on 29 November 1951, and on 15 March the following year it was joined by the second prototype, the YB-52. It was this machine that was the first to fly, on 15 April 1952.

Convair's submission, on the other hand, envisaged a straightforward swept-wing development of the B-36, and was intended to give the US strategic-bombing force an aircraft with the same range and load-carrying ability as the B-36's, but with a greatly improved performance. Originally designated YB-36G, the aircraft was re-designated YB-60 in 1950 and Convair received a contract for two prototypes on 15 March 1951. The first of these (aircraft no. 40-2676, designated YB-60-CF) flew on 18 April 1952, powered by eight Pratt & Whitney J57-P-3 turbojets in four paired under-wing pods. Three quarters of the YB-60's structure was similar to that of the B-36, but it had a revised undercarriage and its fuel capacity was greater. Its wingspan was 206ft (63m), the wing being swept at an angle of 35 degrees at the leading edge. Plans called for the production version to be powered by an uprated version of the J57 engine developing 10,000lb (44.5kN) s.t., which would have given the bomber a maximum speed of 550mph (890km/h) at 55,000ft (17,000m). However the B-52, which had flown three days earlier than the Convair design, proved superior on almost every count and the YB-60 programme was abandoned, the second prototype having never flown.

Chapter 2

Soviet Heavy Bomber Development, 1945–55

The Tupolev Tu-4

In the evening of 30 July 1944, Soviet Yak-9 fighters were ordered to take off from the airfield of Spassk, close to Russia's border with Japanese-occupied Manchuria, to intercept an unidentified aircraft that had just entered Soviet airspace. To their surprise, the fighter pilots discovered that the aircraft was not Japanese, as they had expected, but an American B-29 Superfortress. The aircraft belonged to the 771st Squadron of the USAAF's 462nd Bombardment Group, the first unit to equip with the new type; operating out of Chengtu air base in southern China, it had been part of a force of 100 B-29s which, a couple of hours earlier, had attacked a Japanese steel mill at Anshan in Manchuria. The B-29 had been hit by an anti-aircraft shell over the target and the pilot, realizing that the aircraft would be unable to regain its base on three engines, had decided to follow the laid-down emergency procedure and head for Soviet territory. The Soviet fighters escorted the B-29 to a small airstrip near Tavrichanka, at the northern tip of Vladivostok Bay, and the pilot landed with considerable difficulty, bringing the aircraft to a stop only yards from where the edge of the field dropped away into the sea. A few hours later, the members of the crew were being interrogated by Soviet Air Force officers; it was to be several months before they finally left the USSR on their way home to the United States. They never saw their B-29 again.

As the war in Europe neared its end, the Chief Administration of the Soviet Air Force had plans in hand for a substantial modernization programme, and these included the formation of a modern strategic bomber force. In 1944, however, the only Soviet long-range bombers were the Petlyakov Pe-8 and Ilyushin Il-4, both of which were obsolescent in comparison with Allied types. These types formed the backbone of the Soviet Long-Range Aviation Force, the ADD, which earlier in 1944 had been re-designated the 18th Air Army and turned over to tactical-bombing duties in support of the Soviet ground forces.

With the wartime emphasis very much on the development of tactical bombers, assault aircraft and fighters, Soviet designers had had little time to study long-range bomber projects, and it was obvious that even if work on such projects began in 1944, there would still be a lengthy delay before a modern long-range bomber could be produced in series. The unexpected arrival of the B-29 – which was followed by three more under similar circumstances during the remaining months of 1944 – offered a ready-made answer to the problem. By copying the B-29 in every detail, the Russians hoped to avoid all the technological problems associated with the indigenous development of such an aircraft. The designer chosen for the task was Andrei Tupolev, who had just begun work on the design of a long-range, high-altitude, four-engined bomber called the Tu-64; this never got past the design stage and was abandoned in favour of the B-29 copy. Meanwhile the job of copying the B-29's Wright R-3350 engines went to A.D. Shvetsov.

The work was not easy, involving as it did much reverse engineering; major snags cropped up frequently, particularly in connection with electrically operated equipment such as the B-29's gun turrets. Despite everything, however, construction of the prototype Russian B-29 – designated Tu-4 – was begun in March 1945, and the first three prototypes were ready for flight testing at the beginning

The Tupolev Tu-80 was a developed version of the Tu-4, the Soviet copy of the B-29. It did not enter production. (Tupolev)

of 1947. The following year these three aircraft were publicly revealed at the big Soviet air display at Tushino, near Moscow. By this time series production of the Tu-4 was well under way and the first examples had been delivered to the Soviet strategic bomber force, the Dal'naya Aviatsiya (DA). The aircraft was externally similar to the B-29, except that the standard armament of twelve 0.50in machine guns and one 20mm cannon was replaced by ten NS-23 cannon.

Production of the Tu-4 (which was later allocated the NATO code-name 'Bull') was a very important milestone in the history of the Soviet aviation industry. Plants involved in the aircraft's manufacture had to learn more refined and precise methods; they also learned how to miniaturize certain items of equipment and to impose stringent quality control in turning out material that had to be more finely machined than anything they had encountered so far. With the B-29/Tu-4, the Russians now had the means to deliver a nuclear weapon.

Developments from the Tu-4

Meanwhile, the Tupolev design team had been turning its attention to improving the basic Tu-4 design, the principal object being to increase the bomber's range. Retaining the basic structure of the Tu-4, Tupolev's engineers set about streamlining the fuselage, increasing its length by several feet and redesigning the nose section to replacing the Tu-4's rather bulbous cockpit with a more aerodynamically refined stepped-up configuration. The area of the tail fin was also increased and the fin made more angular in design. To reduce drag, the nacelles of the Ash-73TK engines were redesigned. The outer wing sections were also redesigned and the span increased slightly, allowing for a 15 per cent increase in fuel tankage. Two prototypes of the redesigned aircraft, designated Tu-80, were built and the first flew early in 1949. The operational version, while carrying a similar payload to that of the Tu-4, was to have had a defensive armament of ten 23mm cannon or ten 12.7mm machine guns in remotely controlled barbettes. By this time, however, the Soviet Air Force had begun to think in terms of an aircraft that could compare to the Convair B-36, which was beginning to enter service with Strategic Air Command, and the Tu-80 was not ordered into production. Another Tu-4 derivative, the DVB-202, designed by Vladimir Myasishchev, suffered the same fate.

At this time, several engine design bureaux in the USSR were working on powerful jet and turboprop engines that would power the next generation of Soviet combat aircraft, but it would be some time before these became operational. In the meantime, with relations between East and West deteriorating rapidly – particularly as a result of the Russian blockade of Berlin in 1900 – the race to achieve military parity with the United States assumed a high degree of urgency. This was especially true in the strategic-bombing field: it was of little use if the Russians broke the American nuclear weapons monopoly by building up their

The last Soviet piston-engined strategic bomber was the Tupolev Tu-85. It was overtaken by progress with jet bombers and did not enter service. (Tupolev)

own stockpile of atomic bombs, only to lack the means of delivering them to their targets.

The B-36 had given Strategic Air Command the capability to deliver nuclear bombs deep into the heart of the USSR, but in 1949 the Soviets had no comparable bomber. The Tu-4 had the capacity to lift Russia's early, cumbersome atomic weapons, but only over limited ranges; it could theoretically strike at targets in North America across the Arctic regions, but such a mission would be strictly one-way. A new specification was now issued, for an intercontinental bomber capable of carrying an 5,200kg (11,500lb) bomb load over a combat radius of 8,100km (4,375nm) and then returning to base without refuelling.

In mid-1949, in response to the new specification, Tupolev embarked on the design of the biggest aircraft so far constructed in the Soviet Union, and the last Soviet bomber to be powered by piston engines: a scaled-up version of the Tu-80 powered by new 4,000hp piston engines. In this way, Tupolev succeeded not only in retaining the proven aerodynamic and technical qualities of the Tu-80 and its predecessor, the Tu-4, but also saved time: only two years elapsed between the start of the intercontinental bomber programme and the first flight of a prototype. By way of comparison, it took the Americans five years to produce the B-36, although the latter was somewhat more revolutionary in concept.

The new bomber, designated Tu-85, began flight testing at the beginning of 1951, powered by four Dobronin VD-4K engines producing 4,300hp on take-off. The structure was light, employing a number of special alloys, although for some reason magnesium, which was used in the structure of the B-36, was not incorporated. The long, slender, semi-monocoque fuselage was split into five compartments, three of which were pressurized to house the sixteen-man crew. Defensive armament was the same as the Tu-4's, comprising four remotely controlled turrets each with a pair of 23mm cannon. The roomy weapons bay could accommodate up to 20,000kg (44,000lb) of bombs. With an 5,000kg (11,000lb) bomb load, the Tu-85 had a range of 14,000km (7,500nm) at 550km/h (295kt) and 10,000m (33,000ft); normal range was 10,250km (5,530nm). Maximum speed over the target was 652km/h (352kt). Several Tu-85 prototypes were built and test flown in 1951–2, but the aircraft was not ordered into production.

Times were changing fast: in February 1951, before the Tu-85 began its flight test programme, the US Air Force had decided to order the Boeing B-52 Stratofortress, which was capable of attacking targets in the USSR from bases in the continental USA, and it was clear that the day of the piston-engined bomber was over. The Russians therefore decided to abandon further development of the Tu-85 in favour of turbojet-powered strategic bombers, although they fostered the impression that it was in service by showing the prototypes, escorted by jet fighters, at Aviation Day flypasts.

The First Soviet Jet Bombers

The production of a strategic jet bomber was entrusted to the Tupolev and Myasishchev design bureaux; the latter's efforts were to culminate in the four-engined M-4, which first appeared at Tushino in 1954 and received the NATO code-name

Given the NATO reporting name 'Badger', the Tu-16 was a very successful design that went on to perform a wide variety of tasks. This one bears the legend Otlychnii *('Excellence') on its nose, signifying that its air- and ground crews are top performers. (RAF)*

The Tupolev Tu-95, re-designated Tu-142 in its later versions, has had a front-line service life of over half a century. (RAF)

'Bison'. Although never an outstanding success in the long-range strategic bombing role for which it was intended, the M-4 was nevertheless the Soviet Union's first operational four-engined jet bomber, and was roughly comparable to early versions of the B-52. Its main operational role in later years was maritime and electronic reconnaissance, and some were converted as in-flight refuelling tankers.

Tupolev's strategic jet-bomber design was much more successful. Designated Tu-88 by Tupolev, it flew for the first time in 1952 and entered service three years later as the Tu-16, receiving the NATO code-name 'Badger'. Owing much – in fuselage design, at least – to the Tu-80, the Tu-16 was destined to become the most important bomber type on the inventories of the Soviet Air Force and Soviet Naval Air Arm for over a decade, about 2,000 examples being produced. Tupolev also adopted the Tu-85's basic fuselage structure in the design of a new turboprop-powered strategic bomber, the Tu-95.

To bring the project to fruition as quickly as possible, the Tupolev team married swept flying surfaces to what was basically a Tu-85 fuselage. Development of the Tu-95 and M-4 proceeded in parallel, and it was intended that both types should be ready in time to take part in the Tushino flypast of May 1954. However, some delay was experienced with the Tu-95's massive Kuznetsov NK-12 turboprop engines, and in the event only the M-4 was test-flown in time. Flight testing of the Tu-95 began in the summer of 1954, and seven pre-series aircraft made an appearance at Tushino on 3 July 1955, the type being allocated the NATO code-name 'Bear.'

By this time the importance of the Tu-95 was growing, for the performance of the M-4 had fallen short of expectations and as a result production orders for that type were being drastically cut back. Even though the Tu-95's engines were still causing problems, it was realized that the Tupolev design would form the mainstay of the DA's strategic air divisions for at least the next decade; an ironic turn of events, for in the beginning emphasis had been placed on the production of the M-4 in the mistaken belief that the turboprop-powered Tu-95 would be limited to Mach 0.76. It was even more ironic that the Tu-95 would still be in first-line service half a century later, long after the M-4 had been retired.

Atomic-Powered Bombers

A major red herring in military aircraft development in the years after the Second World War was the concept of the atomic-powered bomber. In 1946, the Fairchild Engine and Airplane Company was awarded a contract to study the feasibility of a nuclear-powered aircraft; the research, which was known by the name NEPA (Nuclear Energy for the Propulsion of Aircraft), was carried out at Oak Ridge, Tennessee. A later study, carried out in 1948 by the Massachusetts Institute of Technology on behalf of the Atomic Energy Commission, concluded that a nuclear-powered aircraft was technically possible, but that it would take at least fifteen years to develop.

In 1951, the USAF Air Materiel Command awarded General Electric a contract covering the development of a nuclear propulsion unit. The principle of such a system was that air would enter a compressor, be heated and expanded as it passed through the reactor unit, and then be exhausted through a jet nozzle. At the same time Pratt & Whitney were contracted to develop an indirect-cycle engine, which would use an intermediate fluid to heat the air, rather than passing it through the reactor core itself.

In 1954, Lockheed and Convair were given contracts for the development of a nuclear-powered aircraft, designated WS-125A, with Pratt & Whitney and General Electric as the primary engine contractors. The WS-125A would in effect be the prototype of a high-altitude bomber, which would cruise at subsonic speed and have a supersonic dash capability (Mach 1.3) over the target.

Meanwhile, a Convair B-36H, serial number 51-5712, had been assigned to the nuclear programme, its function being to test the effects of nuclear reactor radiation on instruments, equipment and airframe, and to study shielding methods. The aircraft was one of several B-36s that had been damaged by a tornado at Carswell AFB in September 1952, and subsequently repaired. A 1,000kW nuclear reactor weighing 35,000lb (16,000kg) was mounted in the aft bomb bay, being cooled by large air intakes and exhaust holes in the rear fuselage. The entire crew was housed in a special compartment in the fuselage nose section, surrounded by lead and rubber shielding. Further protection was provided by a 4-ton lead disc shield, installed in the aircraft's centre-section. Only the pilot and co-pilot could see out through the 1ft-thick (30cm), leaded-glass windshield. A closed-circuit television system enabled the crew to monitor the reactor. In its new guise the aircraft was designated XB-36H.

Its first flight was made on 17 September 1955, with test pilot A.S. Witchell Jr at the controls. All of the test flights were carried out over sparsely populated areas and the reactor was not turned on until the aeroplane was at a safe altitude. Flying alongside the XB-36H on each flight was a C-97 transport aircraft carrying a platoon of armed Marines, ready to parachute down and surround the test aircraft in case it crashed.

In 1956 the XB-36H was re-designated NB-36H, the aircraft making forty-seven test flights in total up to 27 March 1957, when it flew for the last time. By then the USAF had decided to cancel the WS-125A project. The NB-36H was decommissioned at Fort Worth late in 1957 and its nuclear components buried. A projected nuclear-powered version of the B-36, designated X-6, which was to have been equipped with a General Electric R-1 aircraft reactor, was never completed.

In the late 1950s the Soviet Union also carried out studies into the potential of a nuclear-powered bomber, and reactor trials were carried out with a modified Tupolev Tu-95M. This test bed was designated Tu-95 LAL (Letayushaya Atomniaya Laboratoria, or Flying Atomic Laboratory) and was fitted with two normal NK-42MV turboprops and two experimental NK-44As; the latter were powered by an atomic reactor installed in the rear fuselage, just aft of the centre of gravity. The aircraft, which also bore the designation Tu-119, flew for the first time in 1961 at the Zhukovsky Test Centre, and in the following year it made some forty flights over the nuclear test area at Semipalatinsk, in Kazakhstan. The aircraft habitually flew with two crews, one provided by the Ministry of Aircraft Production and the other by the Soviet Air Force, a total of twelve men. Of these two crews, who did not have the benefit of the shielding that surrounded their American counterparts, only three men survived into the 1990s.

The reasons for the failure of the atomic-powered aircraft programmes are not hard to find. Quite apart from the crew protection problems, the sheer weight of the shielding that needed to be installed in the nuclear-powered prototypes caused an unacceptable deterioration in aircraft performance. The loss of altitude and speed caused by the extra weight cancelled out any advantage that might have been gained in endurance.

Part II

Medium and Light Jet Bombers – the First Generation

Chapter 3
The USAF's Medium and Tactical Bomber Force, 1945–55

In April 1944 the USAAF invited design tenders for a medium bomber possessing a tactical radius of 1,000 miles (1,600km), a maximum speed of at least 500mph (800km/h) and an operational ceiling of 40,000ft (12,000m). Four companies – Boeing, Convair, Martin and North American – went to work on the idea and submitted their proposals in December of that year.

The Boeing B-47

The Boeing Company's thinking crystallized, in September 1945, into the design of a strategic jet bomber designated Model 450. The project had undergone many changes since its conception in the previous year, and after assessing German research data the Boeing design team decided to adopt a configuration that was a radical departure from conventional design. It featured a thin, flexible wing based on wartime German aerodynamic research, with an optimum sweep of 35 degrees, six turbojets in underwing pods, and a main undercarriage housed in the fuselage. A full-scale mock-up was completed in April 1946, and a month later the USAF ordered the construction of two prototypes under the designation XB-47. The first of these, now named the Stratojet, flew on 17 December 1947, powered by six Allison J35 turbojets.

The Stratojet, which was to become the mainstay of Strategic Air Command's nuclear strike force in the early 1950s, was a triumph of engineering skill, and its bold conception a tribute to the confidence

The Boeing B-47 Stratojet, seen here in its RB-47H strategic reconnaissance version, was the mainstay of Strategic Air Command's nuclear strike force in the 1950s. (Author)

of Boeing's designers. As it was one of aviation's biggest successes, it does not fall within the scope of this book; however, some projects that evolved from it deserve mention. The first of these, conceived in 1948, involved a proposal for a derivative of the basic B-47 design, with greater wingspan and length, and a higher all-up weight. Originally known as the Model 474, and later as the XB-55, the aircraft was to have been powered by four Allison T40-A-2 turboprops driving contra-rotating propellers. The XB-55, however, never left the drawing board, and neither did a parallel project, the YB-56, which was also known as the YB-47C. This envisaged a much uprated version of the basic

25

Designed in competition with the Boeing B-47, the highly streamlined Convair XB-46 flew for the first time in April 1947. It was outclassed by its rival. (Convair)

B-47 powered by four 9,700lb (43.1kN) s.t. Allison J35-A-23 turbojets, which would give the aircraft a maximum speed of 633mph (1,018km/h) at sea level and a range of 4,800 miles (7,700km).

A turboprop-powered B-47 did actually fly, although it was purely an engine development aircraft and not a military prototype. In 1955, two B-47Bs (51-2046 and 51-2103) were adapted as flying test beds for the Wright YT49-W-1 turboprop; 51-2103 began flight trials on 26 August 1955 with one of these engines replacing each paired inboard turbojet nacelle and driving a four-bladed Curtiss turbo-electric propeller. Both aircraft, designated XB-47D, were extensively tested at the Moses Lake Flight Center, Larson AFB, and reached a maximum speed in level flight of 597mph (961km/h).

The Convair XB-46

The design submitted by Convair in a bid to meet the USAF medium-bomber requirement was the XB-46, which followed a conventional formula but which was aerodynamically one of the cleanest aircraft ever to take to the air. Powered by four 4,000lb (17.8kN) s.t. Allison-built General Electric J35-C-3 turbojets mounted in pairs in large underwing nacelles, the prototype, 45-59582, flew for the first time on 2 April 1947; after initial flight trials it went to Wright Field for service evaluation early in 1948. During the course of these trials, the XB-46 reached a maximum speed of 491mph (790km/h) at sea level and 545mph (877km/h) at 15,000ft (4,500m), and showed its ability to reach a cruising altitude of 35,000ft (11,000m) in nineteen minutes. The bomber carried a crew of three, the pilot and co-pilot being seated in tandem and the navigator/bombardier in the extreme nose. The XB-46's flight trials revealed excellent handling qualities, but the type's performance was considerably outclassed by that of its rival, the B-47, and it was not ordered into production.

The Glenn Martin XB-48

The Glenn Martin Company's submission, the Model 223, also fell short of performance requirements. Bearing the USAF designation XB-48 and powered by six Allison-built General Electric J35-A-5 turbojets mounted in clutches of three

Designed to the same requirement as the B-47, the Martin XB-48 experimental jet bomber was a much more conventional design than the Boeing aircraft. (Martin)

A North American B-45 Tornado using rocket-assisted take-off. (North American)

under the wings, the prototype (45-59585) flew for the first time on 22 June 1947. The XB-48 was of conventional design and carried a three-man crew; like the XB-46, it was designed to carry an 8,000lb (3,600kg) bomb load, although its range of 2,500 miles (4,000km) was less than that of the Convair type; on shorter-range missions, the bomb load could be increased to 20,000lb (9,000kg). Service evaluation soon revealed the type's performance shortcomings in comparison with the B-47, and no production order was placed.

The North American B-45

North American Aviation's design, the XB-45, was regarded as an interim aircraft from the beginning. Its configuration was deliberately kept conventional to avoid any pitfalls that might emerge in advanced aerodynamic design, the idea being that it would yield valuable information that would permit the designers to develop more advanced construction methods and operational techniques. Similar thinking prevailed in the design of Britain's Vickers Valiant, the first of the jet medium

Of unusual configuration, the Douglas XB-42 Mixmaster attack bomber had two 1,800hp Allison engines in the rear fuselage, driving contra-rotating 'pusher' propellers. (McDonnell Douglas)

bombers (the so-called V-bombers) to enter production for the RAF; yet, in service, both types enjoyed a success that was quite unforeseen. The B-45 Tornado proved superior to both the B-46 and B-48; it went into production for the USAF and entered service in 1948, thereafter serving for many years in the tactical bombing and reconnaissance roles.

The Douglas XB-42 and XB-43

The USAF's requirement for a post-war successor to the Tactical Air Command's Douglas A-26 Invader in the high-speed attack role produced two interesting designs. The first of these was the Douglas XB-43, which itself was developed from the wartime XB-42 Mixmaster. The XB-42 was an unorthodox design with two 1,800hp Allison V-1710-125 engines installed in tandem in the fuselage and driving contra-rotating propellers mounted behind a cruciform tail unit. Two prototypes were built, and the second aircraft, the XB-42A, had auxiliary turbojets mounted under the wing.

The XB-43, unofficially named 'Versatile', was a straightforward turbojet-powered conversion of the XB-42 and was fitted with two General Electric J35-GE-3 engines buried in the fuselage and fed via lateral air intakes positioned in the fuselage sides just aft of the cockpit. The XB-43, which made its first flight on 17 May 1946, had a conventional fin and tailplane but was unusual in having two separate cockpit canopies, situated side-by-side, under which the pilot and co-pilot sat; the third crew member was housed in the glazed nose.

The XB-42A was a variant of the XB-42 with auxiliary turbojets mounted under the wings. (McDonnell Douglas)

The XB-43 was a turbojet-powered version of the XB-42, the first of two prototypes flying on 17 May 1946. (McDonnell Douglas)

Originally designated XA-45, the Martin XB-51 was designed to replace the B-26 Invader in the high-speed tactical-bombing role, but lost out to the English Electric Canberra. (Martin)

The aircraft could carry a maximum bomb load of 8,000lb (3,600kg), but no defensive armament was incorporated.

The first XB-43 (44-61508) was followed by a second prototype, 44-61509, which had a solid nose. Both machines were evaluated at the USAF Flight Test Center during 1947, where they showed performance figures that included a maximum speed of 503mph (809km/h) at sea level and a service ceiling of 38,200ft (11,650m). The aircraft had a maximum range of 1,400 miles (2,250km), or 1,100 miles (1,770km) with an 8,000lb bomb load. Flight testing, however, also revealed some undesirable traits, including instability at certain points of the flight envelope, and the XB-43 was not ordered into production. The second prototype, however, went on to play an important part as an engine test bed from 1948, assisting in the development of the J47 turbojet.

The Martin XB-51

The design submitted by Glenn Martin to meet the high-speed tactical bomber requirement, the Model 234 XB-51, was far more radical. Originally designated XA-45, it had a thin, variable-incidence wing swept at an angle of 35 degrees. It was powered by three General Electric J47-GE-13 turbojets, two mounted in pods under the forward fuselage and the third in the tail. The tail surfaces were swept, the tailplane being mounted on top of the fin, and the aircraft had a tandem-wheel undercarriage. Two prototypes, 46-685 and 46-686, were ordered in June 1946; the first flew on 28 October 1949 and the second on 17 April 1950. The XB-51 was fast – its top speed was 645mph (1,040km/h) at sea level – and its maximum range was 1,613 miles (2,595km). The operational version would have been very heavily armed, with a battery of eight 20mm cannon in the nose and up to 10,400lb (4,700kg) of bombs over a 1,000-mile (1,600km) range. The handling characteristics of the XB-51, however, left a lot to be desired, and further development of the type was abandoned when the English Electric Canberra was found admirably suited to Tactical Air Command's requirements. The Canberra was then licence-built by Martin as the B-57.

Chapter 4
The RAF's Early Jet Bombers

Originally designed for the radar-bombing role as a replacement for the de Havilland Mosquito, the English Electric Canberra was the greatest success story of Britain's post-war aviation industry and was still in service in the twenty-first century, more than fifty years after the prototype was rolled out. Four prototypes of the Canberra B.1 were produced and the first of these flew on 13 May 1949, powered by Rolls-Royce Avon turbojets.

Problems with the radar bomb-aiming equipment, however, led to the redesign of the nose with a visual bomb-aiming position, and with this modification the fifth aircraft became the Canberra B.2, the type entering service with No. 101 Squadron RAF Bomber Command in May 1951. By this time a photo-reconnaissance version, the Canberra PR.3, had also flown; this was basically a B.2 with a battery of seven cameras for high-level photo-reconnaissance, and entered service with No 540 Squadron in 1953.

The Short Sperrin

The Canberra was not a strategic bomber, although in its early years it undertook the strategic-bombing role pending the introduction of the RAF's V-bombers, the Valiant, Vulcan and Victor. Like the Canberra, these aircraft are outside the scope of this book, but there was a fourth, much less well-known, aircraft in the equation. This was the Short SA.4 Sperrin, which was developed by Short Brothers to meet the same specification, B.35/46, that produced the other three aircraft; however, because it was a much more conventional aircraft it was quickly realized that it would be more suited to a less demanding specification, B.14/46. The Sperrin's wing, which was uniform in taper from root to tip, was mounted in the high shoulder position on a deep fuselage, while the completely conventional tail unit comprised a single fin and rudder and a tailplane with 13 degrees

The prototype English Electric Canberra, VN799, then known as the A1, seen on roll-out at Warton in May 1949. (BAe)

of dihedral. It had originally been intended to fit the aircraft with a jettisonable nose section to form a safety capsule for high-altitude escape, but tests with models revealed that severe tumbling would occur before the supporting parachutes could deploy, so instead the crew was housed in a normal pressure cabin. In fact, the only unconventional thing about the Sperrin was the arrangement of its four Rolls-Royce Avon turbojets, which were mounted in pairs in nacelles that hugged both upper and lower wing surfaces.

Two Sperrin prototypes, VX158 and VX161, were built using production jigs, and the first aircraft was taken into the air by test pilot Tom Brooke-Smith at Aldergrove, Northern Ireland, on 10 August 1951. After company trials it went to the Royal Aircraft Establishment to carry out operational testing of new high-altitude radar-navigation and bombing equipment that would later be fitted to the V-bombers. The second prototype, VX161, flew on 12 August 1952 and was subsequently employed in aerodynamic weapons testing, dropping concrete 'bomb shapes' in connection with the development of Britain's first operational atomic bomb, the MC.Mk.1 '*Blue Danube*'. It continued flying until 1956, when one of its undercarriage doors was 'borrowed' to replace one that had broken away from VX158 over the sea. VX161 never flew again, and was scrapped early in 1957.

VX158, meanwhile, after its stint with the RAE, had returned to Aldergrove in the spring of 1955 to be developed as a flying test bed for the 15,000lb (30.2kN) s.t. de Havilland Gyron turbojet, first flying in this new configuration on 7 July. In 1957, however, the Gyron engine programme was cancelled, and VX158 was scrapped at Hatfield in 1958.

Had the need arisen, there is no doubt that the Short Sperrin could have been placed into production very quickly, for very few problems were experienced during its test phase and after, and it would certainly have been a very useful weapons-delivery system, having shown its ability to release payloads of up to 10,000lb (4,500kg) from an altitude of 40,000ft (12,000m) and a speed of Mach 0.78. The fact that it was not adopted for production was due solely to the higher all-round performance prospects of another conventional design, the Vickers Type 660.

The Vickers Valiant

Vickers' last design before the end of the war had been the Windsor, a four-engined heavy bomber. Three prototypes had been built and flown, four more were in hand and 300 production aircraft were on order when the war's end brought cancellation, and a halt to piston-engined bomber development. Under the direction of their new designer, George Edwards, Vickers evolved a conventionally configured jet bomber to meet B.35/46, but it fell short of the requirement and was rejected in favour of the more futuristic Avro and Handley Page designs. In 1948, however, it was decided to go ahead with the development of the Type 660 as an 'interim' design, and a new specification, B.9/48, was written around it.

The problem with the development of the new V-bombers, designed to give the RAF a formidable medium-range nuclear strike capability in the 1950s, was that the timescale was all wrong. After the war, the new Socialist government in Britain had assumed that there would be no major war threat in Europe for at least another decade, and everything, including the British military-aircraft development programme, was geared to that assumption. But in 1948, with the Russians blockading Berlin, there was a sudden pressing need to bring advanced aircraft into service far more quickly than had previously been envisaged, and so the Vickers 660 was selected to fill the bomber gap.

Just how adequately it did so is a matter of aviation history. For several critical years, from 1955 until the operational debut of the Vulcan and Victor at the end of the decade, it was the Vickers Type 660 Valiant that formed the backbone of the RAF's medium bomber force. It continued in service until 1964, when the V-Force switched to low-level penetration tactics and this punishing kind of flying created fatigue cracks in the Valiant's main spar, causing it to be prematurely retired.

The sad fact was that a derivative of the Valiant might have continued in service for much longer, had its development potential been fully appreciated. On 4 September 1953, Vickers flew the prototype Valiant B.2, WJ954, which differed substantially from the production B.1s. The fuselage forward of the wing was lengthened by $4\frac{1}{2}$ft (1.37m), the whole airframe strengthened, the fuel

Resplendent in its white anti-flash paintwork, Valiant B.1 XD823 is pictured prior to its delivery to RAF Bomber Command. (RAF)

The all-black Vickers Valiant B.Mk.2, designed for low-level operations. (Philip Jarrett)

tankage increased and the geometry of the undercarriage radically altered, the main units retracting into pods protruding from the wing trailing edges. The B.2 was developed for the target-marking role, and so was designed for high-speed operation at very low level; its makers claimed that it would have a maximum speed of 665mph (1,070km/h) at sea level, although during trials the aircraft only reached 552mph (888km/h). Nevertheless, this was a good 50mph (80km/h) faster than the B.1, and there is little doubt that the B.2 would have been a formidable addition to RAF Bomber Command's striking power. However, the target-making role was made obsolete by advances in the navigation and bomb-aiming equipment carried by 'normal' bombers, and the promising B.2 programme was abandoned. In the mid-1950s it was not known that bombers would soon be confined to operations at extreme low level in order to penetrate enemy defences of growing sophistication.

Flying Bombs

The arming of the V-Force with stand-off weapons had been under active consideration since 1946 when the Air Staff had stated a requirement for a guided bomb. Work on this project – OR.1059 *Blue Boar* – was undertaken by Vickers-Armstrongs at Weybridge, and in 1949 drawings were produced of a television-guided bomb designed to be carried in a bomber's bomb bay, with flip-out wings deployed at launch. It was to be capable of being launched at altitudes of up to 60,000ft (18,000m) and at speeds of up to 600kt (1,100km/h). The guidance system, however, was not to the Air Staff's liking, and in June 1954 *Blue Boar* was cancelled in favour of the development of an inertially guided stand-off weapon with a range of 100nm (185km) and carrying an atomic warhead. An Operational Requirement for this weapon, OR.1132, was issued on 3 September 1954.

Meanwhile, in 1951, there had been strong intelligence indications (which turned out to be unfounded) that the Soviet Union was on the point of carrying out some kind of military operation against the West, probably in 1953, and Winston Churchill, heading a new Conservative government, ordered a complete reappraisal of all Britain's defence capabilities. As far as Bomber Command was concerned, the position was serious: its main equipment was still the piston-engined Lincoln and Washington, with the Canberra just entering service, and, with the Valiant's Initial Operational Capability (IOC) at least four years away, the Command had little in the way of offensive capability.

As a stop-gap measure two companies, Bristol and Vickers-Armstrongs, were invited to submit proposals for an unmanned flying-bomb design in April 1951. The specification (UB109T) required a weapon that could be launched from a ramp and carry a 5,000lb (2,300kg) warhead at 450kt (830km/h) and 45,000ft (14,000m) over a range of 400nm (740km), just enough to enable it to hit targets in East Germany from sites in the United Kingdom. The design submitted by Bristol, the Type 182 Blue Rapier, was built entirely of plastic apart from the steel wing spar, and was intended for cheap mass production. It had a span of 20ft 10in (6.4m), a length of 33ft 10in (10.4m), and an all-up weight of 9,500lb (4,300kg). It had a swept wing and a small delta tailplane mounted on a stubby fin. Launching was to be achieved by means of a steam catapult, the missile cruising to its target under the power of a turbojet mounted under the fuselage. Estimated maximum speed was 550kt (1,020km/h) and the weapon was intended to be barrage-launched.

Bristol estimated that each round would cost only £600, and tentative Ministry of Supply plans called for a production run of 20,000 rounds. Two prototypes were ordered under the designation Bristol 182R; these were to be made of aluminium, equipped with Armstrong Siddeley Viper turbojets. As the prototypes were to be launched conventionally, they were fitted with undercarriages cannibalized from de Havilland Venom fighters.

The Vickers design to UB109T was known as Red Rapier and was built in light alloy, having three Rolls-Royce Soar expendable turbojets mounted on fuselage outriggers. Like Bristol, Vickers began construction of a prototype, but both companies abandoned the project when UB109T was cancelled in 1953. From now on, the emphasis would be on getting the V-bombers into service as quickly as possible, and equipping them with a stand-off missile to enhance their survival chances. In due course, this weapon emerged as *Blue Steel*, which armed five V-Force squadrons (three Vulcan and two Victor) from 1962 until 1969, when the RAF relinquished its nuclear deterrent role to the Royal Navy's Polaris missile submarines.

Chapter 5

France's Post-War Recovery

At the end of the war in Europe, France's aircraft industry lay in ruins, its factories destroyed or dismantled, its designers scattered far and wide. In seeking to establish a leading role in post-war aviation, therefore, France was faced with a mammoth, twofold task. The first priority was an industrial one, to rebuild the factories and reassemble the design bureaux; the second was of a purely technical nature, involving the design and production of new combat types to meet the demands of the French air force, the Armée de l'Air in the jet age.

The second priority was much harder to achieve than the first. Although some French designers had made studies of jet-aircraft projects in secret during the Occupation, they lagged far behind the Germans and the Allies in the field, from the viewpoints of both airframe and engine design. At the war's end, even with the knowledge that turbojet-powered aircraft were the only answer to meeting future high-performance requirements, some designers persisted in launching new piston-engined projects that resulted only in wasting of time and dissipation of resources.

The Jet-Engine Problem

One of the main problems that confronted the French designers was the acquisition of suitable turbojet engines. It would be a long time before turbojets of French design became available, and in the meantime two options were available. The first was to develop an existing German turbojet: the engine selected was the BMW 109-003, an axial-flow turbojet that stemmed from original design work carried out at Spandau by the Bramo Company in 1938. A prototype engine had been tested in 1940, by which time Bramo had been taken over by BMW, and two of the first production batch were used to power the Messerschmitt Me 262V-1. Series-production BMW 109-003-A2s also powered the Heinkel He 162 and Arado Ar 234. In early post-war France, development work on the 109-003 was assigned to a team led by Dr H. Oestrich and consisting of technical personnel who had worked at the Atelier Technique Aéronautique Rickenbach, a BMW plant installed near Lake Constance during the war. The factory's initials gave the new engine its name: Atar.

Production Atar 101s, however, would not be available before 1948, and so the French also had to exercise the second option, which was to build British turbojets under licence. In 1946, therefore, Hispano-Suiza signed a contract with Rolls-Royce for the licence production of the Nene 101 and 102 engines, and it was the latter that was to power France's first generation of jet aircraft. Yet it would be some time before the first Nenes came off the French production line, and in the meantime French designers were forced to make do with Junkers Jumo 004 turbojets to power their early experimental machines. By this time, French engineers and pilots had acquired a limited amount of jet experience with the aid of three captured (and Jumo 004-powered) Me 262s, which had been delivered to the flight-test centre at Brétigny. The first one flew on 16 June 1945, and subsequent test flying had revealed all too harshly the shortcomings of the Jumo 004 on which the French design bureaux, for the time being at least, were forced to rely.

It was a Jumo 004 that powered France's first experimental jet aircraft, the Sud-Ouest SO.6000 Triton, which flew for the first time on 11 November 1946 with test pilot Daniel Rastel at the controls, and also the Arsenal VG-70, which first flew on 23 June 1948. Other experimental jets were powered by Rolls-Royce Derwent engines purchased directly from the UK.

The Aerocentre NC 270 and NC 271

Of all the early post-war French designs, one of the most promising was the Aerocentre NC 270 which – had it reached fruition – would have been the contemporary of the English Electric Canberra, the North American B-45 Tornado and the Ilyushin Il-28. The NC 270 was designed by a government department, Guerre et Transport, which was roughly the equivalent of Britain's Ministry of Supply, under the direction of M. Robin. The aircraft that took shape on the drawing board was very elegant indeed, with a circular-section fuselage, slightly swept wings and tail surfaces, and the tailplane mounted on top of the rudder; power came from two Nene engine nacelles mounted flush with the fuselage sides at the wing roots. The aircraft was to carry a pilot and navigator, the latter also being responsible for the operation of a television-controlled tail turret of German origin and armed with four 15mm cannon. A 5-ton bomb load was to be carried.

The prototype NC 270 slowly took shape in the factory of the Societe Nationale de Construction Aeronautique Centre (SNCAC), which was shortened to 'Aerocentre', at Billancourt. The flight characteristics of the NC 270 were to be tested with the help of two flying scale-models: the NC 271-01, which was a glider, and the NC 271-02, which was to be powered by a liquid-fuel rocket motor. The NC 271-01, first revealed publicly at the 1946 Salon, was of mixed wood-and-metal construction and was a quarter-scale model of the prototype bomber. It was a single-seater, and in an emergency the entire nose section could be jettisoned with the pilot inside. To test the separation system, several test flights were made with a mock-up of the nose section suspended under a Handley Page Halifax.

The NC 271-01 took to the air for the first time in November 1948, mounted on the back of Sud-Est SE 161 Languedoc F-BCUT, and made eleven more captive flights in the next three months. Its first free flight was made on 28 January 1949, with Claude Dellys at the controls; it lasted for seven minutes, the little aircraft reaching a maximum gliding speed of 225km/h (140mph).

Meanwhile, at Billancourt, the second NC 271 had been built. Its rocket motor, a Walter HWK 109-509A, was taken from a Messerschmitt Me 163 *Komet*, and was to have boosted the NC 271-02 to an estimated maximum speed of 900km/h (560mph), slightly more than the full-size bomber was expected to achieve. The latter, meanwhile, was nearing completion; the fuselage was intact, with wings and engines mounted and tail fin in place, while the outer wing sections and tailplane were also complete and awaiting final assembly. The first flight was scheduled for September 1949, after the rocket-powered model had completed its test programme.

The NC 271-02, complete with rocket motor, was taken to Orléans-Bricy in May 1949, where the plan was to mount it on the back of a Heinkel He 274 bomber and launch it at an altitude of 10,000m (33,000ft). While preparations for this flight were under way, however, SNCAC went into liquidation, with the result that both NC 271s were scrapped. So was the full-size NC 270, which was then 85 per cent complete.

The Sud-Ouest SO.4000

Another early Nene-powered light-bomber design was the twin-jet Sud-Ouest SO.4000, which was powered by two Nene 102 engines, mounted side by side in the centre fuselage. The full-size aircraft was preceded by two scale models, the SO.M-1 and M-2. The first of these, a glider, was registered F-WFDJ and was aerodynamically tested on a rig mounted on the back of a Heinkel He 274; it was subsequently mounted on Languedoc F-BCUT at Orléons-Bricy and made its first gliding flight on 26 September 1949 from a height of 5,000m (16,400ft). Before that, however, the SO.M-2 (F-WFDK) had also flown on 13 April 1949, powered by a Rolls-Royce Derwent turbojet. Both scale models were piloted by Jacques Guignard, Sud-Ouest's chief test pilot, and in May 1950 he reached a speed of 1000km/h (620mph) while flying the M-2.

The SO.4000 bomber prototype was rolled out on 5 March 1950. Registered F-WBBL, it was generally similar in configuration to the scale models. The two crew were seated in tandem in a small, pressurized cockpit in the extreme forward fuselage, which was of large oval section. The low-aspect-ratio wing was swept 31 degrees at quarter-chord and was mounted in high-mid position at mid-point on the fuselage, above the weapons bay,

First flown on 16 March 1951, the SO.4000 was France's first jet bomber design. The prototype, F-WBBL, made only one flight. (Musée de l'Air)

and it was planned that production aircraft should also carry an armament of two remotely controlled cannon, mounted in wingtip barbettes. The undercarriage was complex, having four mainwheels, each with independent levered-suspension legs, and a tall, single nosewheel member. The undercarriage, in fact, proved to be too fragile, because it collapsed during taxiing trials on 23 April 1950, causing extensive damage.

Repaired and with a strengthened undercarriage, F-WBBL flew for the first time on 15 March 1951, with Daniel Rastel at the controls. The aircraft proved to be seriously underpowered and unstable, and it never flew again. Sud-Aviation subsequently turned its attention to meeting a French Air Staff specification, issued in July 1951 and calling for an aircraft capable of fulfilling three separate tasks: all-weather interception, close support and medium- and high-level bombing. This was to emerge as the SO.4050 Vautour, which first flew in October 1952 powered by Atar 101B turbojets.

Chapter 6

The USSR's Tactical Bombers and Assault Aircraft

At the end of the Second World War, and for some years afterward, the mainstay of the Soviet Air Force's tactical bomber squadrons was the twin-engined Tupolev Tu-2, and designing a jet-powered replacement for this aircraft was accorded a high priority with the leading Soviet design bureaux. Tupolev met this requirement without expending too much time and effort on it – he was fully occupied with strategic bombers from 1944 onward – by modifying the existing Tu-2 design and powering it with two imported Rolls-Royce Derwent turbojets, slung in underwing nacelles. The resulting aircraft was designated Tu-12 (it was also sometimes known by the manufacturer's designation, Tu-77) and was flown for the first time on 27 July 1947, by test pilot A.D. Perelyot. The Tu-12 carried a crew of four and reached a maximum speed of 787km/h (489mph); a batch of about fifty aircraft was produced, and used to provide a nucleus of Soviet crews with multi-jet experience.

The Tu-12 also served to evaluate the Rolls-Royce Derwent under operational conditions. The Derwent was one of two British turbojets delivered in some quantity to the Soviet Union in 1947 – the other being the Rolls-Royce Nene – and their delivery to the USSR solved one of the biggest dilemmas that had confronted Soviet designers in the post-war years: the difficulty of acquiring efficient jet engines. During the war, the Soviet aircraft industry, although it had investigated rocket-powered aircraft, had paid scant attention to jet propulsion, and although the acquisition of large numbers of German turbojets at the war's end formed a basis for further development, the German engines were generally underpowered and prone to catastrophic failure after a life of about twenty-five hours. German aerodynamic knowledge was gradually being incorporated into new Russian designs, but these were of little use without the right kind of power plant. By the middle of 1946 it was glaringly obvious that, despite all the German expertise, Russian engine technology was lagging a long way behind that of the west.

The supply of British turbojets to the Soviet Union by Britain's post-war Socialist government, naive though it may appear with hindsight to have

A slightly retouched photograph of the Tupolev Tu-12. Also known as the Tu-77, this aircraft was used to provide a nucleus of Soviet aircrew with multi-jet experience, but was never employed in the tactical-bombing role for which it was designed. (Tupolev)

been, was not out of character in the climate of the times, and neither engine was then on the secret list. The Russians asked for the engines and got them, and within weeks were turning out their own accurate copies. The British engines arrived just in time to power the first Soviet bomber designed for jet propulsion from the outset, the Ilyushin Il-22.

Medium Bombers

Originally intended to be powered by four Junkers Jumo 004 turbojets in underwing pods, the Il-22 was in fact fitted with four Derwents before its maiden flight on 24 July 1947 in the hands of test pilot brothers Vladimir and Konstantin Kokkinaki. The sole example caused a sensation in Western circles when it appeared over Tushino soon afterwards, but its career was short-lived, the aircraft being retired after a two-month test programme. The Il-22 had a crew of five and carried a defensive armament of four 23mm cannon, two in a dorsal turret and two in the tail. It could carry a payload of 3,000kg (6,600lb) and reached a top speed of 718km/h (446mph). Service ceiling was 11,108m (36,420ft) and maximum range 1,866km (1,160 miles). In its overall configuration the Il-22 bore a strong resemblance to the German Heinkel He 323 jet-bomber project of the Second World War, and there was speculation that the Il-22 was in fact the He 323 completed and flown by Ilyushin; in reality, however, the Il-22 was a completely original design, and was much larger than the Heinkel machine.

The Il-22 was one of four aircraft designed to a specification that required a medium-range jet bomber capable of carrying an internal bomb load of 3,000kg; the three others were the Tupolev Tu-72, Ilyushin Il-28 and Sukhoi Su-10. The latter aircraft, although conventional in airframe design, had an unconventional engine arrangement in that its four Lyulka TR-1A (Derwent) turbojets were superimposed one above the other on a thin wing. This method was also adopted by Short Brothers in their design of the SA.4 Sperrin, and had the advantage of leaving the wing aerodynamically clean. The Su-10 was designed to carry a crew of four and a bomb load of up to 4,000kg (8,800lb), rocket-assisted take-off equipment being used in an overload condition. Defensive armament was four 20mm cannon, two in a dorsal turret and two

Although the Ilyushin Il-22 bore a strong resemblance to Germany's wartime Heinkel He 323 jet-bomber project, it was in fact a completely new design. (Ilyushin)

in the tail; estimated maximum speed was 940km/h (580mph), and maximum range 2,000km (1,240 miles). The prototype Su-10 was almost complete by the beginning of 1948, when it was abandoned in favour of the more promising Il-28, which had already flown, and the Su-10 was thereafter used as an instructional airframe.

Tupolev's design to meet the medium-range bomber requirement, the Tu-72, was a straightforward aircraft using conventional aerodynamics and was designed to be powered by two Rolls-Royce Nenes. Before building of the prototype began, it was decided to incorporate a third turbojet – a Derwent – in the rear fuselage as an added safety measure in case one of the two main engines failed. Following this and other modifications the aircraft was re-designated Tu-73, and the prototype was flown for the first time by A.D. Perelyot on 27 July 1947. A second prototype was designated Tu-78, and this joined the test programme in 1948. With the initial test phase successfully completed, plans were made for the series production of the aircraft. By this time, however, flight testing of the Ilyushin Il-28, a smaller, lighter aircraft powered by two RD-45 (Nene) turbojets, had shown it to be the better of the two designs in every aspect except range, and the Il-28 was consequently selected to equip the light-bomber squadrons of the Frontovaia Aviatsiya, the Soviet tactical air force. Known by the NATO reporting name 'Beagle', it performed its task admirably for many years and was exported in substantial numbers.

The Tupolev design continued to be developed for service with the Soviet Naval Air Arm, and the

The Ilyushin Il-30 tactical bomber was a swept-wing version of the Il-28, but despite some promise it was not selected for service. (Ilyushin)

prototype of the production version, the Tu-81, flew in 1949. This was powered by the latest Soviet version of the Nene, the Klimov VK-1, which was reliable enough to allow the designers to dispense with the tail-mounted turbojet. Given the in-service designation Tu-14 (NATO: 'Bosun') the jet bomber entered service in the attack role with the Naval Air Arm, and also served in the photo-reconnaissance and electronic-intelligence roles.

In June 1949 Tupolev also produced a swept-wing variant of the basic Tu-14 design, the Tu-82. Only one prototype was built, powered by two VK-1 turbojets, and although it was not a success it was the first Soviet swept-wing jet bomber to fly. Piloted by A.D. Perelyot, the Tu-82 reached a speed of 874km/h (543mph) and had a 2,735km (1,700-mile) range. Aerodynamically, the aircraft left a great deal to be desired, but much experimental flying was undertaken with it and Tupolev envisaged a production variant, the Tu-86, powered by two Mikulin AM-2 engines. This, however, reached the design stage only.

Successors to the Il-28

With the Il-28 firmly established in Soviet Air Force service, meanwhile, the Ilyushin design bureau lost no time in starting work on a potential successor. Designated Il-30, this flew in 1951 and was the first Russian bomber to reach a speed of 1,000km/h (620mph) in level flight. An elegant and aerodynamically clean aircraft, the Il-30 was basically an Il-28 with swept flying surfaces, and was similar in both size and concept to America's Douglas A-3 Skywarrior and B-66 Destroyer. The Il-30, which had a 30-degree leading-edge sweep and carried a crew of four, was the first Soviet aircraft to feature a novel undercarriage arrangement that was later to be used on several operational Soviet types: twin-wheel main undercarriage units, mounted in tandem in the fuselage, and twin-wheel outrigger units retracting into the engine nacelles. The Il-30 was powered by two underslung TR-3 turbojets and defensive armament comprised twin 23mm cannon in barbettes above and below the forward fuselage, with two more 23mm cannon in the tail. The aircraft could carry a maximum bomb load of 3,000kg (6,600lb), range was 3,500km (2,175 miles) and operational ceiling 13,000m (43,000ft). A promising concept, despite the fact that it experienced some stability problems, the Il-30 was nevertheless not selected for series production.

Ilyushin's next design was the Il-46, another Il-28 derivative. The Il-46, which was essentially a scaled-up Il-28, began life as a contender to meet the Soviet Air Force's requirement for a Tu-4 replacement. The prototype was flown for the first time on 15 August 1952 by V.K. Kokkinaki and was powered by two Lyulka Al-5 turbojets, which gave it a maximum speed of 927km/h (576mph) at 3,000m (10,000ft). Normal bomb load on a long-range mission was 3,0000kg, but this could be increased to 6,000kg (13,000lb) over shorter ranges. The bomber carried a crew of three and defensive armament comprised two fixed 23mm cannon in the nose and two in the tail. Maximum range was 5,000km (3,000 miles) and operational ceiling 12,000m 40,000ft). In the event, Tupolev's Tu-16 (NATO: 'Badger') won the contest, being of more advanced design than the Il-46 and possessing a better performance. The Il-46 was offered as a tactical bomber,

Ilyushin's next design after the Il-30 was the Il-46, which was conceived as a replacement for the Tu-4. The Tupolev Tu-16 was selected in preference. (Ilyushin)

When it was shown to Western visitors in 1956 the Ilyushin Il-54 was erroneously believed to have entered Soviet Air Force service and was given the NATO reporting name 'Blowlamp'. (Ilyushin)

but this idea was dropped and the aircraft never went into production.

The last of Ilyushin's experimental designs of the 1950s was the Il-54, a three-seat light attack bomber with its wings swept at 55 degrees and two underslung Lyulka AL-7 turbojets. The aircraft was built in 1954 and underwent a thorough flight-test programme in the course of the following year, reaching a maximum speed of 1,149km/h (714mph). The aircraft's range was 3,000km (1,490 miles) and operational ceiling 13,000m (42,000ft). In 1956, the Il-54 prototype was shown to a western delegation led by USAF Chief of Staff General Nathan F. Twining at Moscow's Kubinka Airport; it was immediately allocated the NATO code-name 'Blowlamp' and assumed to be in series production for the FA (*Frontovaia Aviatsiya*, or 'Frontal Aviation' – the Soviet/Russian tactical air force). What the Western delegates did not realise was that the IL-54's career was over and that it was already a museum piece.

A New *Shturmovik*

During the Second World War, one of the most important aspects of Russian combat-aircraft design – and one that had given the Soviets a decided tactical advantage during the armoured battles from

One of the ugliest aircraft ever built, the Ilyushin Il-20 was intended as a replacement for the Il-2/Il-10 Shturmovik series of assault aircraft. (Ilyushin)

1943 onward – was the concept of the *shturmovik*, or heavily armoured assault aircraft. The *shturmovik* in most widespread use during the war was the Ilyushin Il-2, and this was followed into service by the Il-10. A derivative of the latter, produced in 1945, was the Il-16, which was fitted with a Mikulin AM-43 twelve-cylinder liquid-cooled engine, but the type experienced aerodynamic stability problems and by the time these were rectified the Il-16 was already obsolete. Fifty-three aircraft were built before production was abandoned.

The Ilyushin team nevertheless continued their studies of piston-engined *shturmovik* designs, and in 1948 they produced the Il-20, which was certainly the ugliest aircraft ever to emerge from this famous design bureau. Unofficially named *Gorbun* (hunchback), the Il-20 was powered by an AM-47F twelve-cylinder liquid-cooled engine and the pilot's cockpit was perched on top of the engine to give the best possible all-round visibility. The gunner sat behind the pilot, a step lower down, with a pair of NS-23 23mm cannon in a remotely controlled barbette. Offensive armament consisted of four fixed 23mm cannon mounted in the wings outboard of the main undercarriage and up to 1,000kg (2,200lb) of bombs and rockets. During flight testing, the Il-20 reached a maximum speed of 515km/h (320mph); range was 1,680km (1,040 miles) and operational ceiling 7,755m (25,426ft). However, only one prototype was built and no further development was undertaken. The Il-20 designation was later allocated to a civil version of the Il-28 and a military variant of the Il-18 airliner.

Ilyushin's last venture into *shturmovik* design, before the concept was abandoned (at least until it was resurrected in the form of dedicated assault aircraft like the Sukhoi Su-25 'Frogfoot', many years later) was the twin-jet Il-40, which first flew in 1953 and which was allocated the NATO reporting name 'Brawny'. The Il-40 was powered by two AM-5F turbojets mounted side-by-side in the centre fuselage and exhausting aft of the wing trailing edge. The engines were fed via individual circular nose intakes, an arrangement that gave the aircraft a curious, pig-like snout. The thick-section wing was low-mounted, with a 35-degree leading-edge sweep, and carried four 37mm cannon. Defensive armament comprised twin 23mm cannon in a remotely controlled tail barbette; these were operated by a rear gunner seated behind the pilot in a long, armoured cockpit compartment. The Il-40 was very heavily armoured, to the extent that the weight of armour reduced its performance below acceptable levels; manoeuvrability also left much to be desired, and the aircraft would have been hard pressed to survive in a hostile fighter environment. Several prototypes were built and evaluated in 1953–4, and the best performance figures included a top speed at sea level of 965km/h (600mph) and a range of 1,000km (620 miles). So the last of the USSR's *shturmoviks* slipped into oblivion, its role eclipsed by a new generation of strike fighters. These were developed, in the main, from the jet interceptors which, in the early 1950s, were enabling the Soviet Air Force to confront its potential NATO adversaries on an increasingly equal footing.

Part III
Fighter Development, 1945–55

Chapter 7
The USAF: the Supersonic Challenge

German Developments

It was only when they occupied the whole of a defeated Germany in 1945, and had the opportunity to investigate fully the labyrinth of underground facilities built by the enemy, that the Allies came to appreciate the staggering technological advances that had been made by German aeronautical science.

At Leck, in Schleswig-Holstein, they found some fifty examples of a new jet fighter, the Heinkel He 162 *Salamander*, a diminutive aircraft with twin fins and a turbojet mounted in a pod above the fuselage. More He 162s were discovered at Salzburg, where they had been about to go into action alongside the Messerschmitt Me 262s of General Adolf Galland's elite Jagdverband 44. Developed as a last-ditch air-defence fighter in the closing stages of the war, the He 162 – also known as the *Volksjäger* ('People's Fighter') – had progressed from drawing board to first flight in a mere ten weeks. Most of the examples delivered to the Luftwaffe were assigned to Jagdgeschwader 1, the aircraft having been rushed through its operational trials by a special unit, Erprobungskommando 162, under the leadership of Colonel Heinz Bär, one of Germany's top air aces with 220 victories. Sixteen of Bär's victories had been gained while flying the Me 262 – in total, twenty-two Luftwaffe pilots became jet aces, destroying five or more Allied aircraft while flying the Me 262.

But aircraft like the Me 262 and the He 162 were the tip of the iceberg: other, even more advanced fighters were either on the drawing board or in various stages of construction and one – the Dornier Do 335 – was flying in prototype form and had entered production. An unconventional aircraft, the Do 335 was powered by two DB 603 engines mounted in tandem, one forward and one aft with the cockpit in between. Armed with 30mm cannon, the Do 335 was capable of 450mph (720km/h) and would have presented the Allies with a formidable challenge, had it been available in quantity some months earlier.

The First US Jet Fighters

The USAAF's principal fighter assets at the end of the Second World War comprised the later versions of well-tried piston-engined designs such as the P-51 Mustang and P-47 Thunderbolt. America's first jet fighter was the Bell P-59 Airacomet, the prototype of which had first flown on 1 October 1942 powered by two General Electric I-A turbojets, derived from the British Whittle W.2B engine. A higher-powered engine, the 1,400lb-thrust (6.2kN) I-16, was installed in the thirteen trials aircraft that followed. The Airacomet proved to be underpowered and its performance fell far below expectations, so the original order for 100 aircraft was reduced. Twenty P-59As were built with J31-GE-3 engines, and thirty P-59Bs with J31-GE-5s. The Airacomet did not see operational service in the war.

America's first fully operational jet fighter was the Lockheed P-80 Shooting Star, which was of very conventional design and which was to become the workhorse of the American tactical fighter-bomber and fighter-interceptor squadrons for five years after the war, giving excellent service in

The Lockheed P-80 Shooting Star was America's first fully operational jet fighter. (Lockheed)

Fitted with swept flying surfaces, the original XP-86 became the F-86 Sabre, one of the most effective jet fighters of all time. (North American)

Korea. The prototype XP-80 was designed around a de Havilland H-1 turbojet which was supplied to the United States in July 1943, the aircraft being completed in just 143 days and making its first flight on 9 January 1944. In April 1945 two YP-80s were sent to England, where they were attached to the Eighth Air Force, and two more went to Italy, but none experienced any operational flying in Europe before the war's end. Early production P-80As entered USAAF service late in 1945 with the 412th Fighter Group, which became the 1st Fighter Group in July 1946 and comprised the 27th, 71st and 94th Fighter Squadrons. The P-80A was replaced by the P-80B in 1947; the major production version was the F-80C (the P prefix, standing for 'pursuit', having been changed to the much more logical F for 'fighter' in the meantime).

The Sabre

Towards the end of the Second World War, the USAAF, drawing on its combat experience, began to draw up specifications around four quite different fighter requirements. The first involved a medium-range day fighter that could also serve in the bomber-escort and ground-attack roles; the second, a medium-range high-altitude interceptor capable of destroying any bomber that a potential enemy could conceivably deploy over the next fifteen years or so; the third, a long-range 'penetration' fighter to fulfil the dual roles of bomber-escort and interdiction; and the fourth, a night and all-weather fighter.

The first of these requirements awakened the interest of North American Aviation, whose design team was then working on the NA-134, a projected carrier-borne jet fighter for the US Navy. This, like the XP-59A and XP-80, was of conventional straight-wing design and was well advanced, so North American offered a land-based version to the USAAF under the company designation NA-140. On 18 May 1945, North American received a contract for the building of three NA-140 prototypes under the USAAF designation XP-86. At the same time, 100 NA-141s (production developments of the NA-134 naval jet fighter) were ordered for the US Navy as FJ-1s, although this order was subsequently reduced to thirty aircraft. Known as the Fury, the FJ-1 flew for the first time on 27 November 1946 and went on to serve with Navy Fighter Squadron VF-51, remaining in service until 1949.

While construction of the XFJ-1 prototypes got under way, design development of the XP-86 and FJ-1 proceeded in parallel. A mock-up of the XP-86 was built and, in June 1945, was approved by the USAAF. There was, however, one worrying factor. According to North American's estimates, the XP-86 would have a maximum speed of 574mph (924km/h) at sea level, which fell short of the USAAF specification. Fortunately, it was at this point that material on German research into high-speed flight, in particular swept-wing designs, became available. North American obtained a complete Me 262 wing assembly and, after carrying out more than 1,000 wind tunnel tests on it, decided that the swept wing was the answer to the XP-86's performance problems.

45

The first jet-powered aircraft of delta-wing configuration to fly, the Convair XF-92A, owed much to the wartime design work of Dr Alexander Lippisch. (Convair)

The redesigned XP-86 airframe, featuring sweepback on all flying surfaces, was accepted by the USAAF on 1 November 1945 and received final approval on 28 February 1946. In December 1946 the USAAF placed a contract for an initial batch of thirty-three P-86A production aircraft, and on 8 August 1947 the first of two flying prototypes was completed, making its first flight under the power of a General Electric J35 turbojet. The second prototype, designated XF-86A, made its first flight on 18 May 1948, fitted with the more powerful General Electric J47-GE-1 engine, and deliveries of production F-86As began ten days later. These were used for various trials, which were accelerated when East–West tension rose as a result of the Soviet blockade of Berlin, and the first operational F-86As were delivered to the 1st Fighter Group early in 1949. As yet, the F-86A was an aircraft without a name, and one of the 1st Fighter Group's acts was to sponsor a competition to find a suitable one. Seventy-eight names were submitted, and one stood out above the rest. On 4 March 1949, the North American F-86 was officially named the Sabre.

The Convair XF-92

The Sabre went on to become one of the greatest military aircraft success stories of all time. It more than adequately met the first of the USAAF requirements and also – thanks to the outdated nature of the USSR's strategic-bomber forces in the immediate post-war years – was sufficient to meet the second. This gave the USAAF (which became the USAF in September 1947) time to reshape its medium-range interceptor requirement and call for an aircraft that would be missile-armed and incorporate an advanced fire-control system.

In a bid to meet this requirement, Convair was first off the mark with the design of a supersonic mixed-power interceptor. Drawing heavily on the results of wartime German research, the Convair design team decided to employ a delta wing. They received invaluable help in realizing this concept from Dr Alexander Lippisch, designer of the revolutionary Messerschmitt Me 163 *Komet* rocket fighter. At the war's end Lippisch had a number of fascinating projects on the drawing board, among them the piston-engined P.10 bomber. His next project, the delta-wing P.11, was to have been

The Republic XF-91 experimental high-altitude interceptor. Note the unusual, outward-retracting arrangement of the undercarriage, and the rocket motor housings above and below the tailpipe. (Fairchild Republic)

powered by two Junkers Jumo 004 turbojets, while the P.12 was to have had a built-in ramjet unit. This was abandoned in favour of the P.13a, which reached the most advanced development stage, although no prototype was completed. The ramjet for the P.12 and P.13a was to use solid fuel (powdered coal fuel), which would burn and combine with oxygen passing through the ramjet duct. Initial acceleration to the speed at which the ramjet would function would be provided by a booster rocket. The P.14 was another ramjet design, while the P.15 was a projected development of the Me 163 powered by a turbojet.

The Lippisch factory at Wiener Wald had been overrun by US forces in 1945 and its contents, together with Lippisch himself, were taken to the United States. One of his designs, the DM-1 delta-wing research glider, was subjected to extensive wind tunnel testing by the National Advisory Committee on Aeronautics (NACA – later to become NASA) and the information made available to Convair. As a result, Convair, in consultation with Lippisch, decided to build a flying delta-wing model of the proposed interceptor.

The latter, known as the Convair Model 7, was allocated the USAF designation XF-92. In an effort to save time and money, the flying scale-model, designated Model 7-002, used the component parts of five other aircraft. Powered by an Allison J33-A-23 turbojet, it made its first flight on 18 September 1948. The aircraft had a 60-degree delta wing with a thickness/chord ratio of 6.5 per cent, with elevons extending along the whole of the straight trailing edge to provide lateral and longitudinal control, and a large vertical fin to provide stability.

While testing of the Model 7-002 got under way, work proceeded with the development of the XF-92, which was to be powered by a 1,600lb (7.14kN) s.t. Westinghouse 130 turbojet for cruising flight and landing; additional power for take-off and combat was supplied by a Reaction Motors LR-11 four-chamber bi-fuel rocket engine giving 6,000lb (26.7kN) thrust. On 3 June 1949, however, further development was cancelled and the Model 7-002 was turned over to high-speed research work, being allocated the designation XF-92A. In 1951, the aircraft's original J33-A-23 turbojet was replaced by a J33-A-29 with reheat; this raised the XF-92A's loaded weight to 15,000lb (6,800kg), but it reached speeds of up to Mach 0.95 at altitudes of over 45,000ft (14,000m).

The Republic XF-91

The other competitor in the design contest for a high-altitude, missile-armed interceptor was the Republic Company, which in 1949 was heavily engaged in the production of the F-84 Thunderjet

Developed to meet a USAF requirement for a long-range penetration fighter, the Lockheed XF-90 proved to be seriously underpowered. (Lockheed)

and the development of a swept-wing successor, the F-84F Thunderstreak. Designated XF-91, Republic's interceptor design – unofficially dubbed 'Thundercepter' – was unusual in that it had a variable-incidence swept wing, which meant that the wing could be pivoted around its attachment point to the fuselage, allowing the angle of incidence to be adjusted by the pilot for the most effective angle of attack during take-off, cruise and landing. The angle of incidence could be varied between –2 and +6 degrees. The wing also featured inverse taper and thickness – in other words, the chord and thickness were greater at the wingtip than at the root. This arrangement, coupled with leading-edge slots, produced more lift at the outboard wing sections and consequently reduced the danger of the low-speed wingtip stall. Because of the unusual wing design, the XF-91's main undercarriage, positioned at mid-point, retracted outwards into wells situated at the wingtips.

The USAF was sufficiently impressed by the design to order two prototypes, the first of which, serial 46-680, flew for the first time on 9 May 1949. Like Convair's XF-92, the XF-91 was a mixed-power aircraft: as well as a General Electric J47-GE-3 turbojet it had a Reaction Motors XLR-11-RM-9 rocket engine fitted in the rear fuselage to provide additional power for take-off and combat. The rocket motor had four tubes, two above and two below the tailpipe. In December 1951, using both jet and rocket power, the XF-91 became the first American fighter aircraft to exceed Mach 1.0 in level flight. Its maximum speed was Mach 1.71 (1,126mph/1,812km/h) at altitude. The second XF-91 prototype was flown experimentally with a V-type butterfly tail, and the first was refitted with a nose radome housing an APS-6 radar installation similar to that fitted to the F-86D Sabre.

The XLR-11 rocket engine was very reliable and never suffered an in-flight failure. On one test flight, it proved its worth when the J47 jet engine flamed out. Unable to restart the jet engine, the pilot fired the rocket motors and was able to reach Edwards AFB and land successfully. Despite the aircraft's promise, no production order was placed. The second prototype was scrapped, and the first is now in the United States Air Force Museum at Wright Patterson AFB, Dayton, Ohio.

The Lockheed XF-90

In 1946, the newly formed Strategic Air Command issued a requirement for a so-called 'penetration fighter' to support the Convair B-36 heavy bomber: the theory was that the fighters would sweep ahead of the bomber force and tear gaps in the enemy's fighter defences. SAC's escort fighter requirement in these immediate post-war years was in effect a hangover from wartime operations over Germany, when the USAAF had learned to its cost that bombers could not hope to penetrate deeply into enemy territory without suffering appalling losses unless they were escorted by effective long-range fighters. The North American P-51 (later F-51) Mustang adequately filled the escort fighter requirement during the last two years of the war, and

Although unsuccessful as a long-range penetration fighter design, the McDonnell XF-88 was later resurrected as the F-101 Voodoo. (McDonnell Douglas)

although this aircraft continued to equip most of the fighter groups assigned to SAC during the first three years of the Command's existence, the advent of jet combat types left it seriously outmoded.

The Lockheed Aircraft Corporation, whose F-80 Shooting Star was then in full production, put forward a design to meet this requirement. Bearing the company designation Model 153 and the USAF designation XF-90, it was a very graceful and highly streamlined aircraft featuring a wing swept at 35 degrees. Power was supplied by two afterburning Westinghouse J34-WE-11 turbojets. A substantial fuel load, carried internally and in jettisonable wingtip tanks, gave the fighter a combat radius of about 1,100 miles (1,800km) at high altitude, sufficient to penetrate as far as Kiev from bases in West Germany. The XF-90 carried a very heavy armament of four 20mm cannon and six 0.5in machine guns. Two prototypes were built, the first flying on 4 June 1949, but flight trials revealed that the aircraft was seriously underpowered, with a maximum speed of only Mach 0.9 at sea level and Mach 0.95 at 40,000ft (12,000m). This fact, together with a change in the USAF requirement, led to the project being abandoned in 1950.

The North American YF-93A

North American, whose F-86A Sabre was in production in 1948, proposed a variant of this promising aircraft to meet the penetration fighter requirement. Designated F-86C, it had an increased wingspan and a larger fuselage cross-section to accommodate a 6,250lb (27.8kN) s. t. Pratt & Whitney XJ48-P-1 centrifugal-flow turbojet with reheat, this being fed via flush air intakes slotted into the fuselage sides beneath the cockpit. The nose section was completely redesigned and fitted with all-weather radar. The undercarriage was also redesigned, and twin-wheel main units were installed to support the fighter's 25,000lb (11,000kg) loaded weight. The F-86C bore so little resemblance to the parent design that it was given the new designation YF-93A, the prototype flying on 25 January 1950. Flight evaluation produced good results and the USAF placed an order for 118 production F-93As, but this was cancelled following the change in requirement and the penetration fighter project was abandoned.

The McDonnell XF-88

The third contender was the McDonnell XF-88, prototype construction of which began in 1947 under a USAF contract. The first prototype XF-88 was powered by two 3,000lb (13.3kN) s. t. Westinghouse XJ34-WE-13 engines, mounted side-by-side and exhausting just aft of the wing trailing edge under a stepped-up rear fuselage. This aircraft flew on 20 October 1948, and in 1950 it was followed by a second prototype fitted with XJ34 WE-22 engines equipped with short afterburners that could boost the thrust to 4,000lb (17.8kN) for combat manoeuvres. The XF-88 had a very thin

The McDonnell XF-85 Goblin parasite fighter was one of the most unconventional aircraft ever built. (Philip Jarrett)

wing swept at 35 degrees and spanning 38ft 8in (11.79m); length was just over 54ft (16.46m).

The first prototype XF-88 reached a maximum speed of 641mph (1,031km/h) at sea level and could climb to 35,000ft (10,700m) in 4½ minutes. Combat radius, however, was 850 miles (1,370km), much less than the XF-90's, and operational ceiling was only 36,000ft (11,000m). The XF-88 development programme was cancelled in August 1950, when the USAF shelved its long-range heavy fighter plans, but the first prototype – as the XF-88B – went on to have a useful life as a test bed for supersonic propellers.

In 1951, the USAF briefly resurrected its long-range escort fighter requirement as a result of the combat losses suffered in Korea by SAC's B-29s. McDonnell used the XF-88 design as the basis for a completely new aircraft, lengthening the fuselage to accommodate increased fuel tankage and two Pratt & Whitney J57-P-13 engines, giving it a top speed of over 1,000mph (1,600km/h) and a ceiling of 52,000ft (16,000m). In its new guise, it became the F-101A Voodoo, an aircraft that was to serve the USAF well for many years in the tactical support and reconnaissance roles.

The McDonnell XF-85 Goblin

One of the most unorthodox escort fighters ever designed was the McDonnell XF-85 Goblin. The project originated in 1942 as the MX-472, and revolved around the notion of a 'parasite' escort fighter that could be launched and retrieved by the bomber itself. By 1944, the USAAF requirement was more specific in that it called for a parasite fighter that could be carried by the existing Boeing B-29 and the proposed Northrop B-35 and Convair B-36 strategic bombers, and McDonnell Aircraft submitted four separate proposals under the company designation Model 27 in the autumn of that year.

The problems involved in successfully launching and recovering an escort fighter were severe enough, but in January 1945 they were compounded even further by a revised USAAF specification that required the parasite fighter to be completely housed inside the parent bomber. No designer in the world could have produced a fighter small enough to be buried inside a B-29, but the mighty B-36 was quite a different matter, and the McDonnell design team, led by project engineer Herman D. Barkey, set about revising the Model 27 to meet the new demand.

The extraordinary aircraft that gradually evolved resembled nothing so much as a large egg fitted with flying surfaces. A Westinghouse J34-WE-7 turbojet occupied almost the whole of the egg; the pilot sat astride the engine and was virtually surrounded by tanks containing 112 US gallons (424ltr) of fuel, enough for about half an hour's flying. Also packed into the nose of the egg were four 0.5in machine guns. The XF-85's wings were swept 37 degrees at the leading edge, had an anhedral of 4 degrees and folded vertically upward for stowage inside the parent aircraft. The tail assembly was complex, with no fewer than six surfaces. The pilot was equipped with a small ejection seat that was operated by a charge of cordite, and with an oxygen bottle and a ribbon-type parachute, designed to withstand heavy shock loadings at high speeds.

The XF-85 mock-up was approved in June 1946, and in March the following year McDonnell received a contract for the construction of two prototypes. At the same time, the USAAF instructed Convair to modify all B-36s from the twenty-third production aircraft to mount a trapeze for the parasite fighter in the forward bomb bay, the requirement now being for thirty operational F-85s to be purchased during 1949. Two schemes were mooted for the operational use of the F-85: one involved a single fighter to be carried by each B-36; the other suggested that an attacking force of B-36s should be accompanied by a small number of specially modified B-36s, each capable of carrying three F-85s.

In August 1947, following a change in strategic requirements, the USAF (as it now was) cancelled the order for thirty production F-85s. Work on the two XF-85 prototypes continued, however, and a bomber – the EB-29B 'Monstro' (44-8411) – was fitted with a trapeze to engage the little fighter's retractable hook. The first XF-85, 46-523, was flown in a C-47 transport to the Ames Laboratory at Moffatt Field for wind tunnel tests and suffered an immediate mishap when it was dropped from a crane. By June 1948 it had been repaired and taken to Muroc AFB for flight testing together with the second XF-85, 46-524.

On 23 August 1948, after making five captive flights, the second XF-85 was taken aloft by the EB-29 for its first free flight, with test pilot Edwin Schoch at the controls. At 20,000ft (6,000m), with the trapeze fully lowered, Schoch started the XF-85's engine and successfully unhooked himself from the parent aircraft, diving away to carry out a series of manoeuvres at speeds of 180–250mph (290–400km/h). Attempts at hooking up, however, presented severe problems because of turbulence, and on the fourth attempt Schoch overshot, striking the trapeze and shattering his canopy. With his helmet and oxygen mask ripped away by the airflow, he had no alternative but to dive sharply away and head for Muroc, where he touched down successfully at 160mph (260km/h) on the steel skid beneath the Goblin's fuselage.

Schoch spent the best part of the next two months practising approaches to the EB-29 in a Lockheed F-80 Shooting Star before taking the XF-85 into the air again on 14 October 1948. On this occasion he successfully engaged the trapeze on his second attempt and was hoisted aboard the parent aircraft. Two more flights, made on the following day, were also successful, but then a new problem arose. Until now, the XF-85 had flown with its hook extended all the time, the well into which it was to be recessed on retraction being faired over. With the fairing removed, however, the aircraft proved to be so unstable due to turbulence around the well that a hook-up was impossible.

Flight testing was temporarily suspended while modifications were carried out: vertical surfaces were fitted at the wingtips to improve stability, and a metal fairing was fitted along the sides of the well to smooth the airflow. On 18 March 1949, after two captive flights, Schoch and the second XF-85 were launched in free flight again, but trouble struck immediately when part of the trapeze fouled the XF-85's nose and broke away. Schoch took the XF-85 back to Muroc for yet another hair-raising skid landing on the dry lake bed. It was the last time the second XF-85 ever flew.

The first XF-85, which returned to Muroc in March 1948 after modification, was destined to make only one flight. This took place on 8 April, the aircraft flying back to Muroc after three unsuccessful attempts to hook on. Further testing of the type was suspended, at least until the trapeze had been redesigned, both the USAF and McDonnell quite rightly believing that if a pilot of Schoch's experience was unable to achieve a successful hook-up, the average fighter pilot would stand little chance of doing so. In the event the XF-85 never flew again, although McDonnell proposed a more conventional development capable of a speed of Mach 0.9. The second XF-85 was eventually presented to the Air Force Museum at Wright-Patterson AFB, while the first

THE USAF: THE SUPERSONIC CHALLENGE

A Republic F-84 Thunderjet hooks up with its B-36 parent aircraft during trials. (Author)

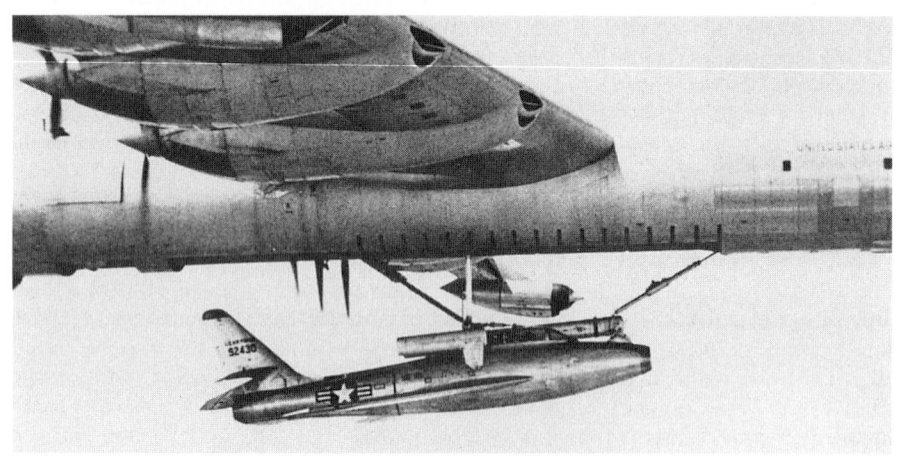

An F-84F Thunderstreak is raised into the B-36's bomb bay after hook-up. (Author)

went to the Air Museum at Orange County Airport, Santa Ana. Between them, the two aircraft had accumulated a total flight time of 2 hours 19 minutes, the highest recorded speed being 362mph (583km/h) – it would have been interesting to see whether the XF-85 would have been capable of coming anywhere near its rather optimistically estimated maximum speed of 664mph (1,068km/h) at sea level.

The FICON Programme

In 1951, the USAF, concerned about the losses inflicted by MiG-15 jet fighters on unescorted B-29 bombers over North Korea, resurrected the parasite fighter programme under the title FICON (Fighter Conveyor). The plan now was to use a Convair B-36 to carry a Republic F-84 Thunderjet, and an RB-36F (the reconnaissance version of the huge bomber) was suitably modified and re-designated GRB-36F. This made its first contact flight with the fighter on 9 January 1952, which was followed, on 23 April, by the first in-flight retrieval and launch of an F-84E. On 14 May the first composite flight was made, with the Thunderjet positioned in the bomb bay during take-off and landing.

By 20 February 1953 the composite GRB-36F/F-84E had completed 170 airborne launches and retrievals, paving the way for further trials with a swept-wing F-84F Thunderstreak. The idea now was that the B-36 could be used to carry an RF-84F

THE USAF: THE SUPERSONIC CHALLENGE

During Project Tom-Tom *trials, a Republic RF-84F Thunderflash joins up with a GRB-36's wingtip. (Author)*

Thunderflash reconnaissance fighter. The latter would be launched at some point outside hostile territory, up to 2,800 miles (4,500km) from the B-36's base, at an altitude of 25,000ft (7,600m); it would then fly 1,180 miles (1,890km) to make a dash over the target at high speed (580mph/930km/h at 35,000ft/10,700m or 630mph/1,000km/h at sea level), after which it would be retrieved by the parent aircraft. It was a desperate idea born of desperate times.

In May 1953, contracts were awarded to Convair and Republic for the modification of ten B-36Ds into carrier aircraft and twenty-five RF-84s as parasites, the types being re-designated GRB-36D and RF-84K. The latter weighed 29,503lb (13,364kg) and was armed with five cameras and four 0.5in machine guns. The GRB-36D retained its cameras and tail armament, all other defensive weapons being deleted, and its electronic countermeasures (ECM) equipment was moved aft to make room for installation in the bomb bay of an H-shaped cradle that was lowered to launch or retrieve the RF-84K. The Thunderflash could be refuelled in the bomb bay, and the pilot could leave the cockpit if necessary.

In December 1954 the 91st Strategic Reconnaissance Squadron (Fighter) was activated and attached to the 407th Strategic Fighter Wing at Great Falls AFB, the pilots being trained on standard F-84F Thunderstreaks. On 24 January 1955 the 71st SRW (F) was activated at Larson AFB, Washington, with two squadrons, the 25th and 82nd SRS (F) of basic RF-84Fs, and the 91st SRS joined them there with its RF-84Ks in July. Meanwhile, the

modified GRB-36Ds were being delivered to the 99th SRW at Fairchild AFB, which was nearby, and operational training between the two units was under way by the end of the year. The system presented continual difficulties, however, and the partnership lasted less than a year, the 91st SRS (F) exchanging its RF-84Ks for RF-84Fs and reverting to conventional reconnaissance operations late in 1956. It remained part of the 71st SRW (F) until the latter was deactivated on 1 July 1957.

Project *Tom-Tom*

In 1952–53, parasite fighter trials were also carried out in connection with Project *Tom-Tom*, a concept that involved two F-84F fighters hooking up to an assembly fitted to a B-36's wingtips. This also started life as a fighter conveyor project, but was subsequently adapted to the strategic reconnaissance role. The aircraft used in these trials were RB-36F 49-2707 and RF-84Fs 51-1848 and 51-1849. Modifications included podded, articulated arm assemblies on the RB-36F and articulated jaw-like clamps on the RF-84Fs, to hold the parasites in position. The first hook-up was made early in 1953, using only one RF-84F, after a series of trials to determine the best approach methods. Several more hook-ups were made subsequently, but because of the enormous slipstream and wingtip vortices generated by the RB-36 the operation was extremely dangerous. The operation was terminated late in 1953 after severe oscillation caused an RF-84F to tear loose from the parent aircraft's hook-up arm.

Chapter 8
United Kingdom: Transition to Transonic

Vampire FB.5 fighter-bombers of No. 608 Squadron, Royal Auxiliary Air Force, seen at RAF Thornaby in the 1950s. (Ken McCreesh)

At the end of the Second World War, RAF Fighter Command had one jet fighter in operational service. This was the Gloster Meteor which, apart from one or two idiosyncrasies, had turned out to be a very good fighter. The Mk III version, which eventually equipped fifteen squadrons of RAF Fighter Command in the immediate post-war years, and which had been operationally tested in a ground-attack role in Belgium with Nos 616 and 504 Squadrons in the closing weeks of the war, was followed into service by the Meteor F.IV. Powered by two Rolls-Royce Derwent 5s, the F.IV first flew in April 1945 and subsequently, in November, set up a new world air speed record of 606mph (975km/h). The second British jet fighter, the de Havilland Vampire, was also of conventional design, and was of simple configuration, comprising a nacelle housing the engine and cockpit, a very straightforward wing with slightly tapered leading and trailing edges, twin tail booms and twin fins.

Design work on the DH.100 Vampire had begun in May 1942, the prototype flying on 20 September 1943, and in the spring of 1944 it became the first Allied jet aircraft capable of sustained speeds of over 500mph (800km/h) over a wide altitude range. The first production Vampire flew in April 1945 and the Vampire F.I was delivered to Nos 247, 54 and 72 Squadrons in 1946. It was followed by the Vampire F.3, a long-range version with extra internal fuel and the ability to carry underwing tanks; both marks were powered by the de Havilland Goblin 2 turbojet. (Note that all British aircraft designations changed from Roman to Arabic numbers on 1 January 1948.)

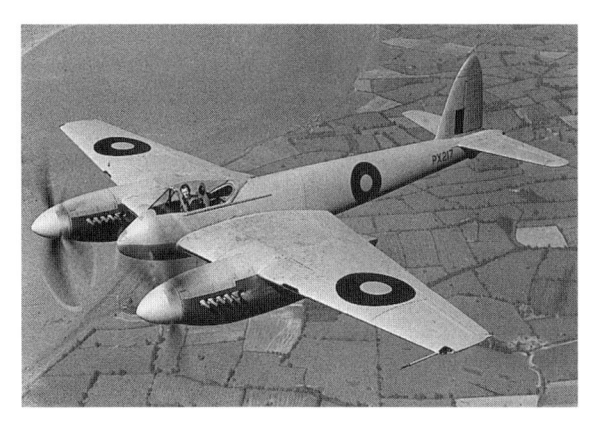

The de Havilland Hornet was the fastest twin piston-engined fighter ever to see operational service. (Hawker Siddeley)

Apart from the Meteor and Vampire, the squadrons of RAF Fighter Command and 2nd Tactical Air Force in Germany in the immediate post-war period were equipped with piston-engined types such as the Tempest Mk 2, which had a Bristol Centaurus radial engine, the Sabre-engined Tempest Mk 6 and the later marks of Spitfire. Perhaps the ultimate in British piston-engined fighter design was the de Havilland Hornet, the fastest twin piston-engined fighter in the world. The Hornet began life as a private venture in 1942 to meet the need for a long-range escort fighter for service in the Far East, but major orders for the Hornet F.I were cancelled at the end of the war and only sixty were built, entering RAF service in 1946. These were followed by 132 Hornet F.3s, which served with four first-line RAF air defence squadrons until they were withdrawn in 1951. Many were subsequently sent to the Far East, where they were used in the ground-attack role against communist terrorists in Malaya.

The Miles M.52

Despite the very conventional equipment that formed Fighter Command's first-line strength well into the post-war era, there had been no lack of forward thinking during the war years. In the autumn of 1943, the Ministry of Aircraft Production had issued Specification E.24/43, astonishing for its day, calling for an aircraft capable of flying at 1,000mph (1,600km/h) at 36,000ft (11,000m) – in other words, a machine advanced enough to make the jump from the subsonic speeds of early jets like the Meteor to a velocity far beyond Mach 1, cutting out the transonic phase altogether.

After negotiation with various airframe and engine companies, the Ministry selected Miles Aircraft to work on the design of the supersonic project; though rightly famous for its range of sport and training aircraft, Miles had also produced several ingenious experimental prototypes over the years. The aircraft's gas turbine engine was to be developed by Power Jets Ltd, under the direction of Group Captain (later Air Commodore Sir) Frank Whittle.

Miles received an Instruction to Proceed on 8 October 1943 and started work at the company's Woodley factory under conditions of strict secrecy. The project had to be as self-sufficient as possible, so Miles set up its own foundry for the production of the necessary metal components and also built a high-speed wind tunnel. The aircraft itself was allocated the company designation M.52. The design that gradually evolved featured a bullet-like fuselage of circular section, 5ft (1.5m) in diameter, constructed of high-tensile steel with an alloy covering. The power plant, a Power Jets W.2/700, was centrally mounted and fed by an annular air intake, the cockpit forming a centre cone. The whole cockpit cone, in which the pilot sat semi-reclined, could be detached in an emergency by firing small cordite charges; the pilot would then bale out normally when the capsule had descended to a safe altitude.

The M.52 was fitted with bi-convex section wings, mounted at the mid-point on the fuselage. A full-scale wooden mock-up of this unique high-speed wing design was built and tested on a Miles Falcon light aircraft in 1944. As design work progressed, various refinements were incorporated. Split flaps were fitted, together with an all-moving tailplane. The addition of rudimentary afterburners in the form of combustion cans situated at the rear of the engine duct was calculated to produce much greater thrust at supersonic speed. The position of the undercarriage presented some headaches: because of the very thin wing section, the wheels had to be positioned to retract into the fuselage in a narrow-track arrangement which might cause landing problems, as the M.52 had an estimated landing speed of 170mph (270km/h). At one stage, it was suggested that the M.52 might be air-launched, landing on a skid at the end of its flight, but this was rejected.

Detail design work on the M.52 was 90 per cent complete by the beginning of 1946, and the jigs were ready for the assembly of three planned prototypes. No snags were envisaged in construction, and it was expected that the first M.52 would fly within six to eight months. Then, in February 1946, quite without warning, F.G. Miles received word from the Director General of Scientific Research at the Ministry of Aircraft Production, Sir Ben Lockspeiser, that all work on the M.52 project was to cease at once. Secrecy surrounded the cancellation of the M.52, just as it had surrounded its design, and it was not until September 1946 that the British public were made aware that their aircraft industry had been within sight of flying the world's first supersonic aircraft, only to have the chance snatched away.

The stated reason behind the decision to cancel the M.52 was that it had already been decided, early in 1946, to carry out a supersonic research programme with the aid of unmanned models developed by Vickers Ltd. The department responsible was headed by Dr Barnes Wallis, designer of the special mines that had breached the Ruhr dams in 1943. Between May 1947 and October 1948 eight rocket-powered models were launched, only three of which were successful. The first attempted launch failed when the Mosquito launch aircraft got out of control in cloud and the model broke away, but in all the other unsuccessful launches it was the rocket motor that failed, not the airframe. The irony was that most of the models were based on the design of the M.52, and the double irony was that, in the light of current knowledge, the full-size M.52 would almost certainly have been a success.

However, to this day a rumour persists that the M.52 was cancelled as part of a secret deal struck between the British and US governments. As part of a larger package, the M.52 would be abandoned, and the lead handed to the Americans, in exchange for the release of certain nuclear research material by the United States to assist the British in the creation of their own nuclear weapons programme. It is known that such collusion did exist, and it is entirely possible that the M.52 fell victim to it.

One authority who remained convinced that the M.52 was an entirely viable prospect was the man selected to fly it, Commander (later Captain) Eric Brown, Chief Test Pilot with the Royal Aircraft Establishment. In Brown's opinion, and that of many others, the abandonment of the M.52 was nothing short of a catastrophe for British aviation. It was now left to the Americans to seize the supersonic high ground, which they did only a year after the M.52's cancellation was made public, when the USAF's Major Charles Yeager made the first manned supersonic flight in the rocket-powered Bell X-1 research aircraft.

The Gloster E.1/44

Although all the major British aircraft companies had embarked on studies of turbojet-powered aircraft during the war, few reached fruition. The notable exceptions were the Gloster Meteor and the de Havilland Vampire, both of which showed a considerable degree of development potential and went on to render invaluable service with many air forces in the day fighter, night fighter and photo-reconnaissance roles.

While they were engaged in the development of the Meteor, Gloster also designed and built a small single-jet fighter, the G.42, which became better known by its specification number, E.1/44. Powered by a Rolls-Royce Nene, it had clean lines and featured lateral air intakes, with square-cut wings and a three-piece cockpit canopy, similar to that fitted to the Meteor F.IV. The first prototype, SM809, was to have flown in August 1947, but was damaged while in transit by road to the Aircraft & Armament Experimental Establishment (A&AEE) at Boscombe Down, so the maiden flight was made by the second aircraft, TX145. This was followed by a third prototype, TX148, which had a tail unit similar in configuration to that of the Meteor F.8. A fourth aircraft, TX150, was allocated to ground testing, and two more fuselages were partially built. The third prototype, TX148, saw lengthy service as a research aircraft at the RAE. A swept-wing version was projected under Specification 23/46, but no work went ahead with this and no production orders were placed.

The CXP-1001

Meanwhile, in 1946, a Chinese Nationalist Government delegation had arrived in the United Kingdom to investigate the possibility of setting up design and production facilities in Britain for the construction of turbojet-powered combat aircraft. The Chinese team entered into negotiations with

Gloster Aircraft, who agreed to assist in the design of a single-seat fighter, and drawing offices were set aside for that purpose at Gloster's Hucclecote factory, on the outskirts of Gloucester. The fighter project was given the designation CXP-1001 and joint work on the design went on for several months, during which time a full-size mock-up and several components were completed. The collapse of the nationalist regime on mainland China in 1949, however, led to the project being abandoned.

The Hawker P.1035 and P.1040

Hawker Aircraft, who had taken piston-engined fighter development to the ultimate with the Tempest, had investigated several jet-powered projects during the war. In 1940, the company had carried out preliminary design work on a new piston-engined high-speed bomber, the P.1005, which was to have been powered by two Napier Sabres, and when this was cancelled in 1942 – by which time a mock-up was almost complete – Hawker briefly studied the possibility of equipping the airframe with two Power Jets gas turbines.

Another scheme, proposed at about the same time, envisaged a single-seat fighter with one Power Jets engine. Both these schemes came to nothing, but with the advent of more powerful turbojets in 1943 Hawker was encouraged to go ahead with other projects, mostly designed around the Rolls-Royce B.40 and B.41 engines. These were: the P.1031, a scheme for a B.40-powered night fighter; the P.1034, which was the old P.1005 bomber scheme resurrected with two B.41s; the P.1035, which involved the fitting of a B.41 turbojet into a Hawker Fury airframe; and the P.1038 and P.1039, which were once again variations on the B.1005 bomber theme.

The P.1035 showed more promise than any of the others, and detailed proposals were submitted to the Ministry of Aircraft production in December 1944, by which time the original design had undergone some changes. The B.41 engine, which was positioned in the fuselage aft of the cockpit and fed by air intakes built into the wing roots, was originally intended to exhaust under the tail, but to minimize thrust loss Hawker decided to shorten the tailpipe by designing a bifurcated, or split, jet pipe that exhausted on either side of the fuselage, just aft of the engine. With this and other modifications the P.1035 was re-designated

The Hawker P.1040, originally developed for the RAF as a land-based fighter, eventually became the elegant carrier-based Sea Hawk, pictured here. (Ann Tilbury)

P.1040, work on which proceeded during the winter of 1944–45 on a private-venture basis.

By the autumn of 1945, with the Gloster Meteor firmly established in RAF squadron service and the DH Vampire coming along, the RAF's interest in the P.1040 had waned, although it was later submitted to the Royal Navy, who accepted it: it was subsequently developed into the very successful Sea Hawk.

The Boulton Paul P.111 and P.120

In 1946, while aircraft designers in the United States and the Soviet Union were putting captured German research material to good use in projects that would soon take fighter aircraft beyond Mach One, British progress in fighter design remained at a low ebb, partly because of the Labour government's firm conviction that there would be no major war threat anywhere in the world for at least ten years. As a result, most of the specifications for new aircraft issued in 1946 originated in the Ministry of Supply and involved experimental prototypes for aerodynamic research.

The first 1946 specification for a high-speed research aircraft was E.27/46, which resulted in the delta-wing Boulton Paul P.111. The prototype, VT935, did not fly until 6 October 1950, powered by a 5,100lb (22.7kN) s.t. Rolls-Royce Nene turbojet fed via an oval nose intake. The leading edge of the delta wing was swept at 45 degrees. In 1953, the P.111 underwent some modification, four air brakes being fitted on the fuselage aft of the cock-

The Hawker P.1052 was a swept-wing version of the P.1040. Two prototypes were built. (Ann Tilbury)

pit, and in this form it was re-designated P.111A. During trials, the P.111A reached a maximum speed of 650mph (1,050km/h) at sea level and 622mph (1,000km/h) at 35,000ft (10,700m). Today, the aircraft is on display at the Midland Air Museum, Coventry Airport.

On 6 August, 1952, Boulton Paul flew a variant of the basic P.111 design, the P.120, which differed mainly in having a redesigned fin and a high-mounted, all-moving tailplane. The P.120 carried out some 11 hours of test flying, showing a performance similar to that of its predecessor, before being destroyed in a crash caused by tail flutter on 28 August 1952. Boulton Paul Chief Test Pilot A.E. Gunn ejected inverted but survived, his parachute deploying just before impact with the ground.

The Hawker P.1052, P.1067 and P.1081

Two notable exceptions to the specifications issued in 1946 were Air Staff Specifications F.43/46 and F.44/46, which called for the development of modern jet fighters, one a single- and the other a two-seater, to replace the Meteor and Vampire in the day fighter role and the de Havilland Mosquito in the night fighter role. Both specifications, however, left much to be desired in that they were formulated around knowledge of high-speed flight that was, at best, imprecise. They were to undergo profound changes over the next two years and in the end they were completely re-written. This process eventually gave the RAF the fighter aircraft it needed, but only after a costly delay that resulted in the Service having to make do with compromises for some years while other major air forces were operating fighter aircraft tailor-made for their roles.

Early in 1946, both Hawker and Vickers-Supermarine were studying schemes for swept-wing jet fighters. Hawker's early scheme, first tentatively proposed in October 1945, involved a rocket-powered version of the P.1040 with a wing swept at 35 degrees – the optimum angle, as had been revealed by German research. Given the designation P.1047, this scheme was the subject of only limited study, but the Royal Aircraft Establishment showed a good deal of interest in the swept wing idea and in 1946 discussions were held between the RAE, Hawker, Vickers-Supermarine and the Ministry of Supply with a view to carrying swept-wing research a stage further. As a result two specifications were issued, both calling for experimental aircraft fitted with swept flying surfaces. E.1/46, issued to Vickers-Supermarine, was written around a swept-wing version of the Attacker, the Royal Navy's first jet fighter, the prototype of which had flown in July 1946. The other specification, E.38/46, was issued to Hawker and called for a swept-wing version of the P.1040.

Both companies submitted their proposals to the Ministry of Supply in March 1947, and each subsequently received a contract for the building of two prototypes. The Vickers-Supermarine design, which was basically an Attacker with swept flying surfaces and which retained the Attacker's tailwheel undercarriage, was known as the Type 510, the prototypes being allocated the serials VV106 and VV109; the Hawker aircraft was designated P.1052 and the prototypes were allocated the serials VX272 and VX279. Both designs were powered by the Rolls-Royce Nene 2 turbojet, which developed 5,000lb (22.2kN) s.t.

The P.1052 (VX272) was the first to fly, followed by the Type 510 (VV106) on 29 December. Both flights were made from Boscombe Down, where much of the subsequent research flying was to take place. Each aircraft soon showed its ability to reach speeds in the order of Mach 0.9 at altitude, and the performance of the P.1052 was so impressive that at one point, at the end of 1948 – with the Berlin blockade at its height and international tension stretched to breaking point – the Air Staff seriously considered ordering the type into production to replace the Meteor.

Meanwhile, efforts were still being made to find a solution to the Air Staff F.43/46 requirement. During 1947 several schemes were considered by Sydney Camm's design team at Hawker Aircraft Ltd; much depended on the selection of a suitable engine, and the most promising appeared to be the AJ.65 axial-flow turbojet then being developed by Rolls-Royce. Preliminary design work on this engine, which was later to be named the Avon, had begun in the summer of 1945. The AJ.65 was an advanced design for its day; it developed some 6,500lb (28.9kN) s.t., about the same as the combined thrust of the Meteor F.4's twin Rolls-Royce Derwents. It was around this power plant, therefore, that Camm's team set about designing a fighter to meet F.43/46. Unfortunately, no one at that time envisaged how protracted the development of the AJ.65 would be: seven years were to elapse before the AJ.65/Avon became operationally acceptable to the RAF, and even then some snags remained to be eliminated.

The project that developed around the AJ.65 was allocated the Company designation P.1067, and the original design drew heavily on wartime swept-wing research data. The potential of the AJ.65 eliminated any need for the aircraft to have a twin-engined configuration, as had originally been specified in F.43/46, and the design that now gradually evolved comprised a single AJ.65 fed via a nose intake. All flying surfaces were swept at an angle of 40 degrees, the tailplane being mounted on top of the fin. Proposed armament was four 20mm Hispano cannon. All-up weight would be in the region of 12,000lb (5,400kg), and performance included an estimated maximum speed at altitude of Mach 0.88.

The P.1067 proposal, in its original form, was presented to the Air Ministry in January 1948. In

Operational Requirement 228 resulted in one of the most beautiful jet fighters ever built, the Hawker Hunter. (Hawker Siddeley)

the meantime, however, the Air Staff had abandoned F.43/46, and in March 1948 a new and much more realistic specification, F.3/48, was issued. This was dictated by the need for a fighter with a sufficiently advanced performance to enable it to intercept a new generation of jet bombers in the class of the Boeing B-47 Stratojet, the prototype of which had flown in December 1947 – the advent of advanced aircraft such as the B-47 had resulted in a new Air Staff Operational Requirement, OR.228, and it was to this that F.3/48 conformed. It would eventually produce one of the finest jet fighters of the Cold War era, the Hawker Hunter.

Meanwhile, Hawker had been continuing their high-speed research programme with the two P.1052s, VX272 and VX279. The Australian Government was showing considerable interest in this design, and Hawker felt justified in proceeding

The Hawker P.1081 might have seen service with the Royal Australian Air Force, had the sole prototype not been destroyed in a fatal crash. (Ann Tilbury)

with the development of an all-swept variant with a straight-through exhaust. At a meeting with Ministry of Supply representatives on 31 January 1950, the company was made fully aware of the RAAF requirement, which was for a fast, cheap-to-produce interceptor armed with four 20mm cannon that could also double up in the ground-attack role with rockets or bombs. The Australians wanted to build the aircraft under licence, and one of the stipulations was that the prototype had to fly within fifteen months.

Conscious of the urgency, Hawkers went ahead and converted the second prototype P.1052, VX279, which they fitted with a Nene turbojet exhausting through a jet pipe 'borrowed' from a Vickers-Supermarine Attacker; it was planned that the production version would be fitted with the 6,250lb (27.8kN) s.t. Rolls-Royce Tay. The modified aircraft, designated P.1081, was taken into the air for the first time on 18 June 1950 by Squadron Leader T.S. 'Wimpy' Wade DFC AFC, Hawker's chief test pilot. Wade was unable to lower the undercarriage fully and also unable to retract the lowered port main undercarriage because of hydraulic failure; he diverted to RAF Odiham and made an emergency landing on the port mainwheel and the nosewheel, sustaining damage to the starboard wingtip and fairing. The aircraft was flown to the Hawker hangar at Farnborough on 20 June to be repaired.

Results obtained during subsequent flight tests led to some rudder and tailplane modifications, and wing fences were also fitted. The P.1081's performance was spectacular, with a maximum speed of 695mph (1,118km/h) at sea level and a climb to 35,000ft (10,700m) in 9 minutes 12 seconds – the installation of the Tay engine would have improved the rate of climb still further. Unfortunately, things went badly wrong during an air test from Farnborough on 2 April 1951, when some kind of emergency developed during a high-speed run and Wade elected to eject. The cockpit canopy was released at about 9,000ft (2,700m) and the ejection sequence was initiated at 2,000ft (600m), but the non-automatic ML Aviation ejection seat began to rotate violently and Wade was apparently unable to operate the mechanism to release himself from it, being killed on impact with the ground. After flying out of control for a few seconds the P.1081 crashed and caught fire on the South Downs. The cause of the accident was never really established, but reports of a sonic boom in the area at the time indicated that the aircraft may have gone transonic in a shallow dive. As the aircraft was fitted only with conventional tailplane, elevators and trim tabs, Wade would have had little chance of recovery – such controls become extremely stiff as the speed of sound is approached. With the loss of the sole P.1081, Australian interest waned: the RAAF's requirement for a high-speed fighter was eventually met by an Avon-powered version of the North American F-86 Sabre.

The De Havilland DH.108

The famous firm of de Havilland also made a substantial contribution to early post-war high-speed research, but their design was developed to an earlier specification, E.18/45. The aircraft they evolved, the DH.108, was intended to investigate the aerodynamic characteristics of the swept-wing formula throughout the subsonic speed range. Design work started in October 1945 and three prototypes were ordered by the Ministry of Supply. The DH.108 airframe consisted of a standard Vampire Mk I fuselage married to a new wooden wing, which had a leading edge sweep of 45 degrees and featured split trailing edge flaps with elevons mounted outboard. The aircraft was fitted with a conventional swept fin and rudder, and was powered by a de Havilland Goblin 2 centrifugal-flow turbojet, fed via air intakes at the wing root.

The first DH.108, TG283, was designed for low-speed handling trials and was fitted with various safety devices, including anti-spin parachutes housed in wingtip containers and leading edge slots fixed in the open position. It flew for the first time on 15 May 1946, and during the next four years carried out extensive handling trials in the low-speed range of the flight envelope, up to a maximum of 280mph (450km/h).

On 1 May 1950, Squadron Leader G.E.C. Genders, OC Aero Flight, RAE Farnborough, took off in TG283 to carry out low-speed sideslip and stalling trials. During the second stall, with the flaps down, control was lost and the DH.108 went into an inverted spin. The anti-spin parachutes were streamed, but only one deployed and was jettisoned. The cockpit canopy was jettisoned at about 5,000ft (1,500m) and a partial recovery was made at 2,000ft (600m), but the aircraft then flicked into a normal spin from which it did not recover. Genders baled out, but his parachute did not deploy fully before impact and he was killed.

The second DH.108, TG306, had its sweepback increased to 45 degrees, and was intended to investigate the middle of the subsonic speed range. It was fitted with power controls and automatic leading edge slots, and its engine was a 3,300lb (14.74kN) s.t. Goblin 3. This aircraft first flew in June 1946 and was demonstrated at that year's SBAC Show, after which it was decided to use it in an attempt on the world air speed record, which then stood at 616mph (991km/h) and was held by a Gloster Meteor F.4. Piloted by Geoffrey de Havilland Jr, son of the firm's founder, TG306 made several high-speed trial runs in preparation for the record attempt, but on 27 September 1946 it experienced structural failure at a speed of about Mach 0.9 and crashed into the mud banks of Egypt Bay, north-east of Rochester, Kent, the pilot's body being washed ashore a few days later. An examination of the wreckage indicated that both wings had failed at the root attachments following a severe bunt (outside loop).

The third DH.108, VW120, was the high-speed aircraft of the trio and incorporated a number of refinements, including a more streamlined nose and cockpit canopy. On 12 April 1948, this aircraft established a new 100km closed circuit record of 605.23mph (974.02km/h) under the power of its Goblin 4 turbojet and with de Havilland's new Chief Test Pilot, John Derry, at the controls. On 9 September that year, again flown by Derry, VW120 exceeded Mach 1.0 in a steep dive between 40,000–30,000ft (12,000–10,000m), the pilot reporting no problems except for a stiffening of the controls. Despite conflicting claims that rose thereafter, the DH.108 therefore appears to have been the first turbojet-powered aircraft in the world to exceed Mach 1. Unfortunately, this historic machine was totally destroyed in a crash at Birkhall, Buckinghamshire, on 15 February 1950, after disintegrating during high speed trials. The pilot, Squadron Leader J.S.R. Muller-Rowland DSO DFC, was killed.

The Hawker P.1083 and Supermarine Type 545

The first British jet aircraft to fly with sweepback on all flying surfaces was the Vickers-Supermarine Type 510 VV106, which first flew in the hands of the company's Chief Test Pilot, Commander Mike Lithgow, on 29 December 1948. Testing was temporarily halted when Lithgow had to make a wheels-up landing on 16 March 1949, but was resumed after repair on 10 May. This became the prototype of the Supermarine Swift, which equipped two squadrons of RAF Fighter Command alongside the Hawker Hunter before being withdrawn, having proved unsuitable for the interceptor role, although it later enjoyed considerable success as a low-level tactical reconnaissance aircraft. On 8 November 1950, the Type 510, flown by Lt J. Elliot RN, became the first swept-wing aircraft in the world to land on and take off from a carrier, in this case HMS *Illustrious*.

In 1951, as both Hawker and Vickers-Supermarine were preparing for series production of the Hunter and Swift, the design teams of both companies were turning their attention to more advanced successor aircraft, machines that would be capable of speeds of up to Mach 1.5 in level flight. Every other nation with modern combat aircraft technology was doing the same: in the United States, France and the Soviet Union, North American, Marcel Dassault and Mikoyan-Guryevich were developing, respectively, the F-100 Super Sabre, the Super Mystère B.2 and the MiG-19; these were successors to the same manufacturers' F-86 Sabre, Mystère IV and MiG-17, all of which were in the class of the Hunter and Swift.

Hawker Aircraft's proposal for a transonic fighter involved a straightforward development of the P.1067 Hunter, with a lengthened fuselage to accommodate an afterburning Rolls-Royce Avon RA.14 turbojet and a new, thin wing with a thickness/chord ratio of only 7.5 per cent and swept 52 degrees at the leading edge. The project was given the designation P.1083 and detailed design work began in November 1951. This led, on 26 February 1952, to an Instruction to Proceed with the construction of a prototype that was allocated the serial WN470 and which was expected to fly before the end of 1953.

Following a draft specification, which was drawn up around the project and issued on 18 April 1952, a meeting was held on 12 June between representatives of Hawker Aircraft Ltd, the Ministry of Supply and the Air Staff to work out a tentative production schedule. At this time the company had begun modification of the fourth prototype P.1067 to meet the P.1083 requirement and had started building the thin wing, the starboard section of which was completed in October 1952. In the same month a mock-up of the RA.14 engine was successfully mated to a mock-up of the P.1083's rear fuselage. It was now estimated that the prototype would be ready to fly in July 1953, and plans were made to power production machines with the uprated Rolls-Royce Avon RA.19 engine of 12,500lb (55.6kNkg) s.t. – this involved some redesign of the rear fuselage to accommodate the RA.19's bigger jet pipe. Other design changes in the production P.1083 included extra fuel tankage and a slab-type tailplane.

Mindful of the endurance problems that beset the Hunter, Hawker gave a lot of thought to increasing the P.1083's combat radius, and to this end it was decided to install integral wing tanks which, together with the rear fuselage tankage, would give the production version a total fuel capacity of 600gal (2,730ltr), compared with the prototype's 440gal (2,000ltr). The aircraft would be fitted with the standard 30mm Aden four-gun pack, with 150 rounds per gun. With a full load of fuel and ammunition, estimated all-up weight would be in the region of 20,000lb (9,000kg).

A typical flight profile worked out for the P.1083 included a one-minute engine run-up at one-third power, take-off and acceleration to climbing speed at sea level, climb to 50,000ft (15,000m), ten minutes of combat at that altitude and then cruise patrol until 40gal (180ltr) of fuel remained for the descent and landing. Even allowing for the use of reheat for take-off, acceleration, climb and combat, this gave the P.1083 an estimated combat endurance of an hour and a quarter, which was about the same as the Hunter F.1's maximum endurance; it was a vast improvement on the F.1's combat endurance, which was roughly 35 minutes.

At a loaded weight of 17,700lb (8,000kg) with half fuel, the P.1083 had an estimated maximum speed of 820mph (1,320km/h, Mach 1.08) at sea level, 790mph (1,270km/h, Mach 1.2) at 36,000ft (11,000m), and 690mph (1,110km/h, Mach 1.05) at 55,000ft (17,000m). Estimated initial rate of climb was 50,000ft/min (15,000m/min) at sea level, 28,700ft/min (8,750m/min) at 20,000ft (6,000m), and 5,400ft/min (1,650m/min) at 50,000ft (15,000m). Estimated service ceiling was 59,500ft (18,150m), while time to 30,000ft (9,000m) at an all-up weight of 20,000lb (9,000kg) was estimated to be 1 minute 57 seconds, and to 55,000ft (17,000m) 5 minutes 12 seconds, from the start of the take-off roll.

In June 1953 the P.1083 prototype was 80 per cent complete, and Hawker was confident that it would be ready in time to take part in that year's SBAC Show at Farnborough in September. Then the blow fell. On 22 June 1953 Sir Sydney Camm received a visit from Air Vice-Marshal Geoffrey Tuttle, the Comptroller of Supplies (Air), and Air Commodore Wallace Kyle of the Directorate of Military Aircraft Research and Development, who informed him that Air Staff policy had now turned against the use of afterburning engines like the RA.19; it was felt that larger, unreheated engines in the existing Hunter airframe would achieve an acceptable performance increase. Camm argued strongly against this opinion, knowing the limitations of the Hunter airframe, but it was no use: the P.1083 was officially cancelled on 13 July 1953.

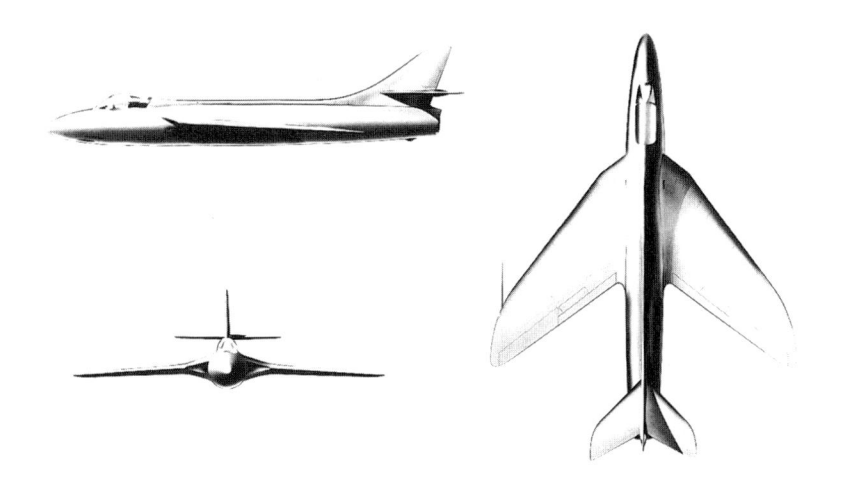

The cancellation of the Hawker P.1083 'Super Hunter' left a gap in the export market that the British military aviation industry was never able to fill. (Hawker Siddeley)

In fact there were two reasons for its cancellation, and they had nothing to do with the hardening of Air Staff attitudes towards afterburning engines. The first was purely one of economy, for the end of the Korean War had resulted in immediate cutbacks in funding for the procurement of new military equipment. The second was that a Vickers-Supermarine design, the Type 545, was considered to have much greater potential than the Hawker aircraft. The Type 545, although based on the Swift, was in fact a complete redesign, with an area-ruled fuselage and a thin, crescent-type wing that featured a leading edge sweep ranging from 50 degrees at the wing root through 40 degrees at mid-point to 30 degrees at the outer section. The chosen engine was the Rolls-Royce Avon RA.14R, developing 14,500lb (64.5kN) s.t. with full reheat.

While work proceeded on the prototype 545, XA181, Supermarine also offered the RAF a follow-on design powered by an RB.106 turbojet. This variant had a lengthened fuselage and a chin-type air intake, and would have had an estimated maximum speed of Mach 1.68 at 36,000ft (11,000m). In 1955, however, all development work on the Type 545 was halted and the prototype cancelled. By this time the Air Staff had decided to bridge the gap from subsonic to truly supersonic by developing a high-speed research aircraft, the English Electric P.1, into a complete weapon system – a formidable and challenging step that would result in the operational deployment of the Lightning F.1 in the summer of 1960.

The export market that might have been captured by the 'Super Hunter' went to its American counterpart, the North American F-100 Super Sabre. (North American)

The problems experienced with the Swift had no small influence on the decision to cancel the Type 545, but the decision to cancel the P.1083 was wrong. Although the type would probably have fallen short of its performance estimates, at least in its initial production version, it would have been a better all-round combat aircraft than the F-100 Super Sabre. Apart from Britain, no fewer than sixteen other countries went on to use the various marks of the Hawker Hunter; but when some of them, particularly those in NATO, came to look for a supersonic successor in the late 1950s, they chose the F-100 because Britain had no 'Super Hunter' to offer them.

For the British aviation industry, however, there was much worse to come.

Chapter 9
France's Road to Success

France's first post-war jet fighter design, the SO.6020 Espadon (Swordfish), was powered by a Rolls-Royce Nene turbojet. The photograph shows the rocket-assisted SO.6025 version. (Musée de l'Air)

As related in Chapter 5, France's initial experiments with jet aircraft relied mostly on captured German engines. When Rolls-Royce Nenes became available, they were earmarked to power a trio of naval fighters – the Aerocentre NC 1080, the Arsenal VG-90 and the Nord 2200 – as well as a twin-jet naval strike aircraft, the NC 1071. Nenes were also to have powered several land-based types: the Sud-Ouest SO.6020 Espadon fighter, the twin-jet Sud-Est SE 2400 attack aircraft, and the SO.4000 and NC 270 twin-jet bombers. In the event, only one early Nene-powered French design ever achieved series production: this was the Dassault MD.450 Ouragan, the first French jet fighter to be ordered in quantity.

The *Espadon*

It was Sud-Ouest who were responsible for the manufacture of France's first post-war jet fighter, the SO.6020 *Espadon* (Swordfish). Its designer was Lucien Servanty, and the first prototype, the SO.6020-01 (F-WFDI) flew for the first time on 12 November 1948, powered by a Rolls-Royce Nene 102 turbojet fed through a ventral air intake under the rear fuselage. This intake arrangement caused many problems and the second prototype, the SO.6020-02 (F-WFDV), which first flew on 15 September 1949, had flush air intakes under the wing trailing edges. A third prototype, the SO.6020-03 (F-WFRG), flew on 28 December 1949 and was fitted with a long ventral air intake,

The prototype SE.2410 Grognard I, which flew for the first time on 30 April 1950. (Musée de l'Air)

a fairing at the rear of which housed an SEPR 251 liquid-fuel rocket motor; it was re-designated SO.6025 shortly afterwards. The fourth prototype, the SO.6021 (F-WFKZ), flew on 3 September 1950 and featured a lighter structure, servo controls and an increased wing area.

In 1952, the SO.6020-01 was retrospectively fitted with a ventral air intake and a Turboméca Marboré turbojet was also installed at each wingtip. The SO.6020-02 was fitted with an SEPR 251 rocket motor, fed from wingtip fuel tanks: in its new guise it was re-designated SO.6026, and on 15 December 1953 it reached Mach 1.0 in level flight over Istres. By this time, however, Dassault's Ouragan and Mystère II fighters, powered by the Atar 101, were coming off the production line, and further development of the Espadon was abandoned.

The *Grognard*

The other early Nene-powered, land-based design, the Sud-Est SE.2400 attack aircraft, developed into the SE.2410 *Grognard* ('Grumbler', a name originally bestowed upon the soldiers of Napoleon's Old Guard). The prototype, the SE.2410 *Grognard* I, first flew on 30 April 1950, powered by two Hispano-Suiza Nene 101s mounted one above the other in the rear fuselage and with wings swept at an angle of 47 degrees. The aircraft reached a maximum speed of 1,040km/h (645mph) at 1,500m (5,000ft). The second prototype, the SE.2415 *Grognard* II, flew on 14 February 1951 and was a two-seater with a sweepback of 32 degrees. This aircraft attained a maximum speed of 959km/h (596mph), but trouble was experienced with tail flutter and then the aircraft was damaged in a belly landing as a result of a false fire warning in the air.

While trials with the two prototypes progressed, albeit at a much slower rate than had been anticipated, Sud-Est's designers were working on the details of the production version, which was designated SE.2418 and which was to have been powered by two Rolls-Royce Tay turbojets. The finalized aircraft had an estimated maximum speed of 1,090km/h (675mph) at sea level, and armament was to have comprised two 30mm DEFA cannon and a combination of rockets and bombs. Sud-Ouest's promising *Vautour* design, however, was

First flown on 25 June 1955, the Dassault MD.550 Mirage I was designed in response to a requirement for a lightweight interceptor. (Dassault)

adopted to meet the Armée de l'Air's ground-attack requirements, and further development of the *Grognard* was abandoned.

The Dassault Jet Fighters

It was Marcel Dassault who won the race to give the Armée de l'Air a series of interceptors that brought France to technical parity with any other nation in the world during the 1950s. Dassault was already a very experienced designer: he was formerly Marcel Bloch, whose fighter and bomber designs had been in the Armée de l'Air's front line at the outbreak of the Second World War. His refusal to co-operate with the Germans after the fall of France, together with the fact that he was Jewish, resulted in his arrest and incarceration in Buchenwald concentration camp in 1944. After the war he changed his name to Dassault, which had been his code-name in the French Resistance.

Dassault's first jet fighter, the Ouragan, was designed, built and flown in fourteen months, and from there it was a relatively simple step to produce a follow-on aircraft based on the Ouragan's design, but with fully swept flying surfaces. This emerged as the Mystère I, which first flew in February 1951 powered by a Nene 104B, and it was followed by two further prototypes designated Mystère IIA, powered by Tay 250 turbojets. Three pre-production machines were also Tay-powered, but the remainder were fitted with the Atar 101; this engine also powered the production aircraft, which entered Armée de l'Air service as the Mystère IIC. Problems with the aircraft soon became apparent, however, and it experienced a series of fatal crashes caused by structural failure. It was consequently overtaken on the production line by the more advanced Mystère IVA, which had been developed in parallel with the Mystère IIC and which proved to be a superb combat aircraft.

In the mid-1950s, the lesson that French combat aircraft were becoming world-beaters was underlined by the first flight, on 2 March 1955, of the Super Mystère B.1, powered by an Avon RA.7R; the next day, it became the first aircraft of European origin to exceed Mach 1.0 in level flight, attained while flying at 12,000m (40,000ft).

More surprises, illustrating the advanced thinking of Dassault's design team, were on the way. In 1952, to meet a Ministry requirement for a lightweight, high-altitude, rocket-assisted interceptor capable of using grass strips, Dassault had begun the design of a small single-seat delta designated MD.550. Renamed the Mirage I, it flew for the first time on 25 June 1955, powered by two Bristol Siddeley Viper turbojets. In May 1956 the Mirage I reached Mach 1.15 in a shallow dive, and on 17 December 1956, with the additional boost of an

SEPR 66 rocket motor, it attained Mach 1.3 in level flight.

The Mirage I, which was too small and lacked sufficient power to be an effective interceptor in its own right, was regarded by Dassault as the development aircraft for the Mirage II, which was to be powered by two Turboméca Gabizo turbojets fitted with reheat. Before the Mirage I had begun its transonic trials, however, Dassault had already decided to abandon the Mirage II in favour of a larger and more powerful variant, powered by an afterburning SNECMA Atar 101G-2 turbojet. This aircraft eventually flew in prototype form on 17 November 1956, as the Mirage III-01.

The Nord 1500 Griffon

The Mirage I, progenitor of one of the world's most successful lines of combat aircraft, was in direct competition with two government-backed projects, the Nord 1500 Griffon and the SO.9000 Trident. Like Dassault, Nord Aviation based its design on a delta-wing configuration, also following Dassault in first building a high-speed research prototype, the Nord 1402 Gerfaut I. This machine, which made its first flight on 15 January 1954, was the first high-powered jet delta-wing aircraft to fly in France, and on 3 August 1954 it became the first European aircraft to exceed Mach 1.0 in level flight without the use of an afterburner or rocket power. The diminutive aircraft had a wingspan of only 6.4m (21ft), and was powered by a SNECMA Atar 101D3 turbojet. A second prototype, the Gerfaut IB, had larger wings; it exceeded the speed of sound in level flight for the first time on 11 February 1955. An uprated version, the Gerfault II, flew on 17 April 1956 and subsequently made many supersonic test flights. The Gerfault II's rate of climb was quite startling: it was able to reach 15,000m (49,000ft) in 3 minutes 56 seconds from a standing start.

The Nord 1500 Griffon was essentially a research aircraft too, although it had definite interceptor potential. From the outset, it was designed to test an airframe design capable of being equipped with a combined turbojet-ramjet propulsion unit. The prototype 1500-01 Griffon 1 made its first flight on 20 September 1955, powered only by a SNECMA Atar 101F turbojet with afterburner. After the completion of the first phase of testing, the airframe was modified to take a propulsion unit consisting of an Atar 101E engine and a Nord ramjet; under this new guise, the aircraft was re-designated 1500-02 Griffon II. It flew for the first time in its new configuration on 23 January 1957, and on 17 May it exceeded Mach 1.0 in level flight with its ramjet ignited, although the full power of the unit was not used. As far as it is known, this was the first time that a piloted ramjet-powered aircraft exceeded the speed of sound. No combat aircraft was developed from the Griffon, however, which went on flying into the 1960s under a US research contract.

The SO.9000 Trident

Sud-Ouest's design, the SO.9000 Trident, was based on the potentially lethal combination of turbojet and rocket power. Design studies began as early as 1949, and building of the first prototype, the SO.9000-01 Trident I, began at Courbevoie in October 1951. At a time when swept or delta wing planforms were considered mandatory for supersonic flight, the Trident's designer, Lucien Servanty, took the bold step of selecting a short, thin, unswept wing spanning less than 9m (30ft), mounted on a bullet-like fuselage and having a Turboméca Marboé II turbojet attached to each wingtip.

The prototype Trident I flew for the first time on 2 March 1953 at Melun-Villaroche, under the power of its wingtip-mounted Marborés; it appeared publicly at Le Bourget in July that year, where it failed to make much of an impression alongside more exotic swept-wing types. Meanwhile, a second prototype, the SO.9000-02, was also nearing completion, and this machine made its maiden flight on 30 August 1953: it was also its last, because it crashed and was a total write-off.

In the meantime, Dassault had been building the prototype of a more advanced version, which was to be the forerunner of a fully operational variant. Designated SO.9050 Trident II, this machine made its first flight – under turbojet power only – at Melun-Villaroche on 17 July 1955. A second Trident II prototype, the SO.9050-002, was destroyed on its first flight that same month, but test pilot Charles Goujon went on to fly -001 to a speed of Mach 1.7 (1,805km/h/1,122mph), at that time the highest speed attained by any piloted aircraft in Europe. In January 1956 an order for six pre-production machines was placed by the French Air Ministry, and the first of these flew on 3 May 1957.

The SO.9000 Trident combined turbojet- and rocket-powered interceptor, seen here with the rocket motor lit, was a radical design. (Musée de l'Air)

Another experimental French interceptor of the mid-1950s was the Sud-Aviation Durandal, which took its name from the legendary sword wielded by Roland, France's national hero. (Musée de l'Air)

The extraordinary Leduc 021 was designed as a research vehicle for a ramjet-powered interceptor. A more advanced prototype, the Leduc 022, was also built and flown. (Musée de l'Air)

Then came tragedy. On 21 May 1957, Trident 001 was destroyed during a test flight when its highly volatile rocket fuels, furaline and nitric acid, became accidentally mixed and caused an explosion. The pilot, Charles Goujon, was killed. Further development of the Trident was halted shortly afterwards.

The Leduc Ramjets

Some of the most radical research aircraft developed during this period were the product of designer René Leduc, who specialized in ramjet-powered designs. His experiments with ramjet-powered aircraft dated back to 1937, and a small research ramjet designated Leduc 010 eventually took to the air in November 1946, mounted on the back of a Bloch 161 transport, making its first gliding flight on 21 October 1947. On 21 April 1949, after a series of gliding trials, it was launched for the first time with the ramjet lit, and on 31 May that year it reached a speed of 905km/h (562mph) at 7,625m (25,000ft). Subsequent testing was not trouble-free; on 27 November 1951 it was badly damaged in a crash-landing, its pilot being seriously injured, and on 25 July 1952, after repair, it struck its Languedoc launch aircraft on release and had to make a belly landing.

Meanwhile, Leduc had been building a larger and more powerful ramjet research vehicle, the Leduc 021. Air tests began on 16 May 1953, with the aircraft mounted above a Languedoc, and several gliding trials were made before the first powered flight on 7 August 1953. Subsequent flight trials were carried out throughout the flight envelope up to a limiting Mach number of 0.85; among other spectacular performance figures the 021 showed an initial climb rate of 200m/sec (39,4000ft/min) and a ceiling of 20,000m (66,000ft). A second Leduc 021 was built, and this flew under its own power for the first time on 1 March 1954.

The 021's pilot was accommodated semi-reclined in a bullet-like nose fairing that protruded from the main engine tube; this could be jettisoned in an emergency, a parachute system being located immediately aft of the pilot. Aft of the cabin, the central body contained the Turboméca Artouste I turbine that drove the fuel pumps and generators, together with fuel tanks, batteries and radio. Aft of this central core were twenty-one burners arranged in seven banks through which fuel was sprayed – each bank could be lit separately, depending on the amount of power required.

The Leduc 021 was intended to be the research vehicle for an operational interceptor, and as the next step towards this goal a more advanced prototype, the Leduc 022, was designed and built. The 022 was larger than its predecessors and had swept flying surfaces; it was equipped with an Atar 101D-3 turbojet, installed inside the ramjet duct, that enabled the aircraft to take off under its own power and accelerate to the point where the ramjet could take over. The aircraft flew for the first time on 26 December 1956 and quickly showed enormous performance potential, including an ability to climb to 25,000m (82,000ft) in four minutes. With flight testing of 022-01 well under way, construction of a second prototype was started.

However, the 022's limiting factor was endurance: at an estimated maximum combat speed of Mach 2.4 (it actually achieved Mach 1.5 during its trials) the aircraft could carry sufficient fuel for only 10 minutes' flying. Besides, French Air Ministry requirements were now turning more towards the concept of multi-role combat aircraft, a policy dictated by wildly escalating research and development costs. The day of the pure interceptor was over, and the Leduc 022, one of the most radical aircraft designed anywhere during the post-war years of experiment, was abandoned.

Chapter 10
The USSR's Early Interceptors

With the acquisition of the first captured German turbojets at the end of 1944, various Soviet design bureaux were ordered to begin a 'crash' programme aimed at producing operational fighters designed around these engines. The bureaux involved were Mikoyan and Guryevich (MiG), Lavochkin, Sukhoi and Yakovlev, and by the time initial design studies were nearing completion, copies of the German engines were already in production, the BMW 003 as the RD-20 and the Jumo 004 as the RD-10.

The Yak-15

Each design bureau tackled the problem in its own fashion, all from a starting point in February 1945. While its rivals all built new designs of various sorts, Yakovlev opted for an adaptation of their existing and well-proven Yak-3 fighter. The resulting aircraft, designated Yak-15, flew for the first time on 24 April 1946 and deliveries to Soviet Air Force fighter squadrons began early in 1947. Production aircraft retained the tailwheel undercarriage of the Yak-3 and were powered by the RD-10 engine; about 280 were built. At the time of its introduction the Yak-15 was the lightest jet fighter in the world, the lightweight structure of the Yak-3's airframe compensating for the relatively low power of the engine. The Yak-15's NATO reporting name was 'Feather'.

The I-300/MiG-9

The MiG design was the I-300, the I standing for *Istrebitel*, or interceptor. Although the aircraft was powered by a pair of BMW 003A engines mounted side-by-side in the centre fuselage, it was by no means heavy, the loaded weight being in the region of 5,000kg (11,000lb). The I-300 featured the first tricycle undercarriage installed on a Soviet-built aircraft, the narrow-track mainwheels retracting outwards into the wings. Three I-300 prototypes were built, the first of which flew on 24 April 1946 with test pilot Alexander Grinchik at the controls. During subsequent testing the maximum speed was gradually pushed up to 895km/h (566mph). Severe vibration was experienced in the higher speed range, and it took a considerable time before the cause was established. The jet efflux, exhausting under the tail, was buffeting the fireproof sheathing of the rear fuselage undersurface and setting up resonance throughout the airframe.

A month after the aircraft's first flight, Grinchik was carrying out a high-speed, low-level run in the first prototype when the aircraft suddenly developed an uncontrollable pitch and dived into the ground, killing its pilot. Grinchik's place was taken by Mark Gallai who, together with Georgii Shianov, continued the flight test programme with the two other aircraft. Gallai enjoyed enormous prestige with the elite Soviet test pilot fraternity: he came from a Jewish family, which might have been a problem for career advancement under the Soviet system, but his manifest skills as a pilot and engaging personality won him respect everywhere. His flight log included some of the most important aircraft of the period after the Second World War. Gallai flew more than 200 types of aircraft, even taking the controls of the Luftwaffe's dangerous Me 163 rocket-powered interceptor.

Both pilots experienced a high workload, for the I-300 was a difficult and often unpleasant aircraft to fly, many of its problems resulting from the haste with which it had been completed. On one occasion, Gallai almost came to grief when, during a high-speed run at Mach 0.8, the nose of the aircraft pitched down violently. The pilot reduced power and managed to restore full control, but after landing it was found that both the tailplane and elevator had become distorted. In all probability, Gallai had experienced the problem that had killed his colleague Grinchik.

On another occasion, Gallai was carrying out a high-speed run at 600m (2,000ft) when the I-300 virtually went out of control; fortunately the nose went up instead of down and the aircraft gained several thousand feet of altitude, vibrating badly, with the pilot practically helpless in the cockpit. Gallai reduced power and restored partial control; looking back to check the tail, he saw to his dismay that the port tailplane was no longer there and the starboard tailplane was badly distorted. To make matters worse, fuel from a ruptured tank was seeping into the cockpit and there was a severe fire risk. Gallai would have been quite justified in bailing out, but he was a test pilot of the highest calibre. Cutting both engines, he managed to bring the aircraft back for a dead-stick landing.

Despite the problems experienced during its development the I-300, with a redesigned nose to accommodate one 37mm and two 23mm cannon, was ordered into production for the Soviet Air Force as the MiG-9, and was the first Soviet jet type to reach squadron service, the first deliveries being made in December 1946. Although far from technically reliable, it provided Russian fighter pilots with valuable experience in jet operations.

While striving to bring the MiG-9 to production standard, the MiG bureau was also studying other fighter projects. In 1946, they built and tested a rocket-powered, target-defence interceptor, the I-270 (Zh).

The MiG I-270

The first Soviet attempt to produce a short-range, rocket-propelled, target-defence interceptor, designed to have a rate of climb of 10,800m/min (35,400ft/min), had been made some years earlier. This was the Bereznyak-Isayev BI-1. It was to be powered by a Dushkin D-1 rocket motor, which was successfully tested in a glider that had been towed to altitude. Of mixed construction, the BI-1, a small low-wing monoplane, was built in only forty days, and was flown as a glider for the first time on 10 September 1941. The first powered test flight was made on 15 May 1942 and was successful, but shortly afterwards the prototype was destroyed when it crashed during a maximum-power run at low level. Despite this setback seven pre-series aircraft were built and the programme went ahead. However, subsequent flight trials revealed unforeseen aerodynamic problems. This, together with the fact that Dushkin's work on a multi-chamber rocket motor encountered innumerable snags, and the powered endurance of eight minutes was considered insufficient for operational purposes, brought an end to the project.

The I-270 was based on the design of the wartime Messerschmitt Me 263A rocket fighter project. Whereas the Me 263A had been a swept-wing design, the I-270 employed an unswept wing of thin section and slightly swept horizontal tail surfaces, mounted T-fashion on top of the vertical surfaces. The Soviet aircraft was powered by an RD-2M-3V bi-fuel rocket motor, which was a slightly modified version of the German Walter HWK 509C; it was equipped with main and cruising chambers, the former giving a maximum endurance of 4 minutes 15 seconds and the latter 9 minutes 3 seconds. The first airframe, Zh-1, began glider tests in December 1946, towed to its release point by a Tu-2. The Zh-2, rocket-powered with a dual-thrust engine giving 16.2kN (3,640lb) boost power and 3.9kN(880lb) cruise power, first flew in March 1947. However total burn time of the Zh-2's rocket engines was only 255 seconds, and by this time the prototype of the faster and much longer ranged turbojet-powered MiG-15 was nearing completion. Therefore the I-270 was seen as having no military utility, and it was abandoned after the Zh-2 was written off after a hard landing in the spring of 1947. Under test, the I-270 had reached an altitude of 10,000m (32,800ft) in 2.37 minutes, and 15,000m (49,200ft) in 3.03 minutes. Maximum speed was 1,000km/h (620mph), and the proposed armament was two 23mm cannon.

The Yak-25

In the late 1940s Yakovlev built the prototypes of three single-seat fighter designs, none of which came to fruition. The first, in 1947, was the Yak-19, a simple and uncomplicated aircraft with unswept flying surfaces and powered by an RD-500 (Rolls-Royce Derwent) turbojet. The Yak-19 served as the prototype of a more refined design, the Yak-25; this had a similar power plant, but was fitted with swept tail surfaces and wingtip drop tanks. The Yak-25 was intended to fulfil the same tactical role as the Republic F-84 Thunderjet, but it had extremely disappointing performance figures and was consequently abandoned, its designation

Yakovlev's Yak-19 was the first of that bureau's jet fighter designs after the Yak-15. (Yakovlev)

The Yak-30 was built to the same specification as the MiG-15, but during comparative trials the MiG emerged as the better all-round design. (Yakovlev)

being allocated to a later – and vastly more successful – fighter type, the Yak-25 'Flashlight'.

The other Yakovlev jet fighter design of the 1940s was the Yak-30, a swept-wing fighter built to the same specification as the MiG-15 – by which it was eclipsed. Powered by an RD-45 turbojet, the Yak-30 first flew in 1948; maximum speed was 1,000km/h (640mph), service ceiling 15,000m (50,000ft) and range 1,450km (900 miles). The Yak-30 underwent comparative trials with the MiG-15, from which the Mikoyan/Gurevich fighter emerged as the better aircraft on all counts.

The Su-9

In the original race to produce a jet fighter in 1945–6, Mikoyan/Gurevich had been ordered to design an aircraft around two Junkers Jumo 004A turbojets; the result, as we have seen, was the MiG-9, the first jet fighter to enter Soviet service. Another designer with the same brief was Pavel Sukhoi, whose Su-2 ground-attack aircraft had filled a dangerous gap during the war until the deployment of the Ilyushin Il-2. His subsequent designs, however, though often advanced and sometimes aerodynamically better than others that achieved production status, had laboured under a series of misfortunes – often caused by the lack of suitable engines – and had consequently never met with the success they deserved. Nevertheless, Sukhoi was one of the USSR's most experienced aeronautical engineers, and it was logical that his expertise should be put to good use in the jet fighter development programme.

Although the Sukhoi Su-9 bore a resemblance to the Me 262, it was a completely new design.

Sukhoi approached the design of his first jet fighter, the Su-9, with a good deal of caution, preferring to adopt a similar configuration to that of the Messerschmitt Me 262, although the aircraft that emerged was by no means a copy of the German fighter. The Su-9's engines were placed in underwing nacelles and the aircraft had an Me 262-style cockpit, but there the resemblance ended. The flying surfaces were less angular and the wings were unswept, while the fuselage was deeper and slimmer than the Me 262's. The only aspect, apart from the engines, which might be said to have been copied from the Me 262 was the tricycle undercarriage, and even here there were distinct differences.

Like the MiG-9, the Su-9 was armed with one 37mm and two 23mm cannon, and for short-field take-offs a pair of solid-fuel booster rockets could be attached under the fuselage. The Su-9 was generally a more refined design than the MiG aircraft: among other items, it featured a compressed-air ejection seat, modelled on German equipment, and a braking parachute. The aircraft flew for the first time in 1946, some months after the MiG-9, and the performance figures for the two aircraft were similar. Although the Su-9 was slightly inferior to the MiG-9 at high altitude, its range performance adequately compensated for this, and it also carried more ammunition. In view of the MiG-9's appalling safety record, there would seem to be no reason why the Sukhoi aircraft should not have been selected in preference.

But there was a reason, and it was an extraordinary one. It appears that other Soviet designers, eager to have their own aircraft accepted, 'ganged up' on Sukhoi at a conference in 1946 and persuaded Josef Stalin that any machine that resembled the Messerschmitt 262 would be unacceptable because the German fighter had proved dangerous to fly. Stalin was by no means an aviation expert, but he had seen photographs of the Me 262, and to his mind the Su-9 was sufficiently like it to be seen in an unfavourable light. In all probability, Stalin's concern was not so much to do with safety concerns but more to do with a desire to show the world that the Soviet regime was capable of producing modern aircraft without being accused of copying those of its former enemy. So, after one brief appearance at the Tushino air display on 3 August 1947, the Su-9 was abandoned and the Soviet Air Force took delivery of the heavy, unwieldy MiG-9, which killed its pilots in considerable numbers.

The Su-15

Following this disappointment, Sukhoi now pinned his hopes on the development of two advanced jet fighter projects, the Su-15 and Su-17. By 1948, the Russians – again relying heavily on German technology – had developed an Airborne Intercept (AI) radar known as *Izumrud* (Emerald), which was intended to equip a new generation of all-weather fighter aircraft. Sukhoi's response to the specification was the Su-15, which was also known as the *Samolyot* ('Aeroplane') P.

Powered by two RD-45 (Rolls-Royce Nene) turbojets, the *Samolyot* P had a mid-mounted wing

The twin-engined Sukhoi Su-15, also known as the Samolyot P, was fitted with a rudimentary AI radar. (Sukhoi)

with a leading edge sweep of 37 degrees, the twin engines being mounted one above the other in a deep centre fuselage and exhausting below the fuselage aft of the trailing edge. The AI scanner was housed in a small radome situated above the nose-mounted air intake, and armament was two 37mm cannon mounted one on either side of the nose. With a loaded weight of 10,400kg (23,000lb) the Su-15 was a very heavy aircraft; nevertheless, its designers estimated that it would have a maximum speed of 1,030km/h (641mph), a service ceiling of 14,000m (46,000ft) and the ability to reach 10,000m (33,000ft) in 6½ minutes. These figures were never proven, because the Su-15 disintegrated following severe vibration on an early high-speed run, the pilot ejecting, and no further prototypes were built.

The Su-17

Work continued in 1949 on the Su-17 supersonic fighter project, which had wings swept at 50 degrees and was to have been powered by a Mikulin TR-3 axial-flow turbojet. Estimated performance figures included speeds of Mach 1.08 at 11,000m (36,000ft) and Mach 1.02 at sea level, with a service ceiling of 15,500m (51,000ft). A novel feature of the Su-17 was that in an emergency the fuselage nose, including the cockpit, was intended to be blasted clear of the rest of the airframe by explosive charges and stabilized by a drogue, the pilot subsequently ejecting in normal fashion. By this time, however, Sukhoi had fallen out of favour with the Ministry for Aeronautical Development and Production and in 1949, on orders from Moscow, his factory was closed down. All work on the Su-17, the airframe of which was partially complete, was brought to a halt and the aircraft was broken up for scrap. Despite these misfortunes, Pavel Sukhoi was later to bounce back into the limelight of Soviet fighter design – confusingly, the designations Su-9, -15 and -17 were later applied to successful Sukhoi-designed interceptors and fighter-bombers of the 1950s, 1960s and 1970s.

The La-150, -152, -154 and -156

The first venture into the jet fighter field by the other leading Soviet designer, Semyon A. Lavochkin, was the La-150, which was powered by a single RD-10 (Jumo 004A) turbojet. The aircraft, which was flown for the first time in September 1946 by test pilot A.A. Popov, featured a 'pod and boom' design, with unswept shoulder-mounted wings and a tricycle undercarriage mounted in the lower fuselage. Armament comprised two 23mm NS cannon, one on either side of the nose. Two prototypes were built, and these reached a maximum speed of 800km/h (500mph) at 5,000m (16,400ft); service ceiling was 12,500m (41,000ft). Three more aircraft were completed and fitted with uprated RD-10F engines, being re-designated La-150M, but the flight characteristics of the Lavochkin design left much to be desired – severe oscillation of the tail boom was only one of its problems – and further development was abandoned in April 1947.

The La-174TK was fitted with a new thin wing, apparent in this photograph. (Author)

The Lavochkin La-168, seen here in a slightly retouched photograph, was the bureau's first really successful jet design, and was the forerunner of the La-15. (Author)

In the meantime, Lavochkin had also begun work on three more fighter prototypes, the La-152, La-154 and La-156, all of which featured a configuration that was closer in style to that of Yakovlev's Yak-15. The fuselage undercarriage arrangement was retained, but the wing was mounted at the mid-point and the cockpit was positioned well aft, over the trailing edge. However, although the handling characteristics of these three aircraft were somewhat better than those of the La-150, their performance was actually poorer and they were used only for experimental flying.

By the middle of 1947, Soviet designers were overcoming an early aversion to the use of sweepback (an aversion that was shared by their British and French counterparts), and Lavochkin decided to fit the basic La-152 fuselage with swept flying surfaces. The result was the La-160, which had a wing swept at the optimum 35 degrees and an armament of two NS-37 cannon. The aircraft flew for the first time in 1947 and was claimed to be the first post-war swept-wing jet fighter, but in fact it was used purely for aerodynamic research and never went into production.

The last of Lavochkin's straight-wing designs was the La-174TK, the 'TK' denoting Tonkii Krylo, or thin wing. Apart from the wing design, the main difference between this aircraft and the La-152, La-154 and La-156 was that it was powered by an RD-500 (Rolls-Royce Derwent) engine and carried an armament of three NS-23 cannon. The La-174TK, which first flew early in 1948, was in fact something of an anachronism, and contributed nothing to Soviet aeronautical knowledge except to underline the fact that the straight, thin wing offered no advantages over the swept planform.

Before the La-174TK even flew, Lavochkin was already studying two infinitely more advanced jet fighter designs, produced to the same specification as the successful MiG-15. The first of these was the La-168, which was intended to be powered by an RD-10 turbojet, but when the Lavochkin team discovered that the MiG design, which weighed about the same as their own, was to be fitted with a much more powerful Nene engine derivative they realized that the La-168's chances of success were very slender indeed by comparison. Lavochkin therefore set about building a second prototype, similar in configuration to the La-168 but powered by the production version of the RD-500. Somewhat confusingly, this aircraft was given the designation La-174.

The prototype of Lavochkin's La-174 flew shortly after the La-168 and, given the service designation La-15, went on to enter Soviet Air Force service in 1949. However, its performance proved inadequate for the interceptor role and only a few ground-attack units were equipped with it, the MiG-15 becoming the standard Soviet interceptor of the late 1940s. About 500 La-15s were built.

The DFS 346

Meanwhile, Soviet aeronautical scientists had been exploring the realms of high-speed, high-altitude flight with the aid of the DFS 346, a German rocket-powered research vehicle built from technical files captured at the end of the war. At

Podberezhye, the Russians set up a research bureau called OKB-2, directed by a German engineer, Hans Rossing, and A.Y. Bereznyak, the man responsible for the BI-1 target defence interceptor of the Second World War. Most of the personnel were German, former employees of the Siebel company, which during the war had been intended to have built the aircraft at Halle, in Germany.

By the time a second group of German engineers arrived at Podberezhye in October 1946 several models of the DFS 346 were under test, and the full-size aircraft was completed in 1947. The aircraft, which was unpowered, was designated 346P and was designed to perfect landing techniques, gliding in to land after being dropped by its parent aircraft. In all other respects it resembled the intended powered version, the fuselage having an unbroken cigar-shaped profile with mid-mounted wings swept back at 45 degrees and a short, broad fin and rudder unit supporting a swept-back, high-mounted tailplane. The pilot lay in a prone position behind a glazed nose cone.

In 1948 the 346P was transferred to the flight test airfield at Toplistan, near Moscow, where several unpowered, towed flights were made by two German test pilots, Rauschen and Motsch. Powered flights were to be made by another German, Wolfgang Ziese, who had been Siebel's chief test pilot. The powered version of the 346 (it is unclear whether this was a new aircraft, or the original one equipped with a rocket motor) was completed in 1949, the aircraft being designated 346D.

On 30 September 1949, the 346D, with Ziese at the controls, was positioned under the starboard wing of its mother ship, a Boeing B-29 called 'Ramp Tramp' (one of three which had made emergency landings in Russia after attacking Japanese targets in Manchuria in 1944). Ziese lit the rocket motor (a Walter HWK-109-509C) a few seconds after the drop and almost immediately experienced control difficulties. Recovering to Toplistan, he touched down at nearly 300km/h (200mph) on the 346D's landing skid, causing damage to the aircraft and injuring himself.

After the aircraft was repaired, testing resumed at Lukhovitsy airfield in October 1950, the pilot being a Russian, P.I. Kasmin. On 10 May 1951, Wolfgang Ziese, now recovered from his injuries, successfully flew the 346D under power, and on 16 June he made a gliding flight in a second aircraft, designated 346-3. On 13 August 1951 Ziese made a powered flight in the 346-3, somewhat disappointed by the knowledge that in the light of wind tunnel tests the aircraft would never fly supersonically and that it was limited to Mach 0.9.

Ziese made another successful flight on 2 September 1951, but during a third flight on the 14th the aircraft went out of control at 6,700m (22,000ft). Ziese had no alternative but to use the 346's novel escape system, in which the whole nose section was jettisoned by firing explosive attachment bolts and the pilot pulled clear by the automatic deployment of a parachute.

It was the end of the 346 test programme. In 1953 the German scientists and engineers were repatriated to East Germany, where they first heard the news, denied to them during their enforced stay in the USSR, that an American research aircraft, the Bell X-1, had already flown faster than sound six years earlier.

Chapter 11
The Heavy Brigade: Long-Range Fighters

The Bell XP-83 was extensively tested and had the potential for further development, but it was overtaken by later designs. (Bell)

The Bell XP-83

The USAF requirement for a long-range night and all-weather fighter originated in a need to replace the Northrop P-61 Black Widow, which was the USAAF's standard specially-developed night fighter at the end of the Second World War. Among possible candidates for the role among the early jet-powered designs was the Bell XP-83, which began life as a heavy, single-seat, long-range fighter and flew for the first time on 25 February, 1945, powered by two 4,000lb (17.8kN) s.t. General Electric J33-GE-5 turbojets. Two prototypes were built and extensively tested, their performance figures including a maximum speed of 567mph (912km/h) at sea level and 525mph (845km/h) at 45,000ft (14,000m), together with a range of 1,730 miles (2,780km) at 30,000ft (10,000m). The proposed armament for the XP-83 was six 0.50in machine guns, with either four 20mm or four 37mm cannon as alternatives. The XP-83's airframe had the potential for conversion to a two-seat configuration and the inclusion of AI radar, but there would have been a substantial weight penalty and the existing engines were not powerful enough. This, together with the fact that the XP-83 was outclassed by later designs, led to development being abandoned.

The Curtiss XP-87

As an interim measure, pending the development of a suitable jet-powered night fighter, the North American F-82 Twin Mustang replaced the Black Widow in the night fighter squadrons of Air Defense Command from 1947. Meanwhile, three American aircraft companies, Curtiss, Northrop and Lockheed, were busy working up designs to meet the USAF requirement, which called for a two-seat radar-equipped aircraft armed with either cannon or machine guns and possessing a top speed of at least 600mph (965km/h) at 40,000ft (12,000m).

The design submitted by the Airplane Division of the Curtiss-Wright Corporation, the XP-87, was the first multi-seat jet combat aircraft specifically designed for the radar-intercept role at night. Developed from an earlier wartime project, the XA-43 attack aircraft, it was powered by four Westinghouse XJ34-WE-7 turbojets, installed in pairs in two nacelles, and was armed with four 20mm cannon. Provision was also made to install 0.5in machine guns in a remotely controlled dorsal turret, but this was never fitted. The XP-87 prototype (49-59600) flew for the first time on 5 March 1948, and work began on a second aircraft, the XP-87A, which was intended to have two General Electric J47-GE-15 engines. The first aircraft was known as the Nighthawk, the second as the Blackhawk. However, the second machine never flew, and an order for eighty-eight J47-powered production aircraft was cancelled to release funds for the development of two more promising designs that were eventually to give the USAF a truly potent night/all-weather capability, the Lockheed F-94C Starfire and the Northrop F-89 Scorpion. The XP-87 passed into aviation history as the last combat aircraft produced by Curtiss-Wright.

The Convair YF-102

In 1950, the USAF formulated a requirement for a night and all-weather interceptor incorporating the latest fire-control system. This was eventually to emerge as the Convair F-102, whose design was based on experience gained during flight testing of the XF-92 delta-wing research aircraft. Two prototype YF-102s were built, the first flying on 24 October 1953. This aircraft was damaged beyond

The Northrop F-89 Scorpion gave the USAF Air Defense Command a true all-weather capability. (Northrop)

repair only a week later, but testing resumed with the second machine in January 1954. Eight more YF-102s were built for evaluation, and it soon became apparent that the aircraft's performance fell short of expectations. After substantial airframe redesign the machine re-emerged in December 1954 as the YF-102A, and the type was ordered into full production. The first F-102A was handed over to Air Defense Command in June 1955, but it was another year before the type was issued to squadrons. As an interim measure, Air Defense Command acquired an interim radar-equipped all-weather fighter, the single-seat F-86D Sabre that mounted a pack of twenty-four 2¾in folding-fin aircraft rockets recessed under the fuselage.

The Avro CF-100 and CF-105

Canada, forming the first line of defence against the threat of bombers attacking the North American continent across the great wastes of the Arctic, was quick to identify the need for a long-range night and all-weather interceptor during the early post-war years. In response to this requirement, Avro Canada designed the CF-100, at that time the largest fighter aircraft in the world. The prototype CF-100 Mk 1 flew on 19 January 1950, powered by two Rolls-Royce Avon RA3 turbojets; production aircraft were fitted with the Avro Canada Orinda. In September 1950 an order was placed with Avro Canada for 124 CF-100 Mk 3s for the Royal Canadian Air Force (RCAF). These

The powerful and heavily armed Avro Canada CF-105 Arrow was an excellent design, but fell victim to escalating development costs. (Avro Canada)

were powered by two Orenda Mk 8s and armed with eight 0.5in Colt-Browning machine guns. In fact only seventy were built, the first entering service with RCAF No. 445 Sqn.

The next production version was the Mk 4A, powered by two Orenda 9s and equipped with a Hughes AGP-40 fire-control radar. This variant could be armed with forty-eight 'Mighty Mouse' High Velocity Aircraft Rockets (HVARs), eight 0.5in machine guns or four 30mm cannon in a ventral pack, plus fifty-eight HVAR rockets in wingtip pods. The first production Mk 4A flew on 24 October 1953 and the aircraft entered service with No. 445 Sqn in the following year. In all, 510 Mk 4As and Mk 4Bs (the latter with Orenda 11 engines) were built, and by the end of 1957 nine RCAF squadrons were operating the type, providing round-the-clock air defence coverage of Canada's far north. Four CF-100 squadrons also served in Germany as part of Canada's NATO commitment, and fifty-three examples of the last production version, the Mk 5, were delivered to Belgium.

The CF-100 was to have been replaced in RCAF service by the very advanced Avro Canada CF-105 Arrow delta-wing interceptor, which flew for the first time on 25 March 1958, powered by two Pratt & Whitney J75 turbojets. Four more aircraft were built, designated CF-105 Mk 1, and another four – designated Mk 2, with 22,000lb (97.9kN) thrust Orenda PS-13 engines – were almost complete when the project was cancelled in February 1959, on grounds of cost. The Arrow was to have been armed with eight Sparrow AAMs.

In the early 1950s the RAF had to rely heavily on night fighter conversions of the de Havilland Vampire (left) and Venom (above). (Hawker Siddeley)

The Gloster GA5 Javelin

During most of the 1950s, the RAF's night and all-weather air defences were sustained by night fighter versions of the Gloster Meteor, culminating in the NF.14, and night fighter variants of the de Havilland Vampire and Venom. Their much-needed replacement, the Gloster Javelin, took nearly a decade between first flight and squadron deployment.

Construction of the Javelin prototype, the Gloster GA5 – the world's first twin-jet delta and an extremely radical design for its day – began in April 1949, and the aircraft flew for the first time on 26 November 1951, powered by two Armstrong Siddeley Sapphires. The maiden flight was attended by a serious snag in the shape of rudder buffeting, and further flight testing was delayed while modifications were carried out. Then, on 29 June 1952, the prototype lost both elevators and was destroyed in a crash landing at Boscombe Down. (The test pilot, Sqn Ldr W.A. Waterton, was subsequently awarded the George Medal for his action in retrieving the vital flight recorder from the blazing wreckage.) Testing continued with the second prototype, WD808, which first flew on 21 August 1952, but this aircraft was also destroyed on 11 June 1953 as the result of a super-stall condition. Three more prototypes had been ordered in the meantime: the third aircraft flew on 7 March 1953 and carried an armament of four 30mm cannon, while the fourth featured a modified wing shape and the fifth, which flew on 20 July 1954, was up to full production standard, with British AI.17 radar.

As the Javelin FAW.1, the new fighter was ordered into 'super-priority' production for the RAF (which was intended to give the highest priority possible to the production of certain military aircraft). The first production aircraft flew on 22 July 1954 and deliveries began to No. 46 Sqn at RAF Odiham in February 1956. Javelin FAW.1s were also issued to No. 87 Sqn, which formed part of 2nd TAF in Germany. In October 1955, a new variant, the Javelin FAW.2, made its appearance. This was basically similar to the FAW.1 apart from its radar – which was the American-designed APQ43 (known in British service as the AI.22) – and avionics, and replaced the earlier production model in No. 46 Sqn. Next on the production line was the FAW.4, the prototype of which was in fact the forty-first FAW.1 fitted with an all-moving tailplane. This variant entered service with No 141 Sqn early in 1957, and except for the tailplane was essentially similar to the FAW.1. Later that year, No. 151 Sqn received the first examples of the Javelin FAW.5, which had a modified wing structure and increased internal fuel capacity, and in 1958 the Javelin FAW.6 – which was basically an FAW.5 with the same radar as the FAW.2 – entered service with No. 89 Sqn.

In November 1956 the Javelin's already formidable combat potential was given an extra boost with the appearance of the FAW.7, which was fit-

THE HEAVY BRIGADE: LONG-RANGE FIGHTERS

The second DH.110 prototype, WG240, was painted gloss black overall. (Hawker Siddeley)

ted with Sapphire ASSa7R turbojets developing 12,300lb (54.7kN) with reheat in place of the 8,300lb (36.9kN) thrust Sapphire ASSa6 engines used in earlier marks. The Javelin FAW.7, which incorporated further structural modifications and increased wing fuel tankage, had an armament of two 30mm Aden cannon and four Firestreak AAMs and entered service with No. 33 Sqn at RAF Leeming in July 1958. The FAW.8, which first flew on 9 May 1958, was externally similar to the FAW.7; it incorporated the AI.22 radar, a simplified afterburning system, a Sperry autopilot, drooped wing leading edges, and dampers on the yaw and pitch axes. The FAW.8 was the last production model of the Javelin, the final aircraft being completed in June 1960, but a number of Javelin FAW.7s were brought up to FAW.8 standard (although with British radar) and designated FAW.9.

The Javelin formed the core of Britain's air defences until the 1960s, when it was progressively replaced by the English Electric Lightning interceptor. Yet the Javelin had plenty of potential for development into a supersonic interceptor in its own right, as will be seen in Chapter 15.

The de Havilland DH.110/Sea Vixen

In its early development phase, the Gloster GA5 faced strong competition from another twin-engined heavy all-weather fighter design, the de Havilland DH.110, which originated in Naval Specification N.40/46. This was issued in June 1946, and two months later it was followed by the RAF's all-weather fighter specification, F.44/46. As the two specifications were generally similar, de Havilland decided to offer the RAF a 'de-navalized' version of the DH.110. During the next two years the specifications underwent a number of changes, the RAF requirement being eventually finalized as F.4/49 and the navy's version as N.14/49, and at the end of 1948 de Havilland received an Instruction to Proceed with the building of two prototypes, one for each service. Early in 1949, however, the Royal Navy changed its requirements and cancelled its order.

Despite this, work proceeded with prototype construction, and the first of the two swept-wing, twin-boom DH.110s, WG236, flew for the first time on 26 September 1951, powered by two 7,300lb (32.5kN) s.t. Rolls-Royce Avons. Six months later, on 9 April 1952, this aircraft became the first twin-engined two-seater to exceed Mach 1 in a dive. The second DH.110 prototype, WG240, first flew on 25 July 1952 and featured modifications that included some strengthening of the wing.

Painted a sinister all black, WG240 was demonstrated by John Derry at that year's Farnborough Air Show on every day except 6 September, when it suddenly went unserviceable. Derry switched to the other DH.110, WG236, and went into his usual display routine. As he was pulling a high-g turn about a mile outside the airfield perimeter the aircraft experienced catastrophic structural failure due to compression buckling and tension stress around the inboard leading edge of the starboard wing; the wing broke away, leading to the complete disintegration of the airframe. Derry and his flight test observer, Tony Richards, were both killed, as were twenty-eight spectators when the engines and other debris plunged into the crowd, a further sixty being injured. As a result of this tragic accident the second DH.110 prototype was grounded, leaving the way clear for the Gloster Javelin to meet the RAF's all-weather fighter requirement.

Yet in some respects, the DH.110 was the better design. It was certainly more manoeuvrable, its handling qualities comparing closely with those of many smaller and lighter single-engined fighters, and it was very stable in a high-g turn right down to the stall, which the Javelin was not. Undeterred,

Despite its unfortunate early career, the DH.110 was developed into the Sea Vixen, which served the Fleet Air Arm well. (Hawker Siddeley)

de Havilland resumed testing with the second DH.110 after further structural modifications, with a renewed naval requirement in mind, and in September 1953 it carried out carrier trials aboard HMS *Albion*. A production order for a developed naval version followed, and this ultimately entered Fleet Air Arm service as the Sea Vixen.

The Mikoyan/Gurevich I-320(R)

During the Second World War, the Soviet Air Force had no aircraft designed specifically for night fighting. During the aerial battles that took place over Moscow and Leningrad in 1941, and later over Stalingrad, some converted Pe-2 dive bombers were used in the night fighter role, as was a heavily armed interceptor variant, the Pe-3, but the Russians had no AI equipment and so had to depend on visual interception techniques. It was not until 1948 that, with the help of German technology, they succeeded in developing a viable AI radar known as *Izumrud* (Emerald), which was intended to equip a new generation of night and all-weather fighter aircraft. As related in Chapter 10, Pavel Sukhoi developed the Su-15, also known as the *Samolyot* P. This could carry an *Izumrud* AI scanner, but following the crash of the prototype, the Su-15 was abandoned.

The other main contenders in the race to produce a Russian night fighter were MiG, Lavochkin and Yakovlev. MiG's design, the single-seat I-320(R), first flew in 1949. It was powered by two Klimov VK-1 turbojets mounted in tandem, one exhausting under the fuselage and one at the tail. The engine installation resulted in a bulky, ungainly aircraft with poor handling characteristics and even worse visibility for the pilot, whose forward view was badly obscured by the long nose and radome.

MiG's I-320(R) all-weather fighter. The aircraft's flight characteristics were poor and it was abandoned.

The La-200B was designed to the same requirement as the Yak-25, to which it proved inferior. With its air intakes below and either side of the massive radome, and large auxiliary fuel tanks under its wings, it was one of the ugliest aircraft ever built.

The Yak-25 'Flashlight', which eventually met the Soviet Air Force's night and all-weather fighter requirement. (Yakovlev)

The Lavochkin La-200

Lavochkin's design, the La-200A, was a better proposition from several points of view, but suffered from having the same engine arrangement as the I-320(R). In both cases, the VK-1 engines were fed via a common nose air intake, but in the La-200A they were installed in tandem, the first exhausting under the fuselage and the second under the tail, and this necessitated some complex ducting that resulted in an inordinately large fuselage. A central air intake cone housed the La-200A's *Izumrud* radar and the fighter was a two-seater, the pilot and radar observer seated side by side. The La-200A had a fuselage-mounted undercarriage and carried an armament of three 37mm cannon, which contributed to the high all-up weight of 10,360kg (22,870lb). Like the I-320(R), the La-200A flew in 1949, and during trials reached a maximum speed of 1,061km/h (660mph) at 5,000m (16,400ft); service ceiling was 18,208m (59,700ft).

Neither the La-200A nor the I-320 underwent extensive operational trials, because in 1950 a developed, lighter version of the *Izumrud* AI radar was successfully installed in a two-seat MiG-15 variant known as the SP-5; both MiG-15s and MiG-17s were subsequently equipped with AI radar. These variants, however, did not meet the urgent requirement for an all-weather fighter fitted with long-range AI radar, and a specification for such an aircraft was issued in November 1951.

Lavochkin set about modifying the La-200A to carry a new radar scanner in a lengthened fuselage nose, and the result was the La-200B, one of the ugliest fighter aircraft ever flown. The massive radome ruled out a single air intake, so the engines were fed by three ducts, one on either side of the nose and one underneath it. Bulky auxiliary fuel tanks were fitted under the wings, and to compensate for the extra weight – the aircraft now weighed 11,211kg (24,750lb) loaded – the undercarriage was strengthened. In the end, preference was given to a far more promising design, the Yakovlev Yak-25, and the La-200B was abandoned.

Part IV
Naval Aircraft Prototypes, 1945–55

Chapter 12
US Naval Prototypes

The Boeing XF8B-1

At the end of the Pacific War, the US Naval Staff had a surprising aversion to the idea that jet aircraft might be successfully operated from aircraft carriers, and was still considering replacing its standard carrier-borne combat aircraft with more piston-engined types, designed around specifications that were dictated by operational requirements in the Pacific. One such aircraft, for example, designed specifically to undertake long-range operations against Japan, was the Boeing XF8B-1, a multi-purpose machine intended to act as a general-purpose fighter, interceptor, light bomber and torpedo bomber. Designed early in 1945, the prototype XF8B-1 flew in 1946 powered by a 2,500hp Pratt & Whitney R-4360 radial fitted with contra-rotating propellers. Its maximum speed was 432mph (695km/h), service ceiling 37,500ft (11,400m) and range 3,500 miles (5,640km). The aircraft, which had a wingspan of 54ft (16.46m) and a length of 43ft 3in (13.18m), could be armed with either six 20mm cannon or 0.50in machine guns and could carry up to 6,400lb (2,900kg) of offensive stores. A promising aircraft, the XF8B-1 nevertheless appeared too late, and a production order was cancelled.

The Ryan XFR-1

One of the most interesting US naval fighters of this period was designed by the Ryan Aeronautical Corporation. Design work on the Ryan Model 28 carrier-borne fighter, also known as the XFR-1 Fireball, was initiated in 1943, and the aircraft was in production before the end of the war in the Pacific. It was the first operational aircraft in which

The Ryan XFR-1 Fireball mixed-power carrier-borne fighter. The aircraft's very small air intakes were positioned just forward of the leading edges. (Philip Jarrett)

a piston engine was combined with a turbojet, using both power plants for take-off, climb and combat, and having the ability to fly and land with either engine shut down. The prototype XFR-1 flew for the first time on 25 June 1944 and the type entered service with Navy Fighter Squadron VF-66 in March 1945. Only sixty-nine were built, the last examples being delivered to VF-1E in June 1947. The type's service career was very brief, the last aircraft being retired at the end of that same month. The XFR-2, XFR-3 and XFR-4 were proposed variants with different engine installations, and a redesigned version, the XF2R-1, flew in November 1946 with a General Electric XT31-GE-2 turboprop in place of the piston engine.

The Curtiss XF15C-1

The Ryan XF2R-1 did not get past the single prototype stage. However, in the early days of the

An experimental carrier-borne fighter, the Chance Vought XF5U-1 had an unusual circular-planform wing. It was rolled out, but never flew. (LTV)

Ryan Corporation's design work on the XFR-1, the Bureau of Aeronautics had been sufficiently impressed by the composite-power concept to allocate further funds to the development of a larger, more heavily armed fighter using the same principle. The design contract for the new machine was awarded to the Curtiss-Wright Corporation, and on 7 April 1944 three prototypes were ordered under the designation XF15C-1. The fighter was powered by a nose-mounted Pratt & Whitney R-2800-34W radial engine rated at 2,100hp and driving a Hamilton Standard four-bladed propeller, while a 2,700lb (12kN) s.t. de Havilland H-1B turbojet, built under licence by Allis-Chalmers, was installed in the rear fuselage aft of the cockpit. The jet engine exhausted beneath a stepped-up tail unit, the tailplane being mounted on top of the fin.

The XF15C-1 had an interesting performance range. On the power of its piston engine only, the aircraft reached a speed of 322mph (518km/h) at sea level and 373mph (600km/h) at 25,000ft (7,600m), but with both engines operating these values increased to 432mph (695km/h) and 469mph (755km/h). The aircraft, which had a wingspan of 48ft (14.64m) and a length of 44ft (13.42m), had a range of 635 miles (1,022km) and an operational ceiling of 41,800ft (12,750m). The first prototype flew on 27 February 1945 on piston power only, but it crashed shortly after the jet engine was installed. The second aircraft flew on 9 July 1945 and was tested until the end of 1946, together with the third prototype, after which further development was abandoned.

The Chance Vought XF5U-1

By the standards of the day, the mixed-power fighters described above were fairly unorthodox – but not nearly as unorthodox as a piston-engined naval fighter design, the XF5U-1, revealed by Chance Vought in 1946. Based on the design of a low-powered predecessor, the V-173, the highly unconventional XF5U-1 prototype naval strike fighter had a roughly circular wing planform and was powered by two 1,350hp Pratt & Whitney R-2000 Twin Wasp engines, buried in the wing and driving large four-bladed propellers via extension shafts. The blades were specially articulated, like those of a helicopter, so that at high angles of attack they would move forward at constant pitch and flatten out to enable the machine to hover. The very low-aspect-ratio wing also housed the fuel tanks and armament, the pilot's cockpit being situated in the extreme nose. It was claimed that the aircraft possessed a speed range of between 40–450mph (64–725km/h). The prototype was rolled out in July 1946 amid much publicity, but it never flew – it having abruptly been decided to

One of America's earliest carrier-borne jet fighters, the Chance Vought F6U-1 Pirate flew for the first time on 2 October 1946. (LTV)

The McDonnell XFD-1 Phantom, which became the US Navy's first fully operational jet fighter, originated in a 1943 design. (McDonnell Douglas)

abandon the project – and was eventually scrapped. Its predecessor, the V-173, is in the Smithsonian Institution's National Air and Space Museum, Washington, DC.

The Chance Vought XF6U-1 Pirate

The US Navy's first jet fighter was the North American FJ-1 Fury, which served from 1947 to 1948 and which was the ancestor of the F-86 Sabre. However, the XFJ-1 Fury prototype was beaten into the air by another jet design, the Chance Vought XF6U-1 Pirate. The first of three prototype XF6U-1 Pirates flew on 2 October 1946, seven weeks before the FJ-1, and a production batch of thirty aircraft was ordered under the designation F6U-1, the first of these flying in July 1949.

The F6U-1 differed from the XF6U-1 in several respects: small auxiliary fins were mounted near the tailplane tips and a large dorsal fillet was fitted, large fillets were attached to the wing trailing edges at approximately quarter-span, and an armament of four 20mm cannon was installed in the fuselage. The F6U-1 made considerable use of Metalite skinning in its structure, this comprising two sheets of high-strength aluminium bonded to a balsa-wood core. After evaluation, however, the Pirate was withdrawn from service. The Pirate, which had a wingspan of 32ft 10in (9.98m) and a length of 37ft 7in (11.43m), could reach a maximum speed of 555mph (894km/h) and had a range of 750 miles (1,200km) with external fuel tanks, but it was inferior to more modern naval jet fighters like the McDonnell F2H Banshee and the Grumman F9F Panther, both of which were to serve the US Navy well during the Korean War.

The McDonnell XFD-1 Phantom

McDonnell, whose name was to become synonymous with naval jet fighter development, in rivalry with Grumman, entered the field with the XFD-1 Phantom, a design that originated in 1943. Initially designated XFD-1, it flew for the first time on 25 January 1945, powered by two Westinghouse J30 turbojets. On 21 July 1946 a pre-series FD-1 carried out the first US jet aircraft carrier trials, and on completion of these an order was placed for one hundred production aircraft, but this was later cut to sixty. On 5 May 1948 Fighter Squadron 17-A, equipped with sixteen FH-1s, became the first carrier-qualified jet squadron in the US Navy, operating from USS *Saipan*. The type remained in first-line service until July 1950, the last unit to use it being Marine Fighter Squadron VMF-122, which operated mainly from *Saipan*.

The Douglas XF5D-1 Skylancer

When the Korean War broke out in 1950, the McDonnell Banshee and the Grumman Panther formed the backbone of the US Navy's fighter-

A development of the Douglas F4D Skyray, the XF5D-1 Skylancer had a speed of Mach 1.5 and an all-weather capability, but did not enter production. (McDonnell Douglas)

attack units. Only four years later, however, the Navy was beginning to receive fighters with a truly supersonic capability. The first of these was the radical Chance Vought F7U Cutlass, which in its day was the heaviest single-seat carrier fighter. It entered service in April 1954, four months after Navy squadrons began to equip with the subsonic North American FJ-2 Fury, a navalized version of the F-86E Sabre. McDonnell's follow-on from the successful F2H Banshee was the F3H Demon, which entered service in 1956, while the Douglas aircraft Company produced the F4D Skyray, a delta-wing design going back to 1948.

The Skyray entered service with the US Navy and Marine Corps in 1956, by which time Douglas were proposing a supersonic successor, the F5D-1 Skylancer. Originally designated the F4D-2N, the first of four Skylancers flew on 21 April 1956 and was followed by the second on 30 June. The aircraft was virtually a scaled-up Skyray, but a higher fuselage fineness ratio (the ratio between length and diameter at the widest point) and a reduced wing thickness–chord ratio produced a greatly improved performance, the F5D-1 reaching a speed of Mach 1.5 at 40,000ft (12,000m) under the power of a Pratt & Whitney J57-P-8 turbojet. Whereas the Skyray had been a short-range interceptor, the Skylancer was intended to have an all-weather capability, and production aircraft were to have been fitted with the latest AI radar and fire-control system, four 20mm cannon and also air-to-air missiles. The Skylancer, however, never went into production because the USN opted instead for the multi-role McDonnell F-4 Phantom, and the four aircraft that were built were passed to NASA for research purposes.

The Grumman XF10F-1 Jaguar variable-geometry carrier-borne fighter was designed as a successor to the F9F Panther. (Grumman)

The Grumman XF10F-1 Jaguar

Meanwhile, Grumman, whose successful F-9F Panther had been followed by the F9F-6 Cougar, a development of the F9F-5 with swept flying surfaces, had been experimenting with the variable-geometry concept in the shape of an advanced naval fighter, the XF10F-1 Jaguar. Conceived in 1948 as a successor to the Panther, the original XF10F-1 design featured a delta wing, but a US Navy requirement for a greater fuel capacity, together with the installation of advanced electronic equipment, led to a formidable increase in weight and the Grumman design team eventually opted for a variable-geometry wing that could be swept at angles of up to 40 degrees.

Grumman, benefiting from the experience gained by NACA in testing the X-5, redesigned the wing of the XF10F-1 in 1950, incorporating a two-position configuration with a sweep angle of $13^1/_2$ degrees for take-off, cruise and landing, and $^1/_2$ degree for high-speed flight. The change increased the aircraft's weight in landing configuration by 2,200lb (1,000kg), but resulted in a dramatic decrease in landing speed from 115 to 95kt (213 to 176km/h). In addition to the Jaguar's very advanced wing, the aircraft was fitted with a highly evolved power control system in which movement of the control column mechanically operated a small triangular surface that protruded in front of the all-flying tailplane, actuating the latter and giving enhanced longitudinal control at transonic speeds without excessive stick forces. Spoilers were also fitted for lateral control.

Grumman, however, had seriously underestimated the amount of engineering work involved in perfecting the Jaguar's innovations, and when the prototype eventually flew on 19 May 1953 it was three years behind schedule. The aircraft was tested at Edwards Air Force Base, and problems soon developed with the all-flying delta tail assembly, even though the Jaguar reached a speed of Mach 0.8 with wings fully swept during this phase. It was therefore decided to replace the delta tailplane with a more conventional swept one, and this brought about some improvement in the aircraft's directional stability.

Meanwhile, a second XF10F-1 prototype had been built and the US Navy had awarded Grumman a production contract for 112 Jaguars. Grumman themselves, however, realizing that the design would need much more development – and much more expenditure – before it reached operational status, terminated the contract and the Navy orders were cancelled. The first prototype XF10F-1 went to Johns Naval Air Station, Philadelphia, where it was eventually destroyed in crash barrier tests, and the second aircraft (which had never in fact flown) was used as a gunnery target at the Aberdeen Proving Grounds – a sorry end to what was potentially one of the most potent combat aircraft of its day. Ironically, the one feature of the Jaguar that was truly revolutionary, the variable-geometry wing, never gave any trouble. In the words of the Jaguar's test pilot, Corwin H. Meyer:

With regard to the variable-sweep wing, I never hesitated to use it under any condition, and it was reputed to be able to unsweep itself if the hydraulic power failed. Fortunately, we never had this problem. There was no question that when the wing was swept and unswept, it had the theoretical effect.

So, with the demise of the Jaguar, the US Navy lost the chance to be the first Service in the world to operate a variable-geometry aircraft. It was not until twenty years later that the Navy had its swing-wing fighter, and that was designed by Grumman too: the F-14 Tomcat.

The Convair XF2Y-1 Sea Dart

In the early 1950s the US Navy travelled down another avenue of combat aircraft development in its attempts to develop a viable seaplane jet fighter.

The Bell X-5

The idea of variable-geometry wings ('swing wings') was by no means new. Toward the end of the war in Europe, Messerschmitt had embarked on the construction of a jet fighter prototype, the P.1101, whose wing sweep could be varied on the ground between 35 and 45 degrees. Construction of the prototype was about 80 per cent complete when the war ended. The captured airframe was shipped to the United States, where it and its associated technical drawings were given to the Bell Aircraft Corporation for example. The result was the Bell X-5 variable-geometry research aircraft which, although it bore a close resemblance to the P.1101, was in fact a completely new design.

While the prototype X-5 was being built, the project came under the joint sponsorship of the USAF and NACA, and Bell received a contract to build a second machine. Both aircraft were to have a wing that could be swept at angles of between 20 and 60 degrees, and the basic design was to conform to full USAF tactical fighter requirements so that they could be used for armament trials at a later date.

A variable-geometry research aircraft, the Bell X-5 owed much to the wartime Messerschmitt P.1101 jet fighter project. (Bell)

The first X-5 flew on 20 June 1951, powered by a 4,900lb (21.8kN) s.t. Allison J35-A-17 turbojet. Its wings were swept in the air for the first time during its fifth flight, changes in sweep being electrically actuated. To minimize trim change, which would have resulted if the centre of pressure moved with sweep variation, as the wing was swept back it was also moved forward in such a way that its centre of pressure retained a near-constant relationship with the aircraft's centre of gravity. To achieve the two basic motions of rotating the wing and moving it forward, it was supported on rollers which moved along tracks located on the inboard ends of the wing panels, and sweep from 20 to 60 degrees required only 30 seconds to complete. The principle worked in practice, the X-5 requiring no trim change at 60 degrees sweep. Both X-5s were extensively flight tested by the USAF and NACA, one of them eventually serving as a chase plane until it was retired in October 1955. The prototype X-5 is in the Air Force Museum at Wright-Patterson AFB, Dayton, Ohio.

In the United States, there had been a drift away from flying boat development by 1944, with long-range maritime patrol tasks being increasingly undertaken by land-based aircraft such as the Liberator and Privateer. In the immediate post-war years, however, research into new hydrodynamic shapes, coupled with jet propulsion, led to a belief that many of the earlier limitations of seaplanes could now be overcome. The lion's share of the research was undertaken by the US Navy Bureau of Aeronautics (BuAer), NACA and the Consolidated Vultee Aircraft Corporation (Convair). Convair received a Bureau of Aeronautics contract to develop a flying boat configuration that would result in a waterborne fighter with a performance comparable to that of land-based aircraft.

The Convair design team, under the direction of Ernest Stout, set about proving their theories in practical fashion by devising a series of scale models. The climax was the top secret Project Skate, which involved some of the most advanced aerodynamic designs to be tested in the late 1940s. The later models employed 'blended hulls', the idea being that the aircraft rode so low in the water that its wings aided buoyancy. In these models, wing and hull blended in unprecedented aerodynamic cleanness; spray dams were fitted on either side of the nose to speed take-off by deflecting the spray downwards, keeping it clear of the air intakes. Some models were taxied, taken off, flown and landed under radio control; others were catapult-launched, and yet others were towed behind high-speed motor launches to test spray and aerodynamic characteristics. At the same time, NACA carried out extensive tests to find an acceptable form of undercarriage that would do away with conventional floats and improve hydrodynamic characteristics.

The configuration that seemed most acceptable was the hydro-ski. In this arrangement, twin hydro-skis, fitted flush against the undersurface of the hull, extended like flat seaplane floats under the water, and as the aircraft gathered speed the action of the skis pushed up its fuselage until it was clear of the surface, the machine skimming the waves until take-off speed was reached. When safe flying speed was attained, the skis were retracted, leaving the aircraft aerodynamically clean.

By early 1948, the Convair blended hull concept and the NACA hydro-skis had reached an advanced stage of development, and this led to a BuAer requirement for a full-scale fighter prototype. The requirement called for an aircraft with a maximum speed of Mach 0.95 and an ability to operate in a 5ft (1.5m) swell. A design contest was initiated on 1 October 1948 and two designs were submitted, one by the NACA and the other by Convair; the former embodied hydro-skis and the latter the blended hull principle. The Convair design, which offered a better rate of climb and high-altitude performance, was accepted, but the project went ahead on a relatively low budget; the US Navy's emphasis at the time was on the development of carrier-borne jet fighters.

At this stage, further development concentrated on comparative tests between the hydro-ski and blended hull concepts. By 1950, hydro-ski development had undergone considerable advances, and as a result the Navy's requirement changed; what was now wanted was a faster aircraft fitted with skis, and smaller in overall dimensions than the original Convair proposal. This had envisaged a large twin-engined fighter with swept flying surfaces, based on the later series of Project Skate models; to meet the new requirement, Convair now evolved a smaller delta-wing design, the Y2-2, equipped with twin hydro-skis.

The new design was aerodynamically similar to the Convair F-102 delta-wing interceptor, then being developed for the USAF. Estimated performance figures included a maximum speed of Mach 1.5 and an initial rate of climb of 30,000ft/min (9,000m/min). Power was to be provided by two Westinghouse XJ46-WE-2 turbojets rated at 4,080lb (18.1kN) thrust, but by the time Convair received a letter of intent on 19 January 1951 it had been decided to install 3,400lb (15.1kN) thrust Westinghouse J34-WE-32 engines, the XJ46 development programme having been subjected to some delays.

In August 1951, the Y2-2 was re-designated XF2Y-1, and on 28 August 1952, with work on a prototype well advanced, Convair received a BuAer contract for twelve pre-series F2Y-1s.

In January 1953, the completed prototype XF2Y-1, now known as the Sea Dart, began taxiing trials in San Diego Bay, and it was during these that unexpected problems were encountered with the hydro-skis. The skis worked adequately at up to 60mph (100km/h), but beyond that they were susceptible to a phenomenon known as ski-pounding, with severe vibration that threatened to damage the airframe. Some modifications were made to the shape of the skis and to the shock absorbers

A transonic, delta-wing seaplane fighter, the Convair XF2Y-1 Sea Dart flew for the first time on 9 April 1953. (Convair)

between the skis and the hull, and the Sea Dart eventually made its first true flight on 9 April 1953, the aircraft already having made a 300yd (270m) hop during a taxi run on 14 January.

Meanwhile, problems had been experienced with the proposed XJ46 power plant which, during test runs, had failed to develop the anticipated thrust. This fact, together with some aerodynamic deficiencies which had been belatedly revealed, meant that the Sea Dart would be unlikely to exceed Mach 1. It was therefore proposed to adopt a single Wright J67 or Pratt & Whitney J75 turbojet, but then the designers realized that this would lead to an unacceptable amount of fuselage redesign and the idea was dropped.

By the autumn of 1953, with the hydro-skis still causing problems, the future for the Sea Dart looked anything but rosy. Development of one of the XF2Y-1 prototypes was abandoned in October, and in November the order for ten of the pre-series F2Y-1s was cancelled. The order for the other two pre-series aircraft was cancelled in March 1954, leaving Convair with an order for four YF2Y-1s for evaluation by the US Navy.

During 1954, more than a hundred hydro-ski modifications were tested, using both single- and twin-ski configurations, and it was found that the single-ski arrangement was the more satisfactory. Ski-pounding was reduced, although stability on take-off left much to be desired and there was a tendency to 'porpoise'.

On 3 August 1954, Convair test pilot Charles E. Richbourg took the second Sea Dart through Mach 1 in a shallow dive. This made the Sea Dart the first (and to date the only) seaplane to go supersonic. Since the Sea Dart had been designed before the advent of 'area ruling' in aerodynamics, the aircraft experienced high transonic drag and was unable to exceed the speed of sound in level flight. Flight tests indicated some wingspan-wise

US NAVAL PROTOTYPES

The Saunders-Roe SRA/1

The world's first jet-propelled flying boat was the Saunders-Roe (Saro) SRA/1, the first of three prototypes of which first flew in July 1947. It was powered by two Metropolitan-Vickers Beryl axial-flow turbojets of 3,850lb (17.1kN) thrust. But the heyday of the flying boat was over as the second half of the twentieth century approached, and no production order was forthcoming.

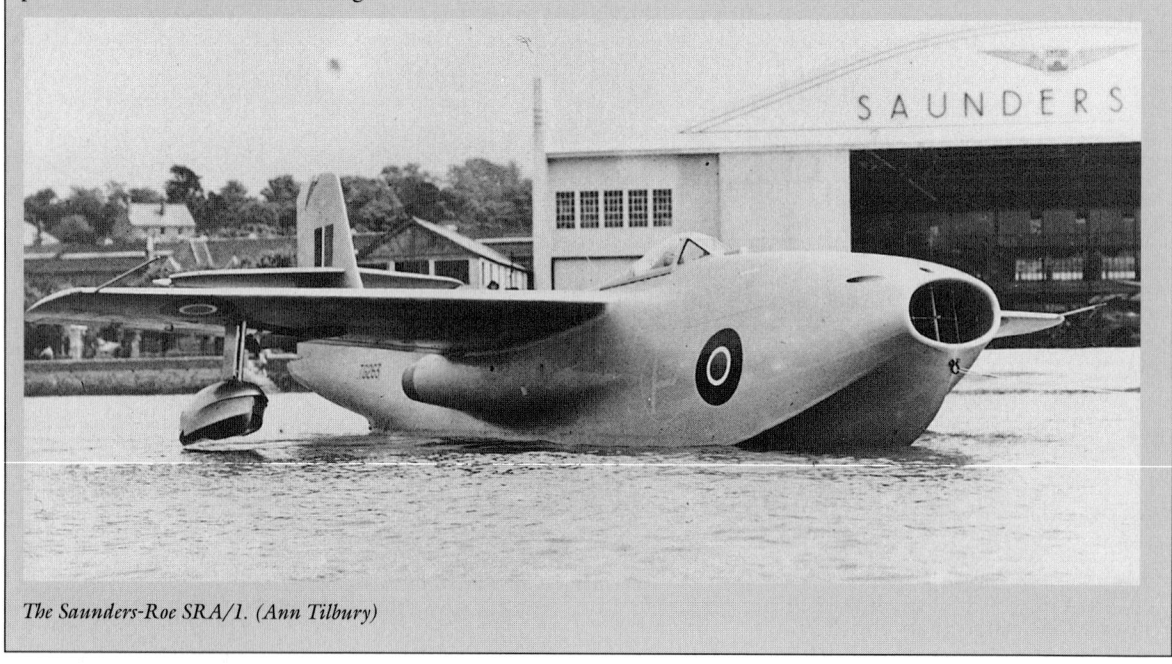

The Saunders-Roe SRA/1. (Ann Tilbury)

airflow, and a single airflow fence was mounted on each upper wing surface near the tip. No other Sea Dart was fitted with wing fences.

The Navy evaluation programme began on 1 November 1954, and was attended almost immediately by disaster. On 4 November, the first of the three YF2Y-1s to be built broke up during a public demonstration over San Diego Bay when Richbourg inadvertently exceeded the airframe limitations. Richbourg was fatally injured, and the evaluation programme was postponed until May 1955. Testing continued with the two remaining YF2Y-1s and the XF2Y-1 prototype, but ski difficulties persisted and the Sea Dart programme was abandoned in 1956.

The Douglas XTB2D-1 Skypirate

For a decade after the Korean War, the standard US Navy carrier-borne attack aircraft was the Douglas AD Skyraider, originally conceived in 1944 for use in the projected invasion of Japan. It stemmed, however, from a design that bore little resemblance to it, the Douglas XTB2D-1. Designed in July 1944, the XTB2D-1 prototype flew for the first time on 18 March 1945 and was followed by a second aircraft. Powered by a 2,500hp (1,870kW) Pratt & Whitney XR-4360-8 radial engine driving contra-rotating propellers, the XTB2D-1, known as the Devastator II and also the Skypirate, was a three- or four-seat aircraft armed with four fixed forward-firing 0.5in machine guns in the wings; production aircraft were to have two more in a dorsal turret and another in a ventral position. The aircraft, which had a maximum speed of 247mph (397km/h) at sea level, could carry four torpedoes or four 1,000lb bombs under the wing roots.

An order for twenty-three Douglas TB2D-1s was cancelled with the end of the Second World War, but the first XTB2D-1 served as the prototype of the AD-1 Skyraider, which entered US Navy service in greatly modified form in 1946.

US NAVAL PROTOTYPES

Known as the Devastator II or Skypirate, the Douglas XTB2D-1 carrier-borne torpedo bomber was intended to replace the Skyraider. (McDonnell Douglas)

The Kaiser-Fleetwings XBTK-1

The Douglas XBT2D-1 was in direct competition with an aircraft which, curiously enough, bore a stronger resemblance to the Skyraider than did the XTB2D-1. This was the Kaiser-Fleetwings XBTK-1, which flew for the first time in April 1945. It was considerably faster than the XTB2D-1, having a top speed of 342mph (550km/h) at sea level, but it carried only one torpedo and eight five-inch rockets as well as a built-in armament of two 20mm cannon. Two XBTK-1s were built and flown, a third aircraft being used for structural testing, but the end of the Pacific war ruled out any prospect of a production order.

The Douglas XA2D-1 Skyshark

Not long after the Skyraider entered service, Douglas embarked upon the design of a turboprop-powered successor, the XA2D-1 Skyshark, which was intended to make use of as many existing Skyraider components as possible. Powered by an Allison XT40-A-2 turboprop, consisting of twin Allison T38 engines mounted side by side and driving co-axial contra-rotating propellers, the prototype Skyshark flew for the first time on 26 May 1950, and during trials reached a speed of 492mph (792km/h) at 27,000ft (8,200m). Maximum speed with a 2,000lb (900kg) bomb load was 442mph (711km/h). Constant troubles were experienced with the Skyshark's contra-prop gearing, and a second prototype was re-engined with an XT40-A-6, but even then the type was plagued by frequent engine failures and a Navy production order was cut back to ten aircraft, these being used for a variety of engine trials.

The Republic XF-84H

The troubles with the Skyshark led to the US Navy seeking another airframe in which to house the XT40 twin turboprop, and the Republic Aviation Corporation came up with a possible solution in

The Douglas Skyshark used many of the Skyraider's components and was powered by a twin turboprop driving co-axial propellers. (McDonnell Douglas)

the form of a turboprop-powered version of its RF-84F Thunderflash. Republic received a contract to convert three aircraft under the designation XF-84H; two of them were to go to the USAF for tests with various supersonic propellers, and the third was to be allocated to the Navy for trials with the XT-40. The first XF-84H, 51-17059, was sent to Edwards AFB for ground tests, and a spate of problems soon developed with the XT40 engine. Apart from that, the propeller, developed by Aeroproducts, rotated at supersonic speed and so set up severe vibrations and resonance that caused acute nausea in anyone standing nearby.

Despite all this, the XF-84H finally took to the air on 22 July 1955, but engine troubles persisted and the project was dropped by both the Navy and Air Force. A second XF-84H was built, but never flew, and in the end the US Navy's requirement for a Skyraider replacement in the attack role was met by a turbojet-powered aircraft that turned out to be an all-round winner – the Douglas A-4 Skyhawk.

The Martin P4M Mercator

The Second World War had hammered home the lesson that it was vital for the US Navy to maintain powerful carrier task forces. However, there remained a pressing need also to maintain a strong element of shore-based naval combat aircraft for anti-submarine warfare and long-range maritime patrol. The first land-based aircraft designed specifically for the long-range maritime reconnaissance role was the Lockheed P2V Neptune, which was destined to be one of the longest-serving military aircraft ever built.

The second was the Martin P4M Mercator, which was designed to meet a US Navy requirement for a long-range maritime reconnaissance bomber, issued in July 1944. The first of two XP4M-1 prototypes flew on 20 September 1946 and a contract was placed for nineteen production P4M-1s, the first entering service with patrol squadron VP-21 in June 1950. A second Mercator squadron, VQ-1, formed in June 1955; this was equipped with P4M-1Q aircraft and was the US Navy's first electronic countermeasures squadron. However, the Neptune adequately filled the roles for which the Mercator was intended, and so this was the limit of the Mercator's operational use.

The Martin XP6M-1 SeaMaster

The US Navy also retained a post-war interest in long-range flying boats, the excellent Consolidated Catalina and Martin Mariner being followed by the Martin P5M Marlin. The prototype XP5M-1 flew for the first time on 30 April 1948, deliveries of the first production aircraft being made to Patrol Squadron VP-44 on 23 April 1952. It was logical, therefore, that Martin should investigate the concept of a long-range jet-powered flying boat, and in October 1952 the Martin Aircraft Company was awarded a contract for the development of such an aircraft, the Model 275 (XP6M-1) SeaMaster. The development programme called for the construction of two XP6M-1 prototypes and six YP6M-1 evaluation aircraft, all of which were to be powered by four Allison J71-A-4 turbojets. They were to be followed by an initial production batch of twenty-four P6M-2s, powered by 15,000lb (66.7kN) thrust Pratt & Whitney J75-P-2 engines.

The XP6M-1 prototype flew on 14 July 1955 and completed seventy-nine hours of taxiing and flight testing before it crashed on 7 December 1955 following a control malfunction. The second SeaMaster flew on 18 May 1956, but that also crashed on 9 November 1956 following a failure in the hydraulic system. The first YP6M-1 evaluation aircraft, with modifications to prevent a recurrence of the disasters that had overtaken the two prototypes, flew on 20 January 1958, and this was followed by the first production P6M-2 on 17 February 1959. In all, as well as the two prototypes, six YP6M-1s and four P6M-2s were completed, but by the spring of 1959 the US Navy's research and development budget was being allocated to other programmes that were thought to be more important. Testing of the SeaMaster had revealed numerous technical problems – water seepage through the rotary weapons bay door in the hull was one, although this was later solved – and the cost of the programme had risen to three times the original estimate.

The first P6M-2 SeaMaster during its take-off run. Note the position of the air intakes high on the wings, and slightly set back, to prevent spray from entering the engines. (Philip Jarrett)

By this time, the number of P6M-2 SeaMasters on order had been reduced to eight, which were to have formed a single US Navy squadron. Only three P6M-2s, however, were taken on charge, and these were eventually broken up for scrap at the Patuxent River Naval Air Test Center, Maryland.

Basically, the SeaMaster's biggest drawback had been its advanced concept. It was potentially a very versatile aircraft with a high performance; maximum speed, for example, was 654mph (1,052km/h, or Mach 0.92) at 21,000ft (6,400m), and unrefuelled range was 1,500 miles (2,400km) with a 30,000lb (13,600kg) payload. With its ability to carry mines, bombs, torpedoes or a camera pack, the SeaMaster would have been capable of performing many roles; however, its operational use would have needed considerable logistical support, and most of the tasks it was designed to carry out could be done equally well by a new generation of advanced carrier-borne aircraft. The demise of the SeaMaster was the final nail in the coffin of combat flying boat development in the United States.

Chapter 13
Britain's Naval Experimentals, 1945–55

Britain's Fleet Air Arm, which had fought its way gallantly through the early years of the Second World War with a variety of obsolescent equipment, ended that conflict with carrier aircraft that compared favourably with any the Americans had. The reason was simple: most of them were American, types like the Grumman Hellcat and Chance Vought Corsair, supplied under Lend-Lease.

Like the US Navy, the British Admiralty initially saw little future in jet aircraft operation from carriers. A few deck landing trials with a Vampire and a Meteor in 1945 had convinced the admirals that jets had too high a landing speed for safe carrier operations, so when the Fleet Air Arm's combat squadrons re-equipped in the late 1940s, it was once again with piston-engined types such as the Hawker Sea Fury and later marks of the Fairey Firefly. Nevertheless, one or two forward-thinking members of the Naval Staff continued to push hard for the development of carrier-borne jets, so the concept was not allowed to stagnate entirely.

The notion of a swept-wing carrier jet fighter was considered to be almost foolhardy, but a conventional straight-wing jet design was treated with much less suspicion. Since both the Meteor and the Vampire were deemed to be unsuitable for various reasons, the Admiralty turned to a new design – the Vickers-Supermarine E.10/44, which had originally been proposed as a land-based fighter for the RAF but which had been ousted by the Gloster Meteor and de Havilland Vampire. Supermarine therefore offered a navalized version to the Admiralty, who wrote Specification E.1/45 around it. The prototype first flew in its navalized form on 17 June 1947 and, as the Vickers-Supermarine Attacker F.1, entered service with the Royal Navy, sixty aircraft being acquired. The Attacker did not enter squadron service until 1951, by which time the Navy's piston-engined Sea Furies and Fireflies were battling against MiG-15 jets over Korea under every possible disadvantage.

The Supermarine Types 505, 508, 525, 529 and 544

The Admiralty's phobia about operating jets from carriers was expressed in a curious requirement, originating at the end of 1945, for a shipboard fighter without an undercarriage. This would have been catapult-launched in the normal way, but would have skid-landed on a flexible flight deck – the idea being to eliminate the considerable weight of the substantial undercarriage required for conventional deck landings. Supermarine worked up a project around the requirement and submitted it to the Admiralty in 1946 under the designation Type 505; it was a straight-wing design with a V-type 'butterfly' tail, and power was provided by two Rolls-Royce Avons. At the same time, Supermarine also offered the RAF a land-based version with a conventional tricycle undercarriage, increased fuel tankage and two 30mm cannon. Six prototypes of the Type 505 were ordered in the summer of 1946, but then the requirement for an undercarriage-less fighter was cancelled and Supermarine were ordered to proceed with the development of a more conventional variant with greater endurance and better performance.

Supermarine accordingly took the basic Type 505 design and scaled it up slightly, giving it an armament of four cannon and cramming in more fuel space. Three prototypes of the new aircraft, designated Supermarine Type 508, were ordered in September 1947 and the first of these, VX133, flew for the first time at Boscombe Down on 31 August 1951. VX133 carried out a series of deck

The Supermarine Type 508 – note the unusual 'butterfly' tail configuration. (Ann Tilbury)

landing trials on HMS *Eagle* in May 1952. Meanwhile, the second prototype, VX136, had undergone various internal modifications, and although it remained externally similar to the Type 508 it was re-designated Type 529. VX136 first flew on 29 August 1952 and immediately embarked on trials alongside its sister aircraft.

In June 1949, Supermarine had submitted a swept-wing version of the basic Type 508 design to the Air Staff for consideration as a twin-engined fighter under the designation Type 525. The Air Staff did not take up the offer, but by this time the Navy had at last woken up to the potential of a swept-wing carrier fighter, and Supermarine received a contract to convert the third prototype Type 508, VX138, to Type 525 standard. In this form, and now fitted with a conventional tailplane, it flew for the first time on 27 April 1954, and two further prototypes had meantime been ordered under the designation Type 544. The latter aircraft embodied several refinements, such as a blown flap system, which was first tested on the Type 525.

VX138 was destroyed in a crash on 5 July 1955 when it failed to recover from a flat spin during low-speed handling. The pilot, Lt Cdr T.A. Rickell RN, ejected through the canopy at 200ft (60m), but his parachute failed to deploy fully and he suffered fatal injuries.

The production version of the Type 544 went on to enter service with the Fleet Air Arm as the Scimitar F.1, the Royal Navy's first swept-wing strike fighter. The aircraft it replaced, and which had been the mainstay of the Royal Navy's jet attack squadrons during the mid-1950s, was the Hawker Sea Hawk. The prototype that led to the Sea Hawk, VP401, had first flown on 2 September 1947 and had met all the requirements of Naval Staff Specification N.7/46. It was, in fact, none other than a revamped and navalized version of the aircraft developed by the Hawker Company as a private venture in the winter of 1944–45, an aircraft that the RAF had not wanted – the Hawker P.1040, described in detail in Chapter 8.

The Short Seamew

In other areas of carrier aircraft requirement, the Navy seemed to know what it wanted with far greater precision, sometimes with unfortunate consequences. A classic example was Specification M.123, issued by the Naval Staff in 1971 and calling for a simple, robust anti-submarine aircraft

The Short Seamew was intended as a cheap, fixed-undercarriage anti-submarine aircraft for service with both the Royal Navy and Royal Air Force. (Ken Calcutt)

capable of operating from small aircraft carriers in the most adverse of weather conditions. Short Brothers submitted a design, the SB.6, and three prototypes were ordered under the official name of Seamew. The first of these, XA209, flew on 23 August 1953, having been built in the record time of fifteen months, but it was severely damaged on landing at the end of its maiden flight. It was repaired in time for the Farnborough Air Show a few weeks later. XA209 was fitted with an Armstrong Siddeley Mamba As.Ma.3 turboprop; the second prototype, XA213, had a more powerful Mamba As.Ma.6.

This aircraft carried out successful deck landing trials in July and December 1955 on HMS *Bulwark*, by which time it had been announced that the Seamew AS.1 would go into production for the Royal Navy and a land-based variant, the Seamew MR.2, would be built for RAF Coastal Command. Early in 1956, however, the RAF order was cancelled, and Seamew production was cut back to twenty-four aircraft for the Royal Navy. An export sales drive in Europe produced no enthusiasm for the type, which had some vicious handling tendencies that Shorts had been unable to eradicate, and in the end the Seamew programme was cancelled after twenty-one aircraft had been built. All were placed in storage and eventually broken up. All in all, the Seamew was a sorry example of an aircraft in which handling qualities had been sacrificed to achieve economy.

The Blackburn YA.5, YA.7, Y.B.8 and Y.B.1

The Naval Staff had certainly known what it required when it issued one of its first post-war specifications, GR.17/45. This called for an anti-submarine aircraft combining, for the first time, the roles of search and strike that had previously been carried out by separate 'hunter' and 'killer' aircraft. Moreover, the aircraft was to be capable of carrying a formidable war load of mines, depth charges, bombs and torpedoes internally. Blackburn Aircraft and Fairey Aviation, both with considerable experience in the design of naval torpedo bombers, each tendered proposals to meet GR.17/45; the designs they evolved were, perhaps not surprisingly, very similar in configuration.

Blackburn's proposal was the YA.5, a two-seater that was originally intended to be powered by a Napier Coupled Naiad N.Na.C.1 turboprop. Development of this engine was discontinued, however, so Blackburn switched to the best alternative, the Armstrong Siddeley Double Mamba, which had also been selected by Fairey Aviation. The Double Mamba, in fact, had been designed as the result of a suggestion by Fairey that two Mamba engines, suitably coupled, would be ideal for an anti-submarine aircraft, giving single-engined handling qualities together with twin-engined performance and reliability. Cruise range could be extended by shutting down one of the

The Blackburn YA.7, which carried out deck landing trials on HMS Illustrious *in February 1950. (Hawker Siddeley)*

coupled engines, since each unit could be controlled separately, and the arrangement produced none of the problems of asymmetric power that bedevilled more conventional twin-engined machines.

The abandonment of the Naiad programme caused some delay in the YA.5 test schedule, but in the meantime two prototypes were built and fitted with Rolls-Royce Griffon piston engines so that aerodynamic testing could go ahead. The first of these, the Blackburn YA.7 (WB781) made its first flight on 20 September, 1949, and made its first deck landing on HMS *Illustrious* on 8 February 1950. It was followed by the second prototype, the Y.B.8, WB788, which made its maiden flight on 3 May 1950 and its first carrier landing on 19 June.

Meanwhile, the YA.5 had at last received its Double Mamba engine; it had also been modified to take a third crew station, following a revision of the specification, and featured redesigned outer

The last version of the Firebrand was the TF.VA, pictured here in its torpedo-fighter role. (Hawker Siddeley)

The Fairey Gannet, seen here with one of its engines shut down, was the winner of the GR.17 contest. (Fairey)

wing panels with leading edge sweep, a configuration first tested on the YA.8. With these alterations, the YA.5 was re-designated Y.B.1, and the sole prototype, WB797, first flew on 19 July 1950. Generally, however, the Fairey design was the better of the two, and it was ordered into production for the Royal Navy as the Gannet.

The Short SB.3

The other competitor in the GR.17/45 contest was the Short SB.3, which was a modified version of the Short Sturgeon target tug. The SB.3 was, in fact, proposed to meet a revised specification, M.6/49, which called for an anti-submarine search and radar patrol aircraft. Shorts took a production Sturgeon and completely altered the basic airframe, redesigning the front fuselage to accommodate two radar operators in a cabin in front of and below the pilot's cockpit, giving the aircraft a curious-looking 'chin'. The prototype SB.3, WF632, was powered by two wing-mounted Armstrong Siddeley Mamba turboprops driving four-bladed propellers and flew for the first time on 12 August 1950. Flight testing, however, revealed some serious stability problems, and the SB.3 was never assessed operationally. In the long run, the radar search requirement was met by the Gannet AEW.3.

The Blackburn YA.1 Firecrest

Blackburn were also unsuccessful in their bid to replace another of their designs, the Firebrand strike fighter. The Firebrand was designed as a short-range, heavily armed naval interceptor, the first of

The Blackburn YA.1 Firecrest was an unsuccessful contender to replace the Firebrand torpedo bomber. (Hawker Siddeley)

three prototypes flying on 27 February 1942. Nine pre-series aircraft were ordered, designated Firebrand F.I, and following carrier evaluation it was decided to re-develop the aircraft as a torpedo-fighter, designated Firebrand TF.II. Because of a shortage of Sabre engines it was then decided to re-engine the aircraft with a Bristol Centaurus radial, the new model emerging as the Firebrand TF.III. With further modifications the aircraft became the TF.IV and entered service with No. 813 Sqn in September 1945, too late to see action in the Second World War. Only Nos 813 and 827 Sqns were equipped with the Firebrand, 225 of which were built. The last variant was the TF.VA, with powered ailerons.

Blackburn's intention was to replace the Firebrand with a more powerful piston-engined type, the YA.1 Firecrest, designed to Specification S.28/43. Design work began in 1943, but the prototype did not fly until March 1947, by which time the Royal Navy was turning to jet and turbo-prop aircraft to meet its requirements.

Chapter 14
France's Naval Prototypes, 1945–55

The Aerocentre NC 1071 was France's first twin-jet design. It first flew in 1948, powered by Rolls-Royce Nene turbojets. (Musée de l'Air)

The post-war French Admiralty, eager to restore France's once powerful battle fleet to its former strength, was quick to recognize the potential of turbojet-powered naval aircraft, and a new aircraft carrier, designated PA28 and provisionally named *Clemenceau*, was designed to accommodate them. The aircraft were a trio of naval fighters, the Aerocentre NC 1080, Arsenal VG 90 and Nord 2200, and a twin-jet naval strike aircraft, the Aerocentre NC 1071.

In the event, the French Navy decided that the piston-engined F4U Corsair would adequately meet its requirements until the British de Havilland Sea Venom (licence-built in France as the Sud-Est Aquilon) became available. Prototypes of all three did fly, however, though none could proceed until Rolls-Royce Nene engines became available to power them.

The Aerocentre NC 1071 and NC 1080

The first of the Nene-powered shipboard prototypes to fly was the NC 1071 twin-jet attack aircraft, on 12 October 1948. A sole prototype was

The Aerocentre NC 1080 single-engined shipboard jet fighter, accidentally destroyed in 1950. (Musée de l'Air)

produced, and development came to an end when Aerocentre went into voluntary liquidation in the summer of 1949. The company's factory at Bourges was absorbed into the Nord (SNCAN) group, and this company was made responsible for the further development of another Aerocentre design, the NC 1080 single-engined naval fighter, which flew for the first time on 29 July 1949. The prototype, however, was totally destroyed in a flying accident on 7 April 1950.

The Nord 2200

Nord's own shipboard fighter design, the Nord 2200, made its maiden flight on 19 December 1949. Somewhat resembling the Dassault Mystère II in outline, it was not fitted with folding wings or armament, but incorporated catapult attachment points and arrester gear. As a result of initial flight trials, a servo control system was installed, an AI radar fitted and the vertical tail surfaces enlarged. Testing of the sole prototype continued into 1952, but no production order was placed, the projected PA28 aircraft carrier having been cancelled in the meantime in favour of the Aquilon.

The Arsenal VG-70, one of France's early experimental jet aircraft, was of wooden construction and was powered by a Junkers Jumo 004 turbojet. (Musée de l'Air)

The Arsenal VG-70 and VG-90

The third French post-war naval jet fighter design, the Arsenal VG-90, was a direct development of the VG-70 research aircraft. After the end of the war, the Arsenal de l'Aéronautique had been preoccupied with the development of a piston-engined fighter, the VB-10, which was powered by two Hispano-Suiza 12Z engines mounted in tandem. The prototype flew at Lyon-Bron on 7 July

The Arsenal VG-90 was developed from the VG-70 to meet a French Navy requirement for a turbojet-powered strike fighter. (Musée de l'Air)

1945 and, after being taken on charge by the Flight Test centre at Brétigny in May 1946, it made 144 test flights before 25 March 1948, after which it was dismantled and scrapped. Two more prototypes were built, together with two pre-production aircraft, but an initial order for 200 production aircraft, placed in 1945, was reduced to fifty photo-reconnaissance aircraft in the following year and this order, too, was cancelled in 1948.

The cancellation of the VB-10, although predictable in view of jet aircraft development, was a severe blow to Arsenal, and the company's hopes were now pinned on the VG-90. The first prototype, the VG-90.01 (F-WFOE) flew on 27 September 1949, but was destroyed in an accident on 25 May the following year, killing its pilot. The second prototype, the VG-90.02, flew in June 1951, incorporating several modifications that included a taller fin. A protracted test programme continued at Melun-Villaroche, but on 21 January 1952 prototype 02 was also destroyed, the pilot being Claude Dellys. These two prototypes, following the pattern of the VG-70, had been of wooden construction, but the third, 03, used metal and was designed to take the Atar 101F turbojet. This aircraft, however, never flew, and its fuselage was used to carry out various aerodynamic tests in the supersonic wind tunnel at Modane-Avrieux.

The Sud-Ouest SO.8000 Narval

In the late 1940s, two French designers proposed piston- and turboprop-powered strike aircraft to fill the gap until the new generation of naval jet aircraft became available. On 1 April 1949, Sud-Ouest flew the prototype of a twin-boom, long-range naval strike fighter designated SO.8000 Narval, powered by an Arsenal 12H-02 engine (a modified Junkers Jumo 213). A second prototype was flown on 30 December 1949 and both aircraft were extensively tested, but the day of the piston-engined combat aircraft was over and the Narval programme was abandoned.

The Breguet Br.690 Vultur

The design proposed by Louis Breguet, on the other hand, showed far more promise. Named Br.690 Vultur, it was equipped with an Armstrong Siddeley Mamba AS.Ma.1 turboprop and a Nene 101 turbojet, a combination designed to give both good endurance and high performance for combat and for take-off with full loads. The first prototype flew on 3 August 1951 and was followed by a second on 15 September 1952, this aircraft having a more powerful Mamba AS.Ma.3 turboprop and a Nene 104.

France's naval strike fighter was met by the de Havilland Sea Venom (seen here), built under licence as the Aquilon. (Hawker Siddeley)

No production order for the VG-90 was ever placed, and the Aéronavale's requirement for a shipboard fighter was filled by the de Havilland Sea Venom, which was built under licence as the Aquilon by SNCASE and which operated from the carrier *Arromanches*, formerly the British HMS *Colossus*, which was initially leased and then bought outright by the French Navy.

The Breguet Br 960 Vultur was originally developed for the strike role. Two prototypes were built. (Breguet)

FRANCE'S NAVAL PROTOTYPES, 1945–55

In 1954, however, the Aéronavale specification was radically altered with the realization that a naval strike aircraft would have to be capable of engaging shore-based fighters, which the Vultur was not equipped to do. Breguet consequently abandoned the strike fighter idea and decided to modify the second Vultur to serve as the prototype of a new shipboard anti-submarine aircraft. It first flew in this form on 26 March 1955, with the designation Br.695, and was followed by three prototypes of the new anti-submarine aircraft. This was the Breguet Br.1050 Alizé, which went into operational service with the Aéronavale and which was also exported to India.

The Vultur was developed into the successful Breguet Alizé ASW aircraft which, like its British counterpart, the Fairey Gannet, was powered by a Double Mamba turboprop. (Breguet)

Soviet Sea Wings

The Soviet Navy, lacking aircraft carriers, was forced to rely on shore-based aircraft and flying boats for its maritime reconnaissance and attack capability. In the late 1940s, the Beriev Design Bureau began developing an advanced jet-powered flying boat, the Be-R-1. It was a good design from both the aerodynamic and hydrodynamic points of view, with a length-to-beam ratio of 8:1 and a long, narrow planing bottom that greatly reduced drag, both in the air and on the water. Moreover, the Be-R-1 was designed for operation in rough seas. The aircraft was powered by two Klimov VK-1 turbojets positioned above the shoulder-mounted gull wing, their long nacelles projecting a considerable distance forward of the leading edge. Wing and tail surfaces were conventional and unswept.

A twin-jet, high-wing flying boat, the Beriev Be-R-1 first flew in 1949 and was tested until 1951. (Beriev)

Everything in the Be-R-1's design reflected Beriev's desire to keep aerodynamic drag to a minimum; the pilot was seated under a fighter-type blister canopy, offset to port, the stabilizing floats were retracted in flight to lie flush with the wingtips, and defensive armament comprised two 23mm cannon in a streamlined tail barbette.

The Be-R-1 underwent flight trials at Taganrog from 1949 to 1951, but although its performance was promising, including a maximum speed at sea level of 769km/h (478mph), the aircraft was not accepted for service, and it was the far superior turboprop-powered Be-12 *Tchaika* (NATO reporting name: 'Mail') that succeeded the piston-engined Be-6 flying boat in service with the Soviet Naval Air Arm.

Nevertheless, the Be-R-1 provided the Beriev team with invaluable experience in high-speed flying boat design, and in 1961 a twin-jet flying boat was publicly revealed for the first time at the Tushino air display. This was the Be-10, known to NATO as 'Mallow', which subsequently established a number of FAI-approved records for seaplanes. A small number of Be-10s entered service with a Soviet Navy trials unit, but the type's career was brief.

Part V
Great Britain, 1955–65 – the Turbulent Years

Chapter 15
Lost Opportunities

The first prototype English Electric P.1 on a test flight from Warton, Lancashire, in 1954. (BAe)

In 1953, at a time when American research aircraft were already attaining speeds of up to Mach 2.5 and altitudes of over 80,000ft (24,000m), Great Britain still had no aircraft that was capable of exceeding Mach 1 in level flight or of reaching altitudes in excess of 50,000ft (15,000m). It would be the summer of 1954 before the English Electric P.1, precursor of the Lightning, touched these values. The development potential of the P.1 was soon to become apparent; what was by no means apparent, when the prototype flew in August 1954, was that its developed version would become the only operational combat aircraft of all-British design ever to reach a speed of Mach 2.

By 1951, it was already clear to British aircraft designers that a dangerous fighter performance gap was looming on the horizon. The Korean War was proving beyond all doubt that Soviet aviation technology was catching up with that of the West, and in some cases outstripping it; this, together with indications that the Russians were giving high priority to advanced jet bomber development, led to a complete re-appraisal of the RAF's fighter requirements.

The Air Staff envisaged that by 1960, the Russians would be in a position to threaten the west with two principal types of manned bomber: a long-range aircraft cruising at up to Mach 0.9 and a supersonic medium-range type capable of an over-the-target speed of up to Mach 2. Both types, it was believed, would be capable of operating at altitudes in excess of 60,000ft (18,000m). The

The English Electric P.1 was developed into the P.1B, which in turn became the Lightning. (BAe)

RAF requirement for an aircraft to deal with this threat – an interceptor with an initial rate of climb of 50,000ft/min (15,000m/min) and a maximum speed of over Mach 2 – crystallized in OR.301, issued in 1951. It presented a formidable challenge, and designers who rose to meet it naturally turned to the one power plant that had already proven itself in the target defence role under operational conditions: the rocket motor.

The combination of Germany's wartime Messerschmitt Me 163B airframe and Walter HWK509A-2 bi-fuel rocket motor, dangerous and unstable though it had been, had served to demonstrate the potential of the rocket-powered target defence interceptor, and in the years after the war the Ministry of Supply had authorized a limited research programme to investigate the possible use of rocket motors in future RAF fighters. In 1946, Armstrong Siddeley and de Havilland had begun work on two such motors, the Snarler and Sprite, using different propellants. The 2,000lb (8.9kN) thrust Snarler used a combination of methyl alcohol, water and liquid oxygen, while the 5,000lb (22.2kN) thrust Sprite used high-test hydrogen peroxide. In addition to powering a new generation of fast-climbing fighters, it was also envisaged that the rocket motors would provide auxiliary take-off power at overload weights for the new jet bombers that were then on the drawing board.

In 1950 the Snarler was installed in the tail of the prototype Hawker P.1040, which was then re-designated P.1072, and the first powered flight trial was made on 20 November that year. De Havilland's Sprite was test-flown under a Comet in April 1951. Tests with the Snarler produced a considerable performance increase, especially with regard to rate of climb, but some technical problems were encountered and the project was dropped. Armstrong Siddeley, however, went on to develop the Screamer, the first British variable-thrust rocket, while experience gained with the Sprite led de Havilland to start work on their own second-generation rocket motor, the Spectre.

On 21 February 1952, following preliminary design studies, Specification F.124T was written around OR.103 and issued to several leading British aircraft companies. The specification called for a small rocket-powered interceptor armed with a battery of air-to-air missiles and able to take off in a very short distance. Like the Messerschmitt 163, it would glide back to earth after combat. Short, Blackburn, Bristol and Avro all submitted tenders; the Avro design, involving a small tailless delta, was potentially the most promising.

The Saunders-Roe SR.53

At this point another company, Saunders-Roe (Saro), entered the running. Saro, though preoccupied with the SRA/1 jet fighter flying boat and the mighty ten-engined Princess flying boat airliner, had also carried out extensive search into high-speed, high-altitude flight, and had made some studies of a rocket aircraft capable of reaching an altitude of over 80,000ft (24,000m). For some reason the company had not been invited to tender to F.124T – in fact, the specification had not even been issued to it. A protest was made, and in March 1952 a somewhat embarrassed Ministry of Supply invited Saro to submit their design together with the other firms.

In just over a month, Saunders-Roe turned in a detailed design project involving a single-seat fighter powered by an 8,000lb (35.6kN) thrust rocket motor giving it an estimated climb rate of 52,000ft/min (16,000m/min) at 50,000ft (15,000m) and a maximum speed of Mach 2.44 at 60,000ft (18,000m). Unlike the other companies, Saro also proposed equipping the fighter with a small turbojet engine that would enable it to make a powered recovery to an airfield instead of having to make a glide landing.

The Air Ministry liked the idea, and all the companies involved in F.124T were asked to incorporate a similar arrangement in their designs. The amendment came as something of a relief, for the performances of both the Screamer and Spectre rocket motors were falling short of expectations and a mixed power plant seemed an acceptable solution to the problem.

Originally, Saunders-Roe had planned to equip their design with their own rocket motor and an Armstrong Siddeley Viper turbojet, which had been developed to power the Jindivik target drone. As design studies progressed, however, it was realized that further development of Saro's own rocket motor would prove too expensive, and so the Spectre was adopted instead. A scheme to incorporate a jettisonable cockpit was also dropped, and a conventional Martin-Baker ejection seat proposed to replace it. The resulting design was given the designation SR.53.

In October 1952, Saunders-Roe received an Instruction to Proceed with three SR.53 prototypes (XD145, XD151 and XD153). Apart from the provision of a turbojet engine, the finalized aircraft differed considerably from the original concept in having slotted flaps and ailerons instead of combined flaps and ailerons, a tailplane mounted on top of the fin and a straight-through jet exhaust instead of a bifurcated one. The turbojet, which was set high in the fuselage to make room for the rocket motor, was fed via twin intakes set immediately aft of the cockpit. The projected armament was still fifty rocket projectiles in a retractable pack, but in December 1952 this was changed to an armament of de Havilland *Blue Jay* AAMs mounted under the wings. The amended specification, issued at this time, was F.138D. At a later date the *Blue Jays* – renamed Firestreaks – were mounted on the wingtips.

The SR.53 design underwent further changes in the spring of 1953. Aerodynamic research by the Royal Aircraft Establishment indicated that the wing needed greater anhedral, and as a result modifications had to be made to wing, fuselage centresection and undercarriage. It was the end of April before design work was sufficiently complete to be presented to the Ministry of Supply, but after that things moved quickly, and within a week Saunders-Roe had received a formal contract for the production of three prototype aircraft.

It was not long before the design teams at both Saunders-Roe and Avro – who were working on a rival mixed-power interceptor, as described below – realized that the combination of Viper turbojet and rocket motor would not match what was required of the proposed combat aircraft. What was needed was a bigger, more powerful jet engine, one that would sustain the aircraft in high-Mach cruise, leaving the rocket motor to be used for the climb and combat manoeuvres. This, together with extra fuel tankage to meet an extended range requirement and the inclusion of AI radar equipment, would mean a larger and more complex aircraft. Early in 1954, following discussions with the Ministry of Supply, both companies therefore began design studies of bigger, more powerful variants of their original concepts.

Saunders-Roe went ahead as rapidly as possible with work on their SR.53, although it was soon apparent that the aircraft would be nowhere near ready to meet the target date for the first flight, optimistically set for July 1954 (the aircraft, in fact, did not fly until May 1957). At the same time, a new High Speed Development Section was set up to begin work on the design of the more advanced version, which was designated P.177. This aircraft started life as a straightforward development of the SR.53, but as the weeks went by its configuration underwent a series of changes, mainly to meet a requirement that called for its use by both the RAF and Royal Navy. After investigating several turbojet alternatives, Saunders-Roe settled for the 8,000lb (35.6kN) s.t. de Havilland PS.38, which was later named the Gyron Junior. In May 1955 the company received a design contract from the MoS, and this was followed in September by an Instruction to Proceed.

Later that year the Ministry cancelled one of the SR.53 prototypes, XD153, as an economy measure. Work on the other two proceeded, and in the summer of 1955 the United States allocated 1\frac{1}{2}$m toward the project on the basis of an agreement under which US funds were released to support projects of potentially high military value to NATO. Plans were made to test the first prototype at Hurn; a storage building for the HTP fuel was erected, together with other necessary installations, and a Meteor F.8, allocated by the MoS, was flown in to test specialized items of radio equipment.

However, Hurn was never used in the SR.53 test programme. The first prototype, XD145, was taken to the A&AEE Boscombe Down in June 1956 for assembly, and all subsequent test flying was done from that establishment. Ground running of the

The first prototype Saunders-Roe SR.53, XD145. (British Hovercraft Corporation)

installed Spectre rocket motor began on 16 January 1957, followed by similar ground testing of the Viper turbojet on 16 April. Taxiing trials got under way on 9 May, and on 16 May 1957, XD145 took to the air for the first time in the hands of Squadron Leader John Booth DFC, Saro's chief test pilot. In September the SR.53 was demonstrated publicly at the 1957 SBAC Show at Farnborough, and no-one who saw it (including this writer) will ever forget the breathtaking climb that took it from the runway to the clouds almost faster than the eye could follow, a tiny dart streaking upwards at the end of a long black pencil-mark of smoke as Booth cut in the Spectre rocket.

What the crowds did not realize was that the SR.53 had, at the time, accumulated only 2 hours' flying time before it went on display. Normally, a minimum of ten hours was required before an aircraft was permitted to be displayed at Farnborough, but in this case the conditions were waived. Booth flew the aircraft on ten sorties of about 20 minutes each before Farnborough, the last being the delivery flight from Boscombe Down.

On 8 December 1957 the second SR.53, XD151, also joined the test programme. This machine was fitted with a revised HTP tank system and made eleven flights before being totally destroyed in an accident on 5 June 1958. On that day, John Booth was taking off under rocket power to check undercarriage reaction at various speeds when he suddenly cut the Spectre and deployed the braking parachute, which failed to deploy properly. The aircraft overran the runway and collided with a large runway approach light post, disintegrating. The pilot was thrown from the aircraft, still in his ejection seat, and was killed instantly. The circumstances leading to this tragic accident were never fully established, although it was believed that the blind flying panel had become detached and obstructed the control column during the take-off roll, hence Booth's decision to abandon the sortie.

The Avro 720 design drew heavily on data gathered from the Avro 707 series of research deltas. Seen here is the Avro 707A, designed for high-speed research. (Hawker Siddeley)

The Avro 707B was intended for low-speed research into delta-wing aerodynamics. (Hawker Siddeley)

The accident brought the SR.53 test programme to an end. XD145 was grounded while the MoS Accident Investigation Department tried to establish what had gone wrong, and it never flew again. It eventually went to the Rocket Research Establishment at Westcott and is today on public display in the Royal Air Force Museum at Cosford, near Wolverhampton. In all, the two prototypes had completed forty-two sorties.

The Avro 720

In parallel with the SR.53, the Ministry of Supply had also given A.V. Roe and Company an Instruction to Proceed with their own design to OR.301, the Avro 720, which went ahead under the designation F.137D. The Type 720 was to be fitted with a Viper turbojet plus an Armstrong Siddeley Screamer rocket motor, the latter burning liquid oxygen and kerosene.

Aerodynamic experience with the Avro 707 family of research deltas and the Vulcan bomber, which was then flying in prototype form, had convinced Avro that the tailless delta provided the optimum aerodynamic efficiency, offering minimum drag, a low wing loading and the desired handling characteristics over the aircraft's whole speed range up to about Mach 2. To keep drag as low as possible, the smallest possible envelope was designed around the fuel and oxidant tanks, and extensive use was made of honeycomb sandwich structure. The central cylindrical portion of the fuselage was almost entirely occupied by the liquid oxygen tank and the forward fuel tank, a small semi-cylindrical portion being hollowed out at the base to provide accommodation for the Viper turbojet. The latter's air intake was situated under the forward fuselage and the exhaust duct under the rear fuselage, which housed the rear fuel tank and carried the mountings for the Screamer rocket motor, the vertical fin and the air brake reaction points. The nosewheel retracted aft, with the intake ducts for the Viper passing on each side of the well, and the main units retracted forward, turning through 90 degrees to lie flat in the wing. Proposed armament for the Avro 720, like the SR.53, was the two *Blue Jay*/Firestreak AAMs mounted on launching pylons outboard of the main undercarriage members.

As related above, Avro and Saro both realized that their designs were not going to be able to meet the laid-down specifications, and would have to be enlarged. Avro submitted their design for a revamped Type 720 in October 1954, stressing that if a 4,850lb (21.6kN) s.t. Bristol Orpheus turbojet were used as an interim engine, the aircraft could be flying by the end of 1955. The company also proposed a naval version, the Type 728, with increased wing area and a lengthened undercarriage. Rocket power for both variants was to be provided by the Spectre, and developed aircraft were to be fitted with the Gyron Junior turbojet.

Like the P.177, the developed 720/728 was to carry advanced AI equipment. Work on the original Avro 720, which was now intended to be a test bed for the more potent variant, was proceeding at a much faster rate than the development of the rival SR.53, and by the end of 1955 the prototype (XD696) was virtually complete. The full-scale test specimen programme included a complete static test structure that was built before the prototype so that, in the event of any failure of the honeycomb structure under test, the prototype could be suitably modified. In the event, the structure stood up to the static tests very well.

Then, abruptly, the Ministry of Supply cancelled the Avro 720 project on the grounds that the cost of supporting two similar projects was too high and that the proposed rocket fuel combination of liquid oxygen and kerosene would prove dangerous to store under operational conditions, especially on aircraft carriers. High-test peroxide was easier to handle, and better safety measures had been evolved for its use.

The Saunders-Roe P.177

Despite the tragic loss of the SR.53 XD151 and the grounding of its sister, XD145, the future for the bigger operational version, the P.177, seemed promising. The Air Staff viewed the project with enthusiasm, foreseeing a potent interceptor force comprising squadrons of Lightnings and P.177s, to be fully operational in the early 1960s, while the Naval Staff was also keeping a close interest in P.177 development. The requirements of both Services were detailed in two operational requirements, OR.337 for the RAF and NA.47 for the Navy. Saunders-Roe went to great lengths to integrate everything in a single design, which was covered by MoS Specification F.177D.

By the end of 1955, work had already begun at Cowes on the development of jigs and tools for the production of an initial batch of twenty-seven P.177s for the RAF and RN. Sub-contractors were selected for the design and development of various airframe components and parts of the fuel system, and two Service officers, Commander P.S. Wilson RN and Wing Commander P.C. Cleaver RAF, were appointed to liaise with Saunders-Roe throughout the development phase up to the prototype's first flight. The schedule called for the completion of five P.177s, without weapons or AI, by January 1958.

Early in 1957 the P.177 programme was gathering momentum. De Havilland was now heavily involved, having acquired a one-third share holding in Saunders-Roe, and Armstrong-Whitworth had been selected to build the P.177's wing. What was even more promising was the interest being shown towards the project by the West German Defence Ministry, which in 1956 had begun to look for a supersonic interceptor to replace its F-86 Sabres. West Germany's air defence problems were more critical in many respects than the United Kingdom's: because West Germany would have a reduced warning time of an air threat from the east, reaction times needed to be much shorter. What the Luftwaffe needed was an aircraft that could get off the ground and climb to its interception height in seconds, rather than minutes, and in this respect the P.177 seemed the ideal formula.

In the summer of 1956, discussions had started between members of the German Defence Staff and a Saunders-Roe team headed by the Director, Robert Perfect, and M.J. Brennan, the Chief Designer. In November, the British Government agreed to the opening of negotiations with the Federal Republic of Germany with a view to securing an order for the P.177. At this stage, the Germans were indicating that they might want about 200 examples. The Germans sent a technical team to Cowes in January 1957 to assess the project at close quarters, while Bonn and London worked out financial details.

Then, in April 1957, the whole P.177 project was rocked to its foundations with the publication of that year's notorious White Paper on Defence (attributed to Defence Minister Duncan Sandys but actually mostly written before he assumed office), which stated that the English Electric P.1B (i.e. the Lightning) would be the last manned fighter to enter RAF service and that henceforth all efforts would be concentrated on perfecting guided missiles for defence. As a result, the Air Staff immediately cancelled OR.337, which left the entire project resting on the intentions of the Naval Staff and the Germans.

Then, in August, the Navy's requirement was cancelled too. Even so, the P.177 project might have been rescued; Aubrey Jones, the Minister of Supply, authorized the continued development of the first batch of five aircraft in anticipation of a German order, even though Duncan Sandys wanted to see the P.177 programme scrapped in its entirety. Even at this critical stage, the P.177 was undergoing design changes; at the last moment the aircraft was re-designed around the Rolls-Royce RB.133 engine instead of the Gyron Junior and its wing section was made thinner.

The German Defence Ministry, too, was becoming increasingly frustrated by the British Government's lack of interest in the project. Moreover, the Luftwaffe's requirement had been modified: what was now required was a medium- and low-level interceptor. Toward the end of 1957, the Federal German Government informed London that it was no longer interested in the P.177; the Luftwaffe turned instead to the United States, and the Lockheed F-104 Starfighter.

The P.177 project was dead, and in Saunders-Roe the sense of numbed shock was in no way diminished by all the prior indications that the axe had been about to fall. The epitaph for one of the most promising and advanced combat aircraft ever to take shape on the drawing boards of a British aircraft designer came in the form of a statement from the Ministry of Supply in January 1958:

> This aircraft commands general recognition as an excellent and unique design in its class. Unfortunately, it no longer fits into the broad pattern of the United Kingdom defence programme.

The Thin-Wing Javelin

Duncan Sandys' preoccupation with guided weapons at the expense of manned combat aircraft was to cost Britain's military aircraft industry dearly, though in fairness it must be said that Sandys was not wholly to blame in formulating a disastrously faulty air defence policy. Plenty of others in high places agreed with him at the time, and few strong voices were raised against him. The fault in the cancellation of a whole range of promising aircraft projects lay as much with the failure of the industry to present a concerted front against what was clearly an erroneous measure, and with the failure of various government departments not only to liaise with one another effectively, but also to make decisions that still might have secured foreign orders which, in the event, were quickly lost to the United States. It is too easy, with hindsight, to find a single scapegoat for the vacillations of the late 1950s.

As we have seen, the Saunders-Roe P.177 was to have formed part of a mixed interceptor force

With the cancellation of the P.177, the Luftwaffe acquired the Lockheed F-104 Starfighter. (Lockheed)

together with the Lightning, and these two aircraft were to have been the mainstay of Fighter Command until the mid-1960s. After that, according to Air Staff thinking, Britain's air defences would standardize on a supersonic all-weather interceptor with long range and a missile armament. Early thoughts turned to an advanced version of the Gloster Javelin, which in the mid-1950s was in 'super-priority' production for the RAF's all-weather fighter squadrons; the new aircraft, designated P.376, would have a thin wing and would be powered by two 16,000lb (71.2kN) s.t. Bristol Olympus engines giving it a speed in excess of Mach 1.77 at 45,000ft (14,000m). A large aircraft, with a span of over 60ft (18.3m) and a length of 72ft (21.96m), the 'thin-wing Javelin' was to be armed with 30mm cannon and the massive Vickers *Red Dean* AAM. Eighteen examples of the P.376 were ordered under Specification F.153D in January 1955, but eighteen months later both the thin-wing Javelin and the *Red Dean* missile were cancelled.

The Air Staff had decided to take an enormous leap forward and go for an all-weather fighter that would be capable of reaching a speed of Mach 2 at 60,000ft (18,300m). The new Operational Requirement, OR.329, called for an ability to reach that altitude within 6 minutes of take-off. A specification, F.155T, was written around the OR and issued in February 1955.

The Fairey FD.1

There were two principal contenders in the F.155T stakes: one was Hawker, whose response to it is

The Fairey FD.1 was designed to investigate the handling characteristics of a projected ramp-launched fighter. Powered by a Rolls-Royce Derwent turbojet, it also had provision for a rocket motor, although this was never fitted. (Fairey)

described later in this chapter. The other was Fairey Aviation, about whom some background detail must be outlined. This company, noted for its long association with naval aircraft, had entered the high-speed research field in 1947, when it built a series of small delta-wing models designed to be launched from mobile ramps. Tests with these rocket-powered designs continued at Woomera in Australia until 1953, when the Ministry of Supply lost interest in the vertical-launch concept.

In 1947, Fairey had received a specification, E.10/47, for a manned delta-wing aircraft to investigate the full range of flight characteristics of a ramp-launched machine that might eventually be developed into a high-speed interceptor suitable for operations from small ships or aircraft carriers: the result was the FD.1, which flew for the first time at Boscombe Down on 12 March 1951. The original plan was that the FD.1 would be fitted with large booster rockets for vertical or angled take-off from a ramp; control at take-off speeds was to be accomplished by four swivelling jet nozzles in the rear fuselage that could be operated by normal controls. With the waning of MoS interest in the ramp launch idea, however, the FD.1 was fitted with a conventional tricycle undercarriage. Powered by a Rolls-Royce Derwent turbojet, its estimated performance included a maximum speed of 587mph (945km/h) at 40,000ft (12,000m)

and the ability to climb to 30,000ft (9,000m) in 4½ minutes. This all altered when, before the first flight, the aircraft was fitted with a small tailplane mounted on top of the fin, which imposed an airframe limitation of 345mph (555km/h). The FD.1 undertook a great deal of test flying, investigating lateral and longitudinal stability, rolling performance and the effectiveness of braking parachutes. The test programme was terminated in 1953 and this interesting little machine ended its days as a ground target.

The Fairey FD.2

Meanwhile, in February 1949, Fairey had been asked to investigate the design of a single-engined transonic research aircraft, which was covered by Specification ER.103. In December 1949 the company came up with firm proposals for a highly streamlined delta-wing machine that was, in essence a supersonic dart just big enough to house a pilot, engines and fuel. Frontal areas were cut to a minimum and all possible external bulges removed. Maximum clearance between the Rolls-Royce RA.14R engine and the fuselage skin was less than 6in (150mm), while the delta wing, spanning 26ft 10in (8.18m), was as thin as possible, with a thickness/chord ratio of only 4 per cent. Leading edge sweep was 60 degrees.

Fairey received a contract to build two aircraft in October 1950, but considerable delay was caused by the fact that the company was heavily involved in the production of the Fairey Gannet for the Royal Navy, and detailed design work did not start until the summer of 1952. By this time, Fairey had a new Chief Engineer; his name was R.L. Lickley, who had been head of the Department of Aircraft Design at RAE Cranfield. Under his direction, the aircraft – now known as the FD.2, or Delta Two – rapidly took shape, and the first drawings were released to the shops in September 1952.

The finalized FD.2 design differed from the original concept only in minor detail. The biggest modification involved the nose section. To improve the pilot's vision during the landing phase, Fairey's design team devised a 'droop snoot' whereby the whole nose section, including the cockpit assembly forward of the front bulkhead, could be hinged downward at a 10-degree angle. The wing, despite its thinness, was a remarkably solid structure of light alloy, with three main and two subsidiary spars forming a torsion box. Each wing contained four integral fuel tanks which, together with the fuselage collector tank, provided a total capacity of 322gal (1,465ltr). The wing trailing edge carried inboard elevators and outboard ailerons, which were power-operated.

Fairey's Chief Test Pilot was Group Captain Gordon Slade, but it was his deputy, a young ex-Fleet Air Arm officer named Peter Twiss, who took the FD.2 into the air for the first time at Boscombe Down on 6 October 1954. Before the flight, Twiss built up his experience of high-speed flight with supersonic dives in Hunters, Swifts and Sabres. He had also amassed considerable flight time in the FD.1.

Right from the beginning, the FD.2 showed itself to be an aircraft of enormous potential. Twiss made thirteen flights, gradually building up his confidence in the machine, and plans were afoot to begin the real work of high-speed, high-altitude research when, during the fourteenth flight on 17 November 1954, something went wrong. At 30,000ft (9,000m), 30 miles (50km) out from Boscombe Down, the engine failed as the result of an internal pressure build-up that collapsed the fuselage collector tank. Twiss did some rapid calculations and worked out that he had just enough height to recover to Boscombe for a dead-stick landing. He scraped across the boundary fence, selecting undercarriage down at the last moment, but only the nosewheel extended. Twiss said later:

> I no longer doubted that we should finish up in one piece, although I believe it looked quite spectacular from the ground. The nosewheel touched first, and we dragged along on this and the tail end, with sparks streaming off the runway. Fortunately, the engine failure had been caused by a fuel stoppage, so there was no fuel near the engine and little fear of fire. Anyway, we gradually lost speed. Eventually the starboard wing dropped and we began careering towards the control tower at about 100kt. On the grass we slowed quickly and, at about 40kt, the starboard wing dug in and brought us to a grinding standstill.

Twiss escaped with a severe shaking, and later received the Queen's Commendation for Valuable Service in the Air. The Delta Two, however, had sustained damage that put it out of action for eight months, and the test programme was not resumed until August 1955. In September the FD.2 prototype, WG774, took part in the SBAC Show at Farnborough, although Peter Twiss kept it throttled well back to keep its true performance secret. The Fairey team, almost to their surprise, were beginning to learn that the aircraft was capable of very high speeds, and as yet it had not even used its afterburner. The first supersonic flight was made on 28 October 1955, and further supersonic trials confirmed Fairey's view that the Delta Two was capable of speeds well in excess of 1,000mph (1,600km/h). Urged by Gordon Slade and Peter Twiss, the company began to think seriously of using the aircraft in an attempt on the world air speed record, which at that time was held by a North American F-100C Super Sabre.

The idea was put to the Ministry, whose initial attitude was one of flat disbelief that the FD.2 could fly at anywhere near 1,000mph. Grudging approval was eventually obtained after much negotiation on Fairey's part, but the Ministry of Supply made it clear that it did not wish to be associated with the attempt. No finance was forthcoming, and Fairey had to pay for the necessary insurance cover as well as for the services of a team of recording specialists from RAE Farnborough.

The attempt on the record was prepared under conditions of strict secrecy, and on 10 March 1956

The last British aircraft to hold the World Air Speed Record, the Fairey FD.2, or Delta Two, was designed to Specification ER.103, calling for an aircraft capable of flying at up to Mach 1.5. (Fairey)

Twiss took WG774 to a new average record speed of 1,132mph (1,822km/h) at 38,000ft (11,600m) over a 9.65-mile (15.52km) course between Thorney Island and Worthing. It was the first time that the record had been raised above the 1,000mph mark, and it exceeded the previous American-held record by 37 per cent, the biggest leap so far.

The achievement astounded the aviation world, and Fairey felt secure in their belief that the Delta Two's design had proven itself to the point where proposals could be put forward for a family of supersonic fighters based on it. Two FD.2s were now flying – the second, WG777, having flown on 15 February 1956 – and between them the two aircraft had made well over 100 flights by the time Peter Twiss captured the air speed record.

As a first step towards the development of a supersonic fighter based on the Delta Two, Fairey proposed ER.103/B, a variant with a modified fuselage housing a de Havilland Gyron or a Rolls-Royce RB.122 turbojet with reheat. This was to be followed by the ER.103/C, which would be a prototype fighter fitted with AI and armed with Firestreak missiles mounted on the wingtips. It was estimated that the aircraft's performance would include a speed of Mach 2.26 at 55,000ft (17,000m) and Mach 1.8 at 60,000ft (18,000m), with a time to 45,000ft (14,000m) of 1.9 minutes.

At the same time, Fairey considered various proposals to meet the demanding F.155T specification for a supersonic all-weather fighter, and came to the conclusion that the weapons system required by the Air Staff was so complex that it would not be fully developed before 1962, at the very earliest. To bridge the gap, the company proposed a simpler delta-wing fighter that would be capable of meeting any air threat that was likely to develop within that period. It would be powered by an afterburning Gyron, plus two Spectre Junior rocket motors, and would be armed with Firestreak Mk 4 AAMs (later renamed *Red Top*) mounted at the wingtips. The aircraft would have a maximum level speed with reheat of Mach 2.5 at 59,000ft (18,000m). With optimum early warning the fighter would be capable of intercepting a target at

60,000ft (18,000m) 118½ nautical miles (219km) from base. Even under the worst conditions, it would be able to reach an intercept point 50 nautical miles (92km) from base in 9.2 minutes, using reheat and one rocket in the climb and both rockets during the intercept manoeuvre.

Later in 1956, Fairey modified the design somewhat. The overall two-seat delta configuration was retained, but the single Gyron was replaced by two afterburning RB.128 engines and the rockets were deleted. Changing the armament to a pair of the big *Red Dean* AAMs was also considered. As a further carrot, Fairey indicated that the design could be readily adapted to the medium/low-level intercept, strike and reconnaissance roles.

It was all for nothing. On Monday 1 April 1957, Fairey received a strong indication from the Ministry of Supply that they were favourites in the running for F.155T. The following Thursday, Duncan Sandys announced the immediate cancellation of the whole programme.

Meanwhile, as the result of a ban restricting supersonic flying over the United Kingdom to altitudes over 30,000ft (9,000m), Fairey had asked the French flight test centre at Cazaux if the FD.2 might be based there for a time to undergo further high-speed trials. WG774 was accordingly flown to Cazaux on 15 October 1956, and in the course of the following month it made fifty-two flights in a total of eighteen hours' flying. A third of the flying time was supersonic, the aircraft achieving Mach 1.04 down to 3,000ft (900m). The French looked on with interest, and afterward gave new priority to the development of their family of delta-wing Mirage fighters. It was afterwards hinted, somewhat spitefully in certain British government circles, that the French had copied the Mirage concept from the FD.2. This was quite untrue, and a gratuitous slur on the technical ability of Marcel Dassault's excellent design team. In fact, the progenitor of the Mirage family, the Dassault MD.550 Mirage I, had already flown in June 1955.

Testing of the FD.2 continued, and in June 1958 one of the aircraft was flown to Norway for further low-level supersonic flight trials intended to provide design information on the behaviour of an axial compression engine over a wide range of flight conditions. Engine intake design had previously been dependent, to a great extent, on the testing of wind tunnel models, and the main purpose of the trials was to record the pressure distribution in the engine intakes at various altitudes under subsonic and supersonic flight conditions up to the maximum speed of the aircraft, while taking simultaneous measurements of the stresses in the first-stage compressor blades.

Together, the two FD.2 prototypes made an enormous contribution to high-speed aerodynamic research. After its flying career was over, the second prototype, WG777, went to the RAF Museum at Finningley and later to Cosford, where it may be seen today. WG774 was almost completely rebuilt and, fitted with a model of the ogival wing planform that was to be used on Concorde, flew again as the BAC 221 in May 1964 – at about the time, ironically, that the delta-wing Mirage III was capturing markets around the world. The BAC 221 is now on display at the Fleet Air Arm Museum, Yeovilton, Somerset, alongside the British prototype of the Concorde SST; both are on loan from the Science Museum, London.

The Hawker P.1121

Returning to 1955, the other main contender rising to meet the demands of F.155T was Hawker Aircraft, who already had considerable experience in the design of advanced all-weather fighters. In the early 1950s, at a time when the DH.110 and the Javelin were undergoing comparative trials and experiencing many teething troubles, the Hawker team had evolved a two-seat design, the P.1092, which featured a slender delta wing. Hawker claimed that with an afterburning Avon engine this aircraft would achieve a speed of about Mach 1.5 and, using AI equipment then under development, could have been in RAF service by 1957. This project came to nothing, but when F.155T was issued Hawker responded with a new and much larger design, the two-seat P.1103, which was to have been powered by a Gyron engine.

This design appeared to have plenty of development potential, and in 1956, at the instigation of the Air Staff, the Hawker design team under Sir Sydney Camm set about designing two variants, the P.1116 and P.1121, which were, respectively, two-seat and single-seat strike derivatives. In the event Camm's main effort was devoted to the development of the P.1121, which, had it come to fruition, would have emerged as a supersonic multi-role combat aircraft in the same class as the McDonnell F-4 Phantom.

Mock-up of the Hawker P.1121 strike and air-superiority fighter project. It would have been in the same class as the F-4 Phantom. (Hawker Siddeley)

Development of the P.1121 went ahead with considerable enthusiasm during 1957, for it was planned to have a prototype flying in the following year. It was a fairly conventional swept-wing design, with a leading edge sweep of 40.6 degrees; power was to be provided by a single de Havilland Gyron of 17,400lb (77.4kN) s.t. and 23,800lb (105.9kN) s.t. with reheat, although plans were made for the production version to take either the Rolls-Royce Conway or Bristol Olympus. The big engine was fed by an under-fuselage air intake. In the event, the Gyron was found to suffer from critically unbalanced pressure distribution on the intake face so, after some delay, Hawker opted for the Olympus 21R as an alternative.

Work on the P.1121, financed entirely by Hawker, continued after the 1957 Defence White Paper brought an abrupt end to OR.329. By the summer of 1958 the wing and fuselage assemblies of the prototype were complete, but it was becoming increasingly apparent that the Air Staff were no longer interested in the project and that it would be a waste of company funds to fly the prototype of an aircraft nobody wanted any more.

The Hawker Siddeley P.1129

The 1957 Defence White Paper had left the British aircraft industry with only one long-term project for a manned combat aircraft: OR.339, an Operational Requirement for a tactical strike and reconnaissance machine, and along with the other leading British manufacturers Hawker was compelled to change course with the prevailing wind. Taking a proposed variant of the basic P.1121 design – the P.1125, which was to have been powered by two RB.133 engines – Camm enlarged it and completed an initial design tender for submission in January 1958. Later in the year, however, with the emergence of the Hawker Siddeley Group, the design was modified to incorporate features from a separate design submitted by Avro.

Work on the Hawker Siddeley OR.339 submission, designated P.1129, continued throughout 1958. Then, towards the end of the year, it was learned that a rival design, submitted by the Vickers/English Electric consortium, had been adjudged the winner. Its name was TSR2.

Chapter 16
TSR2: The Assassination of an Aircraft

A Canberra B.6 of No. 617 Sqn, RAF Binbrook, demonstrates its agility. (BAe)

Aircrew boarding a Canberra before a night sortie. (BAe)

In May 1951, when the English Electric Canberra first entered squadron service, it was beyond doubt the world's finest light jet bomber. With some justification, the Air Staff felt that Bomber Command possessed a tactical aircraft that would remain capable of delivering a wide variety of weapons against targets in Eastern Europe with a high probability of survival for the best part of a decade.

Only a year later, the picture had changed. The fighter squadrons of the Soviet Union and her allies were re-equipping with the MiG-15, which had already proved itself in combat in Korea, and there was an unvoiced but growing feeling that, if the Canberra had to go to war – especially in daylight – the tragedy of May 1940, when the RAF's Fairey Battle light bombers were shot out of the sky over France by the Luftwaffe's fighters, might be repeated.

The Early Specifications

In 1952, therefore, the Ministry of Supply issued Specification B.126T, calling for design studies of a bomber capable of carrying a six-ton nuclear store over a combat radius of 1,500 nautical miles (2,800km) at very low level and high subsonic speed, not less than Mach 0.85. Several firms submitted proposals, but the requirement was well in advance of existing technological capabilities and it was shelved. However, the contest remained open for a low-level naval strike aircraft capable of operating from existing aircraft carriers and delivering a kiloton-range nuclear weapon against land and sea

Although the Buccaneer was an excellent low-level aircraft, it was deemed not fast enough to meet the requirements of Air Staff target B.126T. (Hawker Siddeley)

targets by the toss-bombing method. This requirement was covered by Specification M.148T, which was written around Naval Air Staff Target NAST.39, and in 1955 the design competition was won by Blackburn Aircraft with their B.103. A development batch of twenty aircraft was ordered in July that year, and the robust B.103 went on to enter service with the Royal Navy as the Buccaneer.

On the face of it, the Buccaneer might have seemed the ideal aircraft to meet the RAF's requirement for a Canberra replacement. In fact, although its airframe was quite adequate for the kind of low-level precision strike work envisaged by the RAF, its systems as they existed at the time were not. Admittedly, there was plenty of room for further development, but the Buccaneer was not fast enough. By 1956 the Air Staff had modified B.126T, which had been resurrected, to include an over-the-target speed at low level of Mach 1.3 and the incorporation of an inertial nav/attack system that would enable the aircraft to deliver conventional weapons with pinpoint accuracy.

A year later, in the aftermath of the 1957 Defence White Paper, the RAF's requirement was formalized as General Operational Requirement (GOR) 339. Eight firms were invited to submit tenders by the end of January 1958; the eight did not include the Hawker Siddeley Group, which had already submitted preliminary drawings of the P.1125 project and which was well in the running with its P.1129 variant. The other firms were left in no doubt that they would have to get together and submit joint proposals if they were seriously to contest Hawker Siddeley; GOR.339 was likely to be the only major British military aircraft project for the foreseeable future, and it was too complex to be tackled by the resources of any single company. GOR.339 spelt the beginning of the end for the traditional structure of Britain's aircraft industry.

The English Electric P.17A

English Electric, who had already done a lot of research into a Canberra replacement, had a head start with the design of a two-seat delta-wing project known as the P.17A, which was powered by two RB.142 engines. In collaboration with Short Brothers, English Electric's proposal envisaged a vertical take-off assembly in which the P.17A would be mounted on a Short-designed VTO platform designated P.17D; this was to be powered by forty-four fixed RB.108 lift engines, sixteen swivelling RB.108 lift engines and ten RB.108 engines for forward propulsion. Together, the P.17A/17D combination would weigh somewhere in the region of 150,000lb (68,000kg). In addition to its primary role of getting the P.17A into the air and so dispensing with vulnerable runways, the P.17D could be used to transport freight and fuel to forward operating locations. The idea was by no means as far-fetched as one might think. Shorts were at that time heavily involved with pioneer VTOL techniques and their SC.1 VTOL research aircraft had already flown in conventional flight. Apart from technical considerations, the main drawback to the P.17D was that its development costs were likely to prove prohibitive. As well as the low-level strike version of the P.17A, English Electric also proposed a long-range interceptor variant, the P.22.

TSR2 is Born

Bristol Aircraft and Vickers-Armstrongs also submitted their proposals for OR.339. The Vickers entry, the Type 571, was an advanced twin-engined design incorporating an integrated terrain-following nav/attack system; the aircraft was, in fact, a complete weapons system, and although the Air Staff were coming down heavily in favour of English Electric's P.17A they were sufficiently impressed by the Vickers design to want to incorporate certain features of it in the finalized OR.339 requirement. As a result of this a new Air Staff Requirement, ASR.343, was issued in the spring of 1959; it dispensed with the vertical take-off concept, which brought about the end of Short Brothers' participation, and virtually demanded the amalgamation of Vickers and English Electric to bring the required aircraft to fruition. Together with the Bristol Aeroplane Company, they were eventually to form the British Aircraft Corporation in February 1960.

On 1 January 1959, it was announced that Vickers-Armstrongs and English Electric had been awarded the contract to develop a new tactical strike and reconnaissance aircraft, known as TSR2, to replace the Canberra. Its airframe was to be developed from that of the P.17, and it was to be powered by two afterburning Bristol Siddeley Olympus 22R engines. The choice of power plant was pushed through in the face of severe criticism from the Vickers and English Electric design teams, who wanted a Rolls-Royce engine, and as events were to prove it was an unfortunate choice. Nevertheless, at the time the Olympus 22R was the only engine available for immediate development as a massive reheat unit to provide up to 33,000lb (146.8kN) s.t. with an acceptable specific fuel consumption, and with a configuration suitable for installing twin engines in the rear fuselage.

By May 1959 the contractors, the Air Ministry and the Ministry of Supply had all agreed exactly what was required and what was feasible. The most notable of the changes required under ASR.343 was that the low-level height was defined as 200ft (60m) or less, speed at 40,000ft (12,000m) was to be Mach 2 instead of Mach 1.7, ECM equipment was to be added, ferry range was to be increased to 2,500 nautical miles (4,600km) and the aircraft was to be able to operate from firm grass, to allow it to be dispersed away from the large airfields that would inevitably be targets for an enemy early in any confrontation.

Development work proceeded at Weybridge and Warton, and a Management Board comprising representatives of the RAF, the Ministry of Aviation and BAC was set up to control the entire project and sort out any problems. In fact, the very opposite was to be achieved: throughout its development, TSR2 was to be bedevilled by the Board's decisions and compromises. In effect, it was the first time in the history of British aviation that decisions affecting the design of an aircraft were taken away from the design team involved and placed in the hands of a committee.

While the TSR2 airframe gradually took shape, various sub-contractors were given the responsibility for developing the necessary systems. The contract for the automatic flight system went to Elliott Automation, who had amassed an enormous amount of experience in developing the inertial navigation for the V-Force's *Blue Steel* stand-off missile; Ferranti were given the task of developing the terrain-following radar and nav/attack system, and EMI the sideways-looking radar, while Marconi were made responsible for avionics such as the Instrument Landing System (ILS).

By the spring of 1960, it was apparent that the cost of developing the aircraft's advanced electronic systems was going to greatly exceed the estimated figures; this was the first of a series of cost escalations that were to contribute to the project's eventual downfall. Funds were diverted from other cancelled projects to keep TSR2 going, but there was little slowing in the overall upward trend.

The TSR2 and its Missions

By the autumn of 1962 the design of TSR2 had been finalized and BAC was able to provide the Ministry of Aviation with realistic simulated performance figures. These included a cruising speed of Mach 0.9–1.1 at sea level and Mach 2.05 at altitude. Combat radius with external fuel would be 1,500 nautical miles (2,800km), or 1,000nm (1,850km) with a 2,000lb (900kg) internal bomb load on internal fuel only. Initial rate of climb at sea level would be 50,000ft per minute (15,000m/min). A variety of flight profiles was envisaged, most involving lo-lo sorties at heights of not more than 200ft (60m) at Mach 0.9. The aircraft could carry a formidable range of weapons, in both the conventional and nuclear strike roles.

TSR2's main function, had it entered RAF service, would have been to carry out deep reconnaissance and attack missions against targets that required deep penetration of enemy territory, such as large bridges, airfields, missile and radar sites, marshalling yards, communication centres and depots. As a deep penetration system, TSR2 was years ahead of its time; it was also the only strike aircraft in the world capable of a true short-field performance, which would have enabled it to operate in areas of the globe where large stretches of concrete did not exist, as well as increasing its own chances of survival in the event of an enemy attack on its bases. The use of an all-moving tailplane, replacing conventional elevator and aileron control, allowed maximum use to be made of full-span blown flaps as a high-lift device for short take-off and landing; this permitted the aircraft to operate from semi-prepared or low-grade surfaces only 3,000ft (900m) long. Another feature was TSR2's long-stroke undercarriage with low-pressure tyres, specifically designed for operation from rough surfaces. The nosewheel strut could be extended during take-off to position the aircraft in take-off attitude and so shorten its run.

The nav/attack system incorporated in the aircraft, the most advanced of its type anywhere, exploited the latest developments in radar/computer flight-control techniques. Briefly, the system comprised a Doppler/inertial dead reckoning navigation system of very high accuracy which was corrected over 100 miles or so by fixes obtained from the sideways-looking radar. A forward-looking radar enabled the aircraft to follow the contours of the terrain either automatically or manually and regardless of weather at a pre-selected height above the ground, the pilot having the benefit of a head-up display. Data from the navigation and TFR systems was fed by a complex of digital and analogue computers into an automatic pilot that was capable of flying the aircraft to and from a predetermined target, the flight plan being fed into the digital computer on punched tape. Throughout the flight, the ground position of the aircraft was displayed to the crew on a moving map. The particular attack mode required could be pre-selected and carried out automatically, without visual reference to the target.

In the reconnaissance role, TSR2 was designed to carry a very complete reconnaissance pack in a pannier in the weapons bay. Its equipment included the EMI sideways-looking radar, moving target indication that could blot out all returns from stationary objects to disclose any movement in the area, and linescan, which took a TV-type picture by day or night and could be used to transmit information direct from the aircraft to a ground station in the forward area to provide real-time intelligence.

Because of the requirement that called for TSR2 to be capable of supersonic flight at both high and low altitude, much attention was given in design to reducing the aircraft's response to gusts in order to make working conditions for the crew tolerable at very high speed and low altitude. During the initial design phase of TSR2, research into low-level turbulence using Canberras over the Libyan desert at speeds of about Mach 0.7 (Operation *Swifter*) had shown that bumps of ½g could be expected, on average, twenty-seven times a minute, which was more than twice the rate regarded as intolerable for the operating crews. Gust response is a factor of wing loading, and broadly speaking the lower wing loading is, the rougher the ride for a given speed. The optimum solution is variable sweep, but TSR2's designers opted for a delta planform and a small wing area, a leading edge sweep of 60 degrees and a very thin wing section, mounted as high as possible on the fuselage. To minimize the low-speed 'Dutch roll' characteristic of sharply swept wings (in a Dutch roll the aircraft begins to yaw due to a gust or other input, and this develops into a roll) the tip sections were given a sharp anhedral of 23 degrees.

A lot of thought was given to crew comfort and safety in the TSR2's design. The windscreen, for example, which was made of alumino silicate, was designed to withstand a 1lb (0.45kg) bird strike at speeds in excess of Mach 1.0, and the cockpit incorporated a first-class air conditioning system, including refrigeration for high-speed flight. Both crew members had rocket-powered Martin-Baker ejection seats, capable of safe operation through every phase of the flight envelope from the take-off roll.

Progress and Problems

A contract for nine development TSR2s had already been placed in October 1960, and this was followed by a preliminary order for eleven pre-production aircraft in June 1962. At this stage, it was still hoped to fly the first prototype in the autumn of 1963, with delivery of the first batch of pre-production machines to follow two years later. Research and development costs were estimated at £90m in 1960, but by the beginning of 1963 this figure had doubled and the whole schedule had slipped by two years. The problem of too many committees, each responsible for its own slice of the development work, still dogged the project, and even the setting up of a Steering Committee in 1963 to co-ordinate matters more closely did nothing to alleviate it.

Moreover, the project was now beset by worrying technical problems, mainly to do with the

Olympus 22R engine. The fifth Avro Vulcan B.1, XA894, had been allocated to Olympus development work; the engine, fuelled from two tanks in the bomb bay, was mounted in a nacelle beneath the Vulcan's fuselage. The first flight with the Olympus 22R was made on 23 February 1962, and later in the year XA894 was fitted with the more powerful Olympus 22R-1, featuring a high-performance reheat system. All went well until 3 December 1962 when, during a full reheat ground run, the Low Pressure (LP) shaft of the 22R-1 failed and the engine disintegrated, spewing out metal fragments that ruptured both the bomb bay and main fuel tanks. Such was the force of the break-up that the LP turbine disc was hurled for half a mile in bounds of 150 yards, narrowly missing the Bristol 188 research aircraft. There were no casualties, but the Vulcan was completely burned out.

The cause was resonance, which led to the break-up of the LP shaft at a certain RPM, but it was a long time before Bristol Siddeley established what had gone wrong, and in the meantime other Olympus 22R test engines failed, fortunately on the ground. Modifications were made but these, together with other engine design changes, caused severe problems in marrying the Olympus to the TSR2 airframe. The LP shaft problem had not been completely cured when the aircraft made its first flight, and failures were still occurring when the engine was run up to high RPM from a cold start – a procedure that was very necessary in a military aircraft, especially one whose whole effectiveness relied on getting airborne in the minimum time.

By the end of 1963, the writing was already on the wall for TSR2, although neither the Government nor BAC would admit it. Escalating research and development costs had made the project the subject of heated political controversy: the Labour Party, influenced by 'advisors' who had a minimal knowledge of military aviation and even less of the RAF's operational requirements, made political capital out of the funds that were being diverted to keep TSR2 alive, and left the electorate in no doubt about what they would do to the project if they got into power. But there were sinister forces at work within the Ministry of Defence, too: the Chief of the Defence Staff, Lord Mountbatten, made no secret of the fact that he favoured a land-based version of the Buccaneer to meet the RAF's requirement, while the Ministry's Chief Scientific Advisor, Sir Solly Zuckermann, told everyone concerned that he thought that TSR2 was a waste of public money and that better value could be obtained by buying equipment from the United States.

Australian Interest

Predictably, in-fighting such as this had an adverse effect on Government attempts to promote the TSR2 overseas. The Australians, in particular, had shown an active interest in the aircraft since 1960, and two years later were favouring the British machine as a Canberra replacement. The requirement for a new RAAF bomber, as defined by Air Staff Requirement ASR 36, was that the aircraft should have an all-weather capability in both its primary strike and secondary reconnaissance roles, a capability for delivering both conventional ordnance and 'special stores' (in other words, nuclear weapons), a speed of Mach 2 at 50,000ft (15,000m), a desirable radius of action of 1,100 nautical miles (2,000km), and an in-service date with the RAAF of June 1966.

In May 1963 the Australian Government sent a RAAF evaluation team abroad to investigate possible alternatives to TSR2. The evaluation team defined two basic missions for the new bomber. These involved, firstly, joint operations under American command against targets in southern China and North Vietnam, and secondly, providing a credible deterrent against Indonesia, which in practical terms meant operating from overseas and Australian bases against any Indonesian target. (It should be remembered that, in 1963, British Commonwealth forces were involved in serious armed confrontation with Indonesia on the island of Borneo.) Between June and August 1963 the evaluation team investigated the French Mirage IV and the USA's McDonnell F-4C Phantom, North American RA5C Vigilante and General Dynamics TFX, which was later to be re-designated F-111.

Yet there was no sales drive aimed at convincing the Australian Government that TSR2 was the aircraft the RAAF needed, so it was hardly surprising that Australian interest began to wane after Lord Mountbatten, during a tour of South-East Asia, expressed the opinion that mounting costs and complexity would prevent the aircraft ever coming into service.

It was not until the end of 1963 that a British Government delegation led by Hugh Fraser, the

The prototype TSR2, XR219, on a test flight over Cumbria. (BAe)

Wing Commander Roland Beamont, who took the first TSR2, XR219, on its maiden flight on 27 September 1964. (BAe)

Cancellation

The prototype TSR2, XR219, made its maiden flight from Boscombe Down on 27 September 1964 with Roland Beamont at the controls, after carrying out twelve taxi runs. The flying qualities were good, but the pilot experienced strong lateral vibration on touchdown, which interfered with his vision at that critical moment. The problem lay with the complex undercarriage (which had remained down on this first flight), and it took over four months and nine flights before the undercarriage could be retracted successfully. The aircraft went supersonic for the first time on 21 February 1965, and high-speed low-altitude trials began in March. By this time a second aircraft, XR220, was scheduled to join the flying programme and a third, XR221, had successfully completed an initial ground run of the avionics fit. Work was progressing on six more development aircraft, five of which were partly complete.

The Labour Government that had taken office under Prime Minister Harold Wilson shortly after TSR2's first flight had kept the project going so that the aircraft could be evaluated against the General Dynamics F-111. At that time, Wilson – acting on faulty advice – seriously believed that some £300 million might be saved by buying the American aircraft; his Cabinet thought so too, and the final nail in TSR2's coffin was hammered home

Secretary of State for Air, went to Australia to mount a sales drive, but by that time it was too late. Soon afterwards, the Australians decided to meet the RAAF requirement by ordering twenty-four General Dynamics F-111As. The first of these, designated F-111C in RAAF service, were eventually delivered in 1973.

Final act: the first TSR2, XR219, awaits destruction on the gunnery range at Shoeburyness. (PA)

on 6 April 1965, when Chancellor James Callaghan, during his budget speech, announced that the project was to be cancelled forthwith. The assassination was to be complete: no trace of the project was to survive. Orders were issued for the destruction of the completed prototypes and those on the assembly line, and of all the jigs and tools used by the manufacturing companies.

It is fair to say that the decision to cancel TSR2, in its stage of development, was probably the most ill-advised ever made by a British government involving the aircraft industry. Admittedly, there were still snags to be overcome, but fewer snags than those that afflicted the F-111, for which the British Government now opted. Soaring costs and technical problems in the F-111 development programme eventually led to the cancellation of the British order, at considerable cost.

The gap was filled, in 1969, by the Buccaneer S.2, which Blackburn had wanted the RAF to have ten years earlier, and an admirable job it subsequently did. But it was not until 1982, with the debut of the Tornado, that the strike squadrons of the Royal Air Force at last possessed an aircraft capable of carrying out all the tasks for which the ill-fated TSR2 had been intended.

Of the TSR2 airframes, XR219, XR221 and XR223 were taken to the shooting range at Shoeburyness to be destroyed as 'damage to aircraft' targets. XR220 was kept at Boscombe for a year or so and then placed in storage at RAF Henlow after it had had all its internal equipment ripped out (even the wires to equipment were cut rather than disconnected). It was later transferred to RAF Cosford's Aerospace Museum. XR222 was initially to be scrapped but was instead sent to the College of Aeronautics at Cranfield and later saved for restoration and moved to the Imperial War Museum at Duxford. All the other airframes were scrapped. All tooling was destroyed: on the production line, as workers completed assembly of some airframes prior to their transport to the scrap yard, the tooling was being destroyed with cutting torches behind them. A wooden mock-up of the TSR2 was dragged out of the Warton factory and burned while the workers looked on. All technical publications were ordered to be destroyed; even photographs of the aircraft were destroyed. Boscombe Down's official records of test flights were 'lost'. It was an act of vandalism unparalleled in the history of British military aviation.

Part VI
Other Developments, 1955–90

Chapter 17
Lightweight Fighters

The concept of the lightweight fighter pre-dated the Second World War, with French and Italian designers at the forefront of its development. In France, Caudron-Renault developed the CR.710 and CR.714 Cyclone lightweight fighters, the first of which flew in July 1936 and which was derived from Marcel Riffard's famous series of racing aircraft of the early 1930s. The type was in direct competition with the Morane 406, which was selected for major production, but smaller orders were placed for the Caudron fighter. On 10 May 1940 the Armée de l'Air had forty-six C.714s on charge, most serving with GC I/145, manned by Polish pilots. The C.714's operational career was brief, lasting only from 2–13 June 1940, in which time GC I/145's pilots destroyed twelve enemy aircraft for the loss of thirteen Caudrons. Six aircraft were also supplied to Finland during the 'Winter War' of 1939–40. Italy's lightweight fighter proponent was Sergio Stefanutti, whose designs will be described later in this chapter.

Perhaps the most famous lightweight fighter of the Second World War – although it was not designed as such – was the Mitsubishi A6M 'Zero', which owed its lightness of structure in part to the materials used and in part to a complete lack of armour protection. In order to meet an exacting Japanese Navy requirement, weight conservation was of paramount importance, and the A6M design featured several innovations in order to achieve this goal. For example, the wing was built in one piece, eliminating the need for the heavy centre-section fittings that were normally required for joining two separate wing sections together. The one-piece wing combined with the engine, cockpit and forward fuselage to form a single rigid unit, the centre-section of the fuselage being riveted to the upper wing skin and the latter forming the cockpit floor. The rear fuselage, with the tail, was joined to the forward section by a series of eighty bolts, fixed to two ring formers just aft of the cockpit. The aircraft could therefore readily be split into two components, facilitating storage and also providing unobstructed access to the cockpit area from the rear.

Another weight-saving device was the use of a lightweight alloy called Extra-Super Duralumin (ESD) in the construction of the wing main spar. Manufactured by the Sumitomo Metal Industry, it had a tensile strength 30 to 40 per cent higher than any alloy used previously. Although very light in weight (3,704lb/1,680kg empty, compared with the Spitfire I's 4,341lb/1,969kg), a feature that gave the impression that the airframe was structurally weak, the A6M fighter design was actually very strong. As the war progressed, however, the need for more powerful engines and armour plating resulted in the Zero becoming increasingly heavy, so that the advantages it had earlier enjoyed over Allied fighter types were gradually eroded away.

The NATO Lightweight Strike Fighter

In April 1954, the increasing complexity of modern combat aircraft, together with a complete reappraisal of tactical air power requirements in Europe, led to the issue of a specification for a new lightweight strike fighter for service with NATO's tactical fighter-bomber squadrons. The specification, drawn up by the technical staff of the Supreme Allied Commander, Europe – at that time General Lauris Norstad – called for a single-seat aircraft of robust construction, easy to maintain under arduous operational conditions, with equipment that included a gyro gunsight and rocket sight, Distance

Measuring Equipment (DME), Identification Friend/Foe (IFF), radar homing, UHF radio and cockpit pressurization. It had to carry one of three different types of built-in armament (four 0.5in machine guns, two 20mm or two 30mm cannon) as well as a variety of underwing stores such as two 500lb bombs and twelve 3in rockets. The empty weight of the machine was not to exceed 5,000lb (2,265kg). It had to be capable of taking off from a grass strip fully laden to clear a 50ft (15m) obstacle within 1,000yd (915m), and of flying at Mach 0.95 at heights from sea level up to 500ft (150m) for one-third of its mission, the remainder of the sortie to be flown at a cruising speed of 400mph (640km/h). A rate of roll of at least 100 degrees per second at Mach 0.9 was also required.

The Folland Midge

When the specification was issued, Great Britain enjoyed a substantial lead in lightweight jet fighter development. In 1950, W.E.W. Petter, Chief Designer of the Folland Aircraft Company, had initiated design studies of just such an aircraft based on the use of a 3,800lb (16.9kN) s.t. Bristol BE.22 Saturn axial-flow turbojet, which was originally intended to power the *Blue Rapier* guided missile. In the event, the missile project was cancelled and development of the Saturn was abandoned, but Petter persisted in his design work in the knowledge that a suitable power plant would materialize before long. Development went ahead with a low-powered prototype of the proposed fighter, and on 11 August 1954 this aircraft – the Folland FO.139 Midge, fitted with a 1,640lb (7.3kN) s.t. Viper 101 engine – flew for the first time from Boscombe Down in the hands of Squadron Leader E.A. Tennant, Folland's Chief Test Pilot.

Most maiden flights are restricted to a few minutes' duration, but after taking the Midge up to 8,000ft (2,400m) and putting it through various handling checks at speeds of between 120–350kt (220–650km/h) Tennant felt so confident that he remained airborne for over half an hour, carrying out several rolls and high-speed turns before returning to Boscombe Down. During the next five hours he made four successive flights in the little aircraft, culminating in a trip to Chilbolton where the test programme was to be carried out.

Despite its low power, the Midge was later dived at speeds in excess of Mach 0.9. Its performance provided an enormous boost to Folland's morale, the aircraft having been developed as a private venture and a lot of money having been invested in it. The operational version, the Fo.141 Gnat, was to have a much more powerful Bristol Orpheus turbojet. It now seemed certain that the Gnat would have a good chance of acceptance by both the RAF and NATO, even though the competition was stiff, as were the conditions imposed by NATO: whoever received the contract would have to deliver three prototypes and twenty-seven production-standard aircraft by January 1957.

The Dassault Etendard

Nine designs were submitted, of which five were French and two Italian. Apart from Folland, the other British contender was Avro, who proposed the Type 727, a small tailless delta based on the earlier 707 research series. It was the French, however, who appeared to have a head start, for the French Air Ministry had for some time envisaged a requirement for just such an aircraft and had issued a complementary specification calling for the development of a twin-jet strike fighter as well as a single-engined one. The twin-engined machine would be heavier than that required by the NATO specification, but this would be offset by greater reliability. It would offer a similar performance and payload as the lighter single-engined type, and a prototype could be built and flown quickly with existing turbojets.

France, therefore, was able to offer alternative configurations based on the same airframe, and the Ministère de l'Air lost no time in awarding development contracts to the two principal companies involved, Avions Marcel Dassault and Louis Breguet. Dassault, who were already engaged in a private-venture development of their mixed-power plant MD.550 delta, received the go-ahead for the Mystère 22 and 26, the former to meet the French requirement and the latter NATO's. Both aircraft used basically the same airframe, but the 22 was designed to take a pair of existing turbojets while the 26 was to be fitted with the Bristol Orpheus, the engine specified by NATO.

The first prototype Mystère 22, renamed Etendard II, flew for the first time at Melun-Villaroche on 23 July 1956, powered by two Turboméca Gabizo lightweight turbojets. On the following day a second, scaled-up aircraft, the

Etendard IV, made its first flight at Bordeaux-Merignac under the power of a single SNECMA Atar 101E-4 turbojet. A developed version of the Etendard IV was eventually to be produced for the Aéronavale, but the Etendard II was short-lived: trouble was experienced with the Gabizo engines and the Armée de l'Air abandoned the requirement shortly afterwards. The Mystère 26, meanwhile – renamed Etendard VI – was nearing completion, but the Orpheus engine was still not available for installation so Dassault proceeded, at their own expense, to refit the prototype with an Atar 101. It flew in March 1957, and was evaluated alongside the other contenders later in the year.

The Breguet Taon

The other French company involved in the lightweight fighter contest, Avions Louis Breguet, had approached the twin requirement in similar fashion. Their proposal for the NATO contract was the Orpheus-powered Br.1001 Taon (the name means Horsefly, but it is also an anagram of NATO) while to meet the Armée de l'Air requirement they put forward a twin-engined design, the Br.1101.

The Taon was a very promising design which, on the face of it, was significantly superior to the other competitors. Design work started in July 1955, but was halted in February 1956 when, as a result of wind tunnel tests with a mock-up in the United States, it was decided to incorporate area rule in the aircraft's design. (This is the process whereby an aircraft's fuselage is shaped to provide a smooth cross-sectional area from nose to tail in

The highly promising Taon might have been selected to fill the NATO lightweight fighter requirement had the prototype flown earlier. (Breguet)

This photograph, showing the pilot about to enter the Taon's cockpit, gives a good impression of the aircraft's relatively small size. (Breguet)

order to minimise wave drag at high subsonic speeds.) Consequently, although there was a considerable delay before construction of the Taon prototype could begin, the aircraft that took shape was aerodynamically more advanced than the other contenders, all of which were flying by then.

The first metal for the prototype Taon was cut in January 1957. Only seven months later, on 26 July, Breguet test pilot Bernard Witt took the aircraft on its maiden flight. This machine, and two more prototypes, were powered by the Bristol Orpheus B.Or.3 turbojet, although it was planned that the definitive version would have the more powerful B.Or.12. The built-in armament selected for the Taon was four 0.5in Colt-Browning machine guns; external armament comprised two or four 500lb napalm tanks or bombs, or two Nord 5103 beam-riding AAMs, or two Matra 116c pods each containing nineteen 68mm Brandt SNEB rockets.

Preliminary flight trials proved very satisfactory, the Taon meeting every aspect of the NATO requirement, and in September 1957 the first prototype went to the Flight Test Centre at Bretigny for evaluation alongside the other competitors. Meanwhile, the prototype of the Breguet 1101 had also flown on 31 March, powered by two Turboméca Gabizo engines, but the 1100's test programme was halted when the Armée de l'Air withdrew its requirement for a twin-engined strike fighter.

The Aerfer Sagittario, Ariete and Leone

Of the two Italian companies that submitted designs to the NATO specification, it was Fiat who were destined to win the contest with their G.91, which ultimately went into production as NATO's standard tactical fighter-bomber. It was an ironic choice, for the rival design was the work of a man who, for nearly twenty years, had devoted much of his talent as an aircraft designer to perfecting a lightweight fighter, and who had come very close to succeeding.

Sergio Stefanutti, Chief Designer of the Industrie Meccaniche Aeronautiche Meridiolani-Aerfer, had begun studies of a lightweight fighter as long ago as 1939, and after producing some experimental types had designed the SAI.207 Sagittario ('Arrow'), which weighed only 2,262kg (4,993lb) loaded and carried an armament of two 20mm cannon and two machine guns. During tests, it was dived at an indicated airspeed of 750km/h (466mph) at 3,000m (10,000ft), and its performance was so promising that 2,000 examples were ordered for the Regia Aeronautica. However, only a few had been completed by the time Italy signed the armistice in 1943.

Stefanutti resumed his experimental work after the war, fitting his SAI.7 trainer design with swept flying surfaces and testing this configuration as a first step in the development of a lightweight jet fighter. The next step was simple enough. After amassing a considerable amount of aerodynamic information with the aid of a piston-engined test aircraft named the Freccia, Stefanutti replaced its power plant with a little Turboméca Marboré II turbojet. Renamed Sagittario 1, the revamped design flew for the first time on 5 January 1953 and was tested extensively, the upper limit of its flight envelope being dictated by its all-wood construction.

Work went ahead on the development of a definitive fighter variant, the Sagittario 2. This was to have been powered by a Bristol Saturn turbojet, but when the Saturn was cancelled Stefanutti opted for a Rolls-Royce Derwent Mk 9, and it was this engine that powered the prototype Sagittario 2 on its maiden flight from Practica del Mare, Rome, on 19 May 1956. On 4 December that year, piloted by Colonel Giovanni Franchini, it became the first aircraft of Italian design to exceed the speed of sound, reaching Mach 1.1 in a shallow dive.

Although the Sagittario 2 was highly manoeuvrable, could carry the requisite combination of weapons and was able to operate from grass strips, its overall performance did not match the NATO requirement, so, with the help of US funds, Stefanutti took development a stage further and modified the basic design to include a 1,810lb (8.1kN) s.t. Rolls-Royce Soar R.Sr.2 auxiliary turbojet in addition to the Derwent. The configuration of the new prototype fighter, known as the Ariete ('Battering Ram'), was exactly the same as that of the Sagittario except for the rear fuselage, which was made deeper to house the auxiliary turbojet and was 4in (10cm) longer. The Ariete flew for the first time on 27 March 1958, and while flight testing continued Stefanutti's design team was occupied with the third and final development, the Leone ('Lion'). This was to have been powered by either a Bristol Orpheus B.Or.12 or a de

The Aerfer Sagittario 2 was a promising design, but its performance did not match up to NATO requirements. (Ann Tilbury)

The Aerfer Ariete was closer to the definitive prototype of Stefanutti's lightweight jet fighter. (Ann Tilbury)

The NATO lightweight fighter contest was won by the Fiat G-91, seen here in its G-91Y version. (Fiat)

Havilland Gyron Junior turbojet, with a de Havilland Spectre rocket motor replacing the Soar, but the adoption of the Fiat G.91 by the Italian Air Force and NATO brought further work to an end.

The Folland Gnat

Of the two British contenders in the NATO competition, the Avro 727 was adjudged a 'close runner-up' in the original design contest, but it never left the drawing-board. The other aircraft, the Folland Gnat, was to enjoy at least a partial success story as a combat aircraft, but not with NATO. The prototype of the Orpheus-powered Gnat flew on 18 July 1955 and was followed by a batch of six aircraft for the Ministry of Supply, the first of these flying on 26 May 1956. Production Gnat Mk 1s were powered by the Bristol Orpheus 701 turbojet of 4,520lb (20.1kN) s. t. and carried an armament of two 30mm Aden cannon plus up to 2,000lb (900kg) of underwing stores, but despite the promise shown by the diminutive aircraft, which cost far less to manufacture than other combat aircraft of comparable performance, it was not adopted by the RAF or NATO. One hundred Gnat Mk 1s were built under licence in India; the type saw considerable action during the 1971 war between India and Pakistan, and proved quite deadly in high-speed, low-level combat. It therefore adequately fulfilled the role for which it had been originally intended years earlier. It was also supplied to Finland. In the United Kingdom, it was developed into the Gnat T.1 advanced trainer, in which guise it became famous as the mount of the Red Arrows aerobatic team.

Perhaps the real irony about the Gnat, however, was that its development potential was never fully appreciated at the right time, at least in its European context. India's Hindustan Aeronautics Ltd were not slow to realize it, though, and produced an updated version called the Ajeet ('Invincible'), with a redesigned wing, integral fuel tanks and four weapons pylons. The Ajeet entered service with the Indian Air Force in 1977 and served for over a decade, seventy-nine new aircraft being built and ten more converted from Gnats.

Chapter 18
Supersonic Bombers and Reconnaissance Aircraft

Two prototypes of the XB-70 supersonic bomber were built, one being lost as the result of a mid-air collision. (North American Rockwell)

The North American XB-70 Valkyrie

Late in 1954, General Curtis LeMay, at that time Commanding General of the US Strategic Air Command, made a formal request to the Department of Defense for an aircraft to succeed the Boeing B-52 Stratofortress, with a minimum unrefuelled range of 6,000nm (11,100km) and as high a speed as possible. As a result of this request two System Requirements were issued by the Air Research and Development Command: WS-110A, specifying a cruising speed of Mach 0.9 and a supersonic dash capability during a 1,000nm (1,850km) target penetration, and WS-125, a competitive requirement for a nuclear-powered bomber concept, which in the event was short-lived.

The contract for the development of the supersonic bomber, designated XB-70, was awarded to North American, but the entire programme was affected by escalating costs, the target date for the prototype first flight being continually put back. In March 1961, as part of his defence budget speech, President John F. Kennedy asked for a reduction in the XB-70 programme, citing several factors that included the high cost of developing the aircraft, its greater vulnerability compared with that of intercontinental ballistic missiles (ICBMs), and its late projected in-service date, which now coincided with that of operational ICBMs.

The B-70 strategic bomber project was subsequently discontinued, although two prototypes were built for research purposes, the first flying on

21 September 1964. The second XB-70A followed on 17 July 1965, and in January 1966 flew for more than half an hour at Mach 3.0. On 8 June that year, it was lost when an F-104 chase plane collided with it. The first XB-70A continued to serve as a high-speed aerodynamic research vehicle, yielding much information that would later be incorporated in the design of the Rockwell B-1 supersonic bomber. Both XB-70As were powered by six General Electric YJ39-GE-3 turbojets each rated at 31,000lb (137.9kN) s.t.

The Avro 730

Britain's supersonic bomber projects of the 1950s were born of a requirement for a long-range, high-speed reconnaissance aircraft. In 1954, the Ministry of Supply issued Specification R.156T, which was drawn up around Operational Requirement 330. This called for a very long range reconnaissance aircraft with a speed of at least Mach 2.5, an operational ceiling of 60,000ft (18,000m) and a minimum range of 5,000nm (9,300km). Crammed with the latest electronic surveillance equipment, the resulting aircraft would be capable of operating beyond the performance envelope of the latest Soviet fighters and surface-to-air missiles. Its design presented the British aircraft industry with a formidable and unprecedented challenge. (The Americans set about solving the high-level, long-range reconnaissance problem in a different way, and came up with the Lockheed U-2. The first prototype was airborne in August 1955 – at which time the British Ministry of Supply was still studying the first submissions to Specification R.156T.)

Three manufacturers – Vickers, Handley Page and Avro – submitted designs. Vickers opted for a single-seat aircraft, a canard delta with four Rolls-Royce RB.121 turbojets slung under the wing and two more in pods under the forward fuselage. Handley Page also went for the canard delta configuration in their proposal, the HP.100; the Handley Page aircraft, however, had a crew of three and twelve RB.121 engines, boxed in groups of six under the wing. The HP.100 design was subjected to extensive wind tunnel tests and a full-scale mock-up was built, but it and the Vickers project were both dropped in favour of the Avro submission.

This was the Avro 730, detailed drawings of which were submitted to the MoS in May 1955. A prototype contract was awarded a few weeks later. The Avro 730 was a canard design with unswept flying surfaces, employing stainless steel brazed-honeycomb sandwich construction. It was to be powered by four Armstrong Siddeley P.159 turbojets, mounted in pairs close to each wingtip. The principal reconnaissance system built into the design was a sideways-looking X-band radar known as *Red Drover*, with a 52ft (15.9m) antenna running along the fuselage side.

Longitudinal control was effected by an all-moving canard foreplane with trailing edge elevators, the aircraft having conventional ailerons and rudder. Flying control surfaces were actuated by a quadruple electro-hydraulic power unit designed by Boulton Paul and integrated with an electrical 'fly-by-wire' automatic control system designed by Louis Newmark Ltd. The Dowty Company was responsible for the undercarriage, which consisted of a single centre-fuselage main unit with four wheels, a twin-wheel nose unit and outriggers; Dowty also built the engine nacelles. For very high take-off weights, provision was made for four extra wheels on the main undercarriage axles.

The 730's pressure cabin was situated just aft of the canard foreplane and contained a pilot and two navigators, the latter seated side by side and facing aft. All three crew members had lightweight ejection seats. In the prototype aircraft, the pilot was to have been housed under a cockpit canopy slightly offset to starboard, but in the production version he would have been completely buried in the fuselage, seeing out by means of a retractable periscope. During its flight, the 730 was to have been under the control of fully automated systems, leaving the pilot free to perform certain functions that would normally have been the responsibility of a co-pilot.

Avro received an Instruction to Proceed in September 1955 and planned to fly the first of ten prototypes in 1959, followed by the first production aircraft in 1961. In the meantime, the original design had undergone a number of changes. The Air Staff now saw the Avro 730 as a potential successor to the Vulcan and Victor in the strategic bombing role, and OR.330 was amended to give the aircraft a bombing capability. Under a revised specification, RB.156D, a weapons bay was incorporated and provision made for the 730 to carry a stand-off bomb some 50ft (15m) long and containing a thermonuclear warhead. The wing planform

The Avro Ashton, seen here landing at Farnborough, served in an important role as a trials aircraft in the 1950s. (Author)

was also revised and the original P.159 engines were replaced by eight Armstrong Siddeley P.176 engines in rectangular nacelles.

Nothing was left to chance in the Avro 730 development programme. For example, the extreme temperatures that would be encountered by the aircraft in operational use were simulated in a heat-testing building that was capable of accommodating a full-size airframe, while a complete fuselage was to be tested to destruction. Two flying scale models were to be built, one going to Armstrong Whitworth for aerodynamic trials and the other to Bristol Siddeley for engine development. The pilot's periscope was complete and ready to be installed in an Avro Ashton trials aircraft.

Then came 1957, and the notorious White Paper on Defence which, at one stroke, cancelled almost every promising and futuristic British military aircraft project in favour of missiles. The Avro 730 was one of the victims, being cancelled in favour of further development of *Blue Streak*, Britain's intermediate-range ballistic missile (IRBM), itself destined to be short-lived in the military role, as related later in this chapter. The Avro 730, which might have become the first operational bomber in the world capable of Mach 2+, was broken up and its fuselage cut up to become huge metal waste bins in Avro's Chadderton factory.

There was, however, a postscript to the sad tale of Britain's supersonic bomber. On 14 April 1962, a research aircraft called the Bristol 188 took to the air for the first time, powered by two afterburning Gyron Junior turbojets. It had originally been one of the scaled-down Avro 730 research models, differing from the original configuration mainly in having the canard foreplane replaced by a more conventional T-tail. The Bristol 188, made of stainless steel, was to have been used for high-speed research during prolonged flights at more than Mach 2, but its fuel consumption was extremely high and made sustained hypersonic flight impossible.

The *Blue Streak*

Although the *Blue Streak* IRBM does not really fall within the scope of this book, it is worth examining it in some detail, as it formed the very basis of British strategic defence policy in the late 1950s.

The concept of a medium-range ballistic missile (MRBM) to supplement the manned bombers of the V-Force dated from August 1953, when the Air Staff launched a full evaluation of all possible solutions to bringing such a weapon to fruition. In April 1955, after lengthy preliminary studies, the de Havilland Propeller Co. was asked to take on the responsibility of co-ordinating the weapon system and design. The de Havilland Aircraft Company was to be responsible for the airframe, Rolls-Royce for the propulsion system, the Sperry Gyroscope Co. for inertial guidance and Marconi for ground radar and communications links. At the same time, the Saunders-Roe Company was asked to build an experimental re-entry vehicle, designed by the Royal Aircraft Establishment. The concept was formalized on 8 August 1955, when the Air Staff issued Operational Requirement OR.1139, calling for the development of a strategic missile with a 1-megaton warhead (OR.1142) and a range of 1,500–2,000nm (2,800–3,700km). The missile would be operated by Bomber Command and would be deployed to prepared sites in both the United Kingdom and the Middle East.

The missile that began to evolve, named *Blue Streak*, owed a great deal to the technology incorporated in America's first-generation ICBM, the Atlas. Development of the Atlas, the West's original ICBM, began in 1954, when the USAF realised that it had been mistaken in its earlier assessment of the ICBM's potential. The Convair Division of General Dynamics, which had already done a considerable amount of practical work with test vehicles – including one called MX-774, which tested such advanced features as a gimbal-mounted engine, separable nose cone and a structure of very thin stainless steel.

The pattern of the two development programmes, in fact, followed each other closely, except that the Atlas was several years more advanced. Each of the original Atlas strategic missile squadrons to be deployed, in 1958, had six missiles. The latter were sited entirely above ground in long shelters, which had sliding roofs to allow the missiles to be erected for fuelling and launch. The 549th Strategic Missile Squadron, which became operational in 1961, had semi-hardened installations recessed into the ground and was equipped with nine rounds. The RAF Air Staff was aware of American concern about the vulnerability of the Atlas's fixed, above-ground sites, and it was generally accepted that *Blue Streak* would be launched from underground sites.

By the end of 1957 the *Blue Streak* programme was progressing well, and it was estimated that the first test firing of a *Blue Streak* could probably take place from Woomera, Australia, early in 1962. The newly formed Ballistic Missile Division of the RAE exercised technical supervision, and numerous Air Ministry meetings were held to discuss matters concerning the weapon's operational deployment. The plan was for the operational missiles to be deployed in underground silos and raised to the surface immediately before firing. The operational missile sites would need to be at least 6 miles (10km) apart, and about seventy were required for the missile force to be fully effective.

While work proceeded on the *Blue Streak* missile itself, and planning for its deployment reached a fairly advanced stage, trials with its associated systems were also progressing. In May 1957 the warhead assembly (code-named *Orange Herald*) that was to be fitted to the missile was tested at Christmas Island during Britain's first thermonuclear weapons trials, dropped by a Vickers Valiant bomber of No. 49 Squadron (Bomber Command's atomic test unit) and in September 1958 the re-entry test vehicle, *Black Knight*, was launched successfully from Woomera.

However, there was now growing concern over the rising costs of the *Blue Streak* programme. In the summer of 1957, as an economy measure, the Air Staff relaxed the accuracy requirement for *Blue Streak*, permitting the cancellation of two associated contracts: the Marconi radar guidance system and the English Electric backup inertial guidance system. In August 1957, a revised development programme was submitted to the Defence Research Policy Committee, limiting research and development costs to around £80 million, about half what would realistically be needed to complete the R&D programme.

What it all added up to was that the *Blue Streak* programme was now seriously under-financed, with corners being cut everywhere as the purse strings were tightened. With the development programme now proceeding at a dangerously slow pace because of the financial restraints imposed upon it, it was unlikely that the test firing programme, which envisaged twenty-three shots by the end of 1963, would be completed. One area of concern was that more money needed to be spent on the engine test centre at Spadeadam, near Gilsland in Cumberland, where progress was painfully slow. Already, by mid-1958, there was a school of thought that considered the development of *Blue Streak* as an operational weapons system should be abandoned. Various options were considered, including collaboration with the Americans in the development of a strategic rocket using a solid propellant, which would drastically reduce the launch time; another option was to purchase Thor IRBMs (which were then on the point of being deployed in the UK under joint Anglo-American control) outright from the USA and arming them with British warheads. The problem with Thor, apart from its vulnerability and slow reaction time, was that its useful life would not extend beyond 1964, and so there would still be a 'missile gap' before a new Anglo-American weapon could be deployed.

As an interim measure, it would be necessary to proceed with the development of the advanced version of the RAF's air-launched stand-off missile, *Blue Steel* Mk 2, in order to prolong the effective life of the V-Force until 1969 or thereabouts. The British Minister of Defence, Duncan Sandys, a strong advocate of ballistic missiles, continued to argue in favour of *Blue Streak*; but he did not, as has sometimes been suggested, envisage the replacement of the manned bomber force by strategic missiles. Sandys wanted a diversified deterrent – manned aircraft and ballistic missiles – despite the fact that it would not be cheap if *Blue Streak* remained in the programme. Sandys took the operational credibility of the UK deterrent force very seriously, hence the expensive scheme for widespread bomber dispersal airfields, overseas as well as at home, and the adoption of the quick reaction procedures that Bomber Command perfected and demonstrated in training and exercises. He was determined that the deterrent should be seen to be effective as well as politically independent. However, Sandys did all he could to divert funds to the ailing *Blue Streak* programme, and one of the measures he took was to cancel further development of the Avro 730.

At a meeting of the Cabinet Defence Committee in September 1958, it was generally agreed that a land-based missile would be needed to maintain an independent British deterrent in succession to the V-Force's bombers, and that work on *Blue Streak* should continue with a view to its deployment in 1965. There were, however, reservations. The Treasury estimated that the development and deployment of *Blue Streak* might cost as much as £600 million, and that the cost might rise appreciably higher if underground launching sites were constructed. The other options – which by now included Polaris, the submarine-launched ballistic missile in whose development the UK was participating with the US Navy – still merited further investigation. In April 1959 the Air Council endorsed the principle of underground deployment for *Blue Streak*, but Treasury approval for this was not forthcoming.

There were other factors to be considered, too, such as the purely physical one of where the missiles were to be deployed in the UK. A wide dispersal policy was obviously necessary, but the UK enjoyed none of the USA's broad geographical advantages. A geological survey had already shown that much of the eastern half of England was geologically unsuitable, as the underground silos needed to be sited in rock masses 300–500ft (90–150m) thick (which is why the French, at a later date, sited their IRBMs in the Plateau d'Albion, Haute Provence), and there would probably be widespread public opposition to the construction of missile silos elsewhere.

The final battle lines around *Blue Streak* were drawn in July 1959, when a British Nuclear Deterrent Study Group began a thorough assessment of the deterrent's future. The Group's conclusions, in a report at the end of 1959, was that *Blue Streak* would not be vulnerable once it had been launched, but that it would be vulnerable to pre-emptive attack regardless of whether it was deployed above or below the surface. It would therefore be effective only as a first-strike weapon, say in response to a Soviet conventional attack, and in that case it would not strictly be necessary to deploy it underground. The report further recommended that if the UK deemed it acceptable to be totally dependent on the United States for a strategic missile force from about 1965, then an approach should be made to the US Government with a view to arming the V-bombers with the Douglas WS138A Skybolt air-launched IRBM, or to acquiring the Polaris SLBM, together with a number of strategic missile submarines.

Although some, with Duncan Sandys (now Minister of Aviation) at the forefront, continued to argue for the retention of *Blue Streak*, it was effectively doomed as an operational missile. From March 1960, when Prime Minister Harold Macmillan conferred with US President Dwight D. Eisenhower at Camp David, the UK Government set its feet firmly on the road that was to lead to Skybolt and ultimately, when Skybolt was cancelled, to Polaris. *Blue Streak* was cancelled in April 1960, having cost the British taxpayer £89 million in research and development. The rocket itself survived, as a first-stage booster in the European Space Programme, until it was eventually replaced by the French Ariane.

The Myasishchev M-50 and M-52

Rather ironically, it was Soviet Premier Nikita Khrushchev's preoccupation with guided missiles that initially killed off supersonic strategic bomber development in the Soviet Union, too. In 1956, the Myasishchev Design Bureau began working on the development of a supersonic strategic bomber, the M-50, which had a projected range of 10,000km (6,200 miles). It was intended to carry the M-61 stand-off missile, also developed by Myasishchev, which had a range of 1,000km (620 miles). The aircraft was to have been powered by four very advanced turbojets developed by Zubets, but these were subjected to delays during their development and so the first M-50 prototype was fitted with less powerful VD-7 turbojets, two of which were mounted under the delta wing and the other two at the wingtips. The long, slender fuselage provided accommodation for two or three crew members and a large weapons bay, and

Russia's M-52 'Bounder' supersonic bomber. (Philip Jarrett)

the fuselage incorporated the area-rule to reduce transonic drag.

The first M-50 prototype, with its substitute engine installation, served as a technology demonstrator, reaching a maximum speed of Mach 0.99. The second prototype, re-designated the M-52, was equipped with the more advanced engines, which doubled the maximum speed to Mach 1.83. Despite this progress, the programme failed to attract the attention of the Soviet leadership, who had become convinced that bombers had been made obsolete by the development of ballistic missiles. As a result, the M-50/M-52 project was cancelled and the Myasishchev Design Bureau closed in 1960. A surviving example of the impressive M-50 is now on display at the Monino Aviation Museum in Moscow. The M-52 was given the NATO reporting name 'Bounder'.

The Sukhoi T-4/Su-100

The appearance of the North American XB-70 Valkyrie in the 1960s re-awakened Soviet interest in the supersonic strategic bomber concept, and August 1972 saw the first flight of the Sukhoi T-4, also known as the Su-100, which was constructed largely of titanium and stainless steel. It featured a fly-by-wire control system with a backup mechanical system. Although it lacked the XB-70's ability to raise and lower its wingtips, the T-4 did have a lowerable nose section, similar to Concorde's, to provide better visibility from the flight deck during take-off and landing. With the nose raised, a periscope was used for forward vision. A static test aircraft (serial 100S) and a prototype, serial 101, were built. Two further prototypes, 102 and 103, were under construction but not completed. The test pilot for the first flight was Vladimir Ilyushin, son of aircraft designer S.V. Ilyushin.

The T-4 weighed about 102,000kg (225,000lb) and was powered by four Kolesov RD36-41 engines of 156.9kN (35,300lb) thrust with afterburners. It was designed to fly at Mach 3, but is believed to have reached Mach 1.3 or 1.4. Serial 101 only made ten flights, of less than eleven hours' total duration, before the programme was cancelled in 1974 or 1975 and the uncompleted prototypes were scrapped. It was considered an expensive under-performer, with continuing problems with its fly-by-wire system. The prototype, 101, is on show in Russia's Monino Air Force Museum. After the cancellation of the T-4, the Soviet Union devoted its funds to the development of the Tupolev Tu-160, its first operational supersonic strategic bomber, which first flew in December 1981.

Chapter 19
Vertical Take-Off

In 1951, when the US Navy issued a requirement for a small fighter aircraft capable of operating from platforms on merchant ships for convoy protection, Convair and Lockheed both launched into research programmes that were to produce some surprising results in the long run. Each company developed an aircraft with a broadly similar configuration, a 'tail-sitter' using a powerful turboprop engine with large contra-rotating propellers to eliminate torque. The idea was that the aircraft, using a simple two-axis auto-stabilizer, would be flown vertically off the ground and then bunted over into horizontal flight. During landing, it would hang on to its propellers, which would then perform the same function as a helicopter's rotor and lower it down to a landing on its tail castors.

The Lockheed XFV-1

The US Navy specification was finalized in 1950, and in March 1951 contracts were issued for the building of two prototypes, the Convair XFY-1 and the Lockheed XFV-1. The latter aircraft was the first to fly, beginning normal flight trials with the aid of a stalky fixed undercarriage in March 1954. For these tests the XFV-1 was fitted with an Allison T40-A-6 turboprop, although plans were in hand to re-engine it with the more powerful YT-40-A-14 when this power plant had completed its full series of trials.

For vertical take-off and landing the XFV-1 stood on small wheels attached to the tips of its cruciform tail unit, an arrangement that would

The Lockheed XFV-1 being raised into its launch position, with its pilot in the cockpit. (Philip Jarrett)

almost certainly have been unstable on a pitching deck. Projected armament for the XFV-1 was two 20mm cannon mounted in wingtip pods, or forty-eight 2.75in unguided folding-fin rockets The XFV-1 made a number of transitional flights before the test programme was concluded in 1955, but its full performance was never evaluated. Performance figures registered during trials, however, together with wind tunnel data, gave the type an estimated maximum speed of 580mph (933km/h) at 15,000ft (4,600m) and an initial climb rate of 10,820ft/min (3,300m/min).

The Convair XFY-1

The Convair XFY-1 was generally a better design. Its flying surfaces were of delta configuration, the wings having a leading edge sweep of 57 degrees, and the castor-type undercarriage was of much wider track than that of the XFV-1, enabling the aircraft to remain stable on its take-off platform at angles of up to 26 degrees from the vertical. It carried 50 US gallons (190ltr) more fuel than the XFV-1, and proposed armament was four 20mm cannon in wingtip pods or forty-six 2.75in rockets. Like the XFV-1, the XFY-1 was fitted with a gimbal-mounted ejection seat that rotated 45 degrees for vertical flight, then slipped into the conventional position for flying horizontally. The XFY-1 initially flew in a series of sixty-nine tethered test flights that began in April 1954, with cables attached to the nose and tail allowing the aircraft to rise and descend but limiting lateral movement. The first free flight took place at Brown Field, south of San Diego, in November; the XFY-1 rose slowly to 200ft (60m), gradually nosed over into a horizontal position, and flew in level flight for twenty minutes, after which test pilot J.F. 'Skeets' Coleman brought it down for a perfect vertical landing. It was the first successful VTOL fighter flight in history, and it brought Coleman the award of the Harman Trophy, awarded for outstanding personal achievement in aviation.

The XFY-1 underwent a much fuller test programme than the XFV-1, achieving a performance that included a maximum speed of 610mph (980km/h) at 15,000ft (4,600m) and 592mph (953km/h) at 35,000ft (11,000m). Climb to 20,000ft (6,000m) and 30,000ft (9,000m) was 2.7 and 4.6 minutes, respectively, somewhat better

The Convair XFY-1 being readied for take-off during its early flight trials. (Convair)

than the estimated figure for the XFY-1, and operational ceiling was 43,700ft (13,300m). In 1956, however, the US Navy withdrew its requirement and abandoned the VTOL programme; reasons given were technical ones, such as instability during the technical phase, but the real reason was that a powerful lobby of senior officers in the US Navy saw the development of the VTOL concept as a threat to the introduction of newer and larger aircraft carriers. It was to be many years before the VTOL concept returned to the US Navy as an operational reality.

The Ryan X-13 Vertijet pictured during hovering trials. (Philip Jarrett)

The Ryan X-13 Vertijet

In 1947, the Ryan Aeronautical Company of San Diego carried out a series of vertical take-off experiments with an Allison J33 turbojet suspended in a vertical test rig. A rudimentary cockpit, reaction controls and two-axis auto-stabilizer were fitted later, and in its new configuration the machine made a series of tethered flights. In 1953, as a result of these early experiments, Ryan received a USAF contract to build a prototype VTOL jet aircraft, the X-13 Vertijet. This was intended to be launched from its own self-contained servicing trailer, which incorporated an hydraulically operated inclining launch ramp. The X-13 prototype first flew on 10 December 1955, fitted with a temporary undercarriage for normal take-off and landing trials, and its first vertical take-off was made on 28 May 1956. A second aircraft was built, and this went on to make the full sequence of vertical take-off, transition to horizontal flight and transition back to the vertical for a landing on 11 April 1957. Both aircraft were powered by a Rolls-Royce Avon turbojet, and although they carried enough fuel for only about 12 minutes' flying, they had proved that vertical take-off was a feasible enterprise, provided the engine thrust exceeded the weight of the aircraft by a substantial margin.

Experiments in Europe

Meanwhile, vertical take-off experiments were also progressing in other countries, and they were proving far from trouble-free. In Britain, Rolls-Royce started tethered flights of a 'Thrust Measuring Rig' (known more popularly as the 'Flying Bedstead') which had two Rolls-Royce Nene turbojets installed horizontally at opposite ends of the assembly, their tailpipes directed vertically downwards near the mass centre.

In France, SNECMA mounted an Atar turbojet in a special test rig fitted with a four-wheeled undercarriage. After unmanned trials, a piloted version, the Atar Volant, made its first tethered hovering flight on 8 April 1957, followed by a free flight on 14 May. The next step was to enclose the Atar in a fuselage, surrounded by an annular wing to allow the aircraft to change from vertical to horizontal flight: the machine, known as the C-450 Coleoptère, flew for the first time on 17 April 1959, but on 25 July it went out of control as the pilot was trying to stabilize it for a vertical descent. The pilot ejected at 150ft and was badly injured; the Coleoptère crashed and was totally destroyed.

In 1958, the Russians also flew an experimental bedstead-type rig known as the Turbolet, which featured a single vertically mounted turbojet surrounded by a spidery structure and equipped with a fully-enclosed cockpit.

Such was the state of the art in 1958. Four countries were involved in VTOL development; one of them – the United States – had already carried out trials with 'tail-sitter' aircraft, and another – Great Britain – was about to start flight testing of a VTOL research aircraft mounted on a conventional tricycle undercarriage. Its name was the Short SC.1.

The Short SC.1

In 1953, when the Rolls-Royce Thrust Measuring Rig was beginning its vertical flight trials, the Ministry of Supply issued Specification ER.143 for

One of the Short SC.1 prototypes. (Philip Jarrett)

a research aircraft that could take off vertically by jet-lift and then accelerate forward into normal cruising flight. Short Brothers' preliminary design, the PD.11 – a small tailless delta aircraft with five RB.108 engines, four for lift and one for forward propulsion – was judged to be the most promising, and in August 1954 Shorts received a contract to build two prototypes, XG900 and XG905, under the designation SC.1.

The first of these, XG900, was shipped to Boscombe Down in March 1957, and on 2 April test pilot Tom Brooke-Smith took it on its maiden flight, which involved a conventional take-off and landing. XG900 was not fitted with lift engines at this stage, and it was the second Short SC.1, XG905, that began hover trials on 23 May 1958. There followed five months of tethered trials over a raised platform with open-grid decking, and the initial free hovers were also made over this platform, but in November 1958 Brooke-Smith landed away from the platform on a football pitch, which was undamaged apart from a slight scorching of the grass. In September 1959 XG905 made its first public appearance at Farnborough, where it was intended to demonstrate vertical and horizontal flight; however, the demonstration was cut short in rather embarrassing circumstances when the debris guard over the lift engines' air intake became clogged with newly mown grass, causing a sudden power loss that compelled Brooke-Smith to make a rapid descent.

On 6 April 1960, Tom Brooke-Smith achieved the first complete transition from level flight to vertical descent and vertical climb following a conventional take-off from Bedford in XG905. That summer, XG900 rejoined the test programme, complete with its five RB.108 lift engines, and the two aircraft were used to develop rolling take-off techniques from unprepared surfaces, the object being to avoid erosion and also to increase the take-off weight when a short, but not vertical, take-off was possible.

In April 1961 XG900 was handed over to the RAE at Bedford, while XG905 went back to Belfast to be fitted with a new auto-stabilization system designed to compensate for gusts. More than eighty flights were made with the new system, starting in June 1963, the development pilot being J.R. Green, who had joined Shorts from the RAE. On 2 October, Green was returning for a landing when the gyros failed, producing false references that caused the auto-stabilizer to fly the aircraft into the ground. The failure occurred at less than 30ft (9m), giving Green no time to revert to manual control. XH905 went into the ground upside down, and Green was killed. The aircraft itself was repaired and flew again in 1966, carrying out trials with the Blind Landing Experimental Unit.

At no time was the SC.1 intended to lead to the development of a combat aircraft; indeed, when the SC.1 began its trials in 1958 the Air Ministry was showing little or no interest in the concept. The general feeling in the United Kingdom (and, for that matter, elsewhere) was that the use of four or five engines solely to provide lift would result in a prohibitive weight penalty, effectively cancelling out the combat potential of VTOL.

The Hawker P.1127

It was a French engineer, Michel Wibault – whose company had built a range of commercial aircraft during the 1930s – who came up with a possible solution. Wibault's idea envisaged a turbojet using vectored thrust, whereby rotating nozzles could be used to direct exhaust gases either vertically downwards or horizontally aft. Seeking funds to develop his theme, he approached the Paris office of the Mutual Weapons Development Team, which at that time was headed by Colonel Bill Chapman. This was in 1956, at the time when Bristol Siddeley was working on the Orpheus engine to power NATO's lightweight fighter, so Chapman approached Dr Stanley Hooker, Bristol's Technical Director, and sought his views on the Wibault project. Hooker was enthusiastic, and one of his project engineers, Gordon Lewis, was briefed to investigate the possibilities. After preliminary studies, Wibault and Lewis applied for a joint patent covering the design of a vectored-thrust engine known as the BE.52 in January 1957; this was further developed into the BE.53 Pegasus I, which was based on the Orpheus.

In the summer of 1957, details of the proposed engine were passed to Sir Sydney Camm at Hawker Aircraft, who made a preliminary design for an aircraft to go around it. The design was allocated the project number P.1127. It bore no resemblance, at this stage, to the amazing combat aircraft that was ultimately to be developed from it – the Harrier – but it was a firm beginning.

In June 1958, the Mutual Weapons Development Team agreed to pay 75 per cent of the development costs of the Pegasus engine. Funding the airframe, however, proved a tougher obstacle, for research funds had been eaten up by other projects. Hawker had no alternative but to proceed as a private venture while the Air Staff set about drafting an operational requirement to cover the concept. This emerged in April 1959 as GOR.345, and Specification ER.204D was issued to cover the P.1127, but it was not until October 1959 that Hawker received a preliminary contract for the building of two prototypes. It was fortunate that Hawker recognized potential when they saw it, or there might never have been a Harrier.

In Hawker's opinion, the P.1127 was the ideal design to meet a new NATO requirement, NBMR-3 (NATO Basic Military Requirement No. 3), which was issued in 1961 after several revisions and called for a VTOL strike fighter with a sustained speed capability of Mach 0.92 at low level and supersonic speed at altitude. The P.1127 was not supersonic, but it had a vast amount of development potential ahead of it, and so Sir Sydney Camm proposed a modified version, the P.1150, which was to have a thin wing and an advanced Pegasus engine. Hawker could have progressed with the building of a prototype almost immediately, but yet another revision to NBMR-3, requiring greater range and load-carrying capacity, meant that the P.1150 would have been too small. Camm and his team therefore set about designing a scaled-up version, the P.1154, which was to have a BS.100 engine of 33,000lb (146.8kN) thrust; this project is discussed in detail later in this chapter.

The Dassault Mirage III-V

However, the P.1154 had a formidable challenger, at least in theory, in the shape of the Dassault Mirage III-V, whose forerunner, the Balzac VTOL research aircraft, was then under construction. The Balzac used the wings and tail surfaces of the Mirage III-01, married to a fuselage that was completely redesigned except for the main frames and the cockpit section. French research into VTOL, in fact, pre-dated both the Hawker P.1127 and NBMR-3, having been initiated in response to a French Air Force requirement, but the French chose to pursue their experiments with a combination of lift jets and propulsion engine, rather than vectored thrust. Even then, the engines they chose to power the Balzac were British, consisting of eight lightweight Rolls-Royce RB.108 lift engines and a Bristol Siddeley Orpheus B.Or.3 turbojet for forward propulsion. Ironically, the use of British engines of proven design led to a strong lobby in both the Ministry of Aviation and the RAF that favoured concentrating on the development of the Balzac/Mirage III-V as the standard NATO strike fighter at the expense of the P.1154.

The Balzac made its first tethered flight on 12 October 1962 in the rig once used by the ill-fated Coleoptère at Melun-Villaroche, and initial tests were made with a non-retractable landing gear. The aircraft made its first free vertical take-off on 18 October 1962 and the first transition to horizontal flight on 18 March 1963. The test programme continued until 27 January 1964, when the aircraft suffered a critical divergent lateral oscillation during hovering descent and dropped out of the sky like a falling leaf, crashing and killing its pilot. It was rebuilt, but crashed again on 8 September 1965, killing another pilot, and this time it was damaged beyond repair.

The Dassault Balzac used the wings and tail surfaces of the Mirage III-01, seen here during flight trials from unprepared surfaces. (Dassault)

The Mirage III-V supersonic VTOL fighter prototype flew in February 1965. A second prototype, which flew at over Mach 2, was destroyed in an accident. (Dassault)

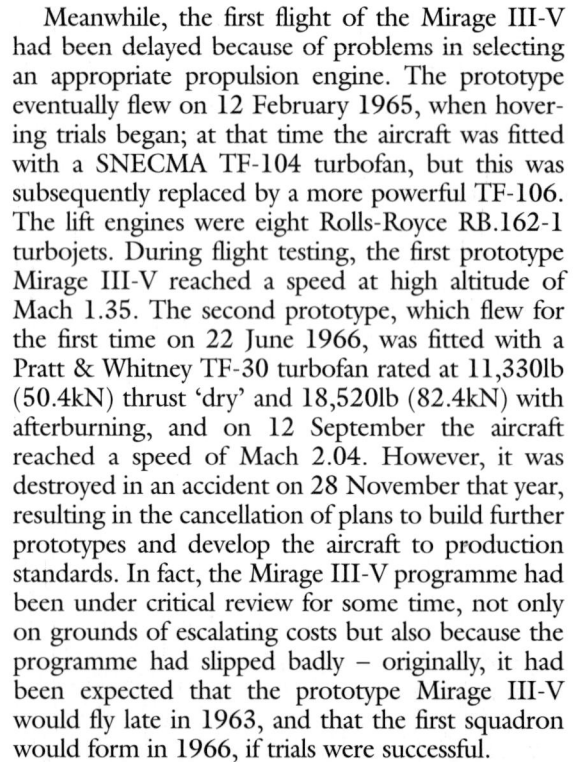

Two views of the VJ-101C during trials. (Philip Jarrett)

Meanwhile, the first flight of the Mirage III-V had been delayed because of problems in selecting an appropriate propulsion engine. The prototype eventually flew on 12 February 1965, when hovering trials began; at that time the aircraft was fitted with a SNECMA TF-104 turbofan, but this was subsequently replaced by a more powerful TF-106. The lift engines were eight Rolls-Royce RB.162-1 turbojets. During flight testing, the first prototype Mirage III-V reached a speed at high altitude of Mach 1.35. The second prototype, which flew for the first time on 22 June 1966, was fitted with a Pratt & Whitney TF-30 turbofan rated at 11,330lb (50.4kN) thrust 'dry' and 18,520lb (82.4kN) with afterburning, and on 12 September the aircraft reached a speed of Mach 2.04. However, it was destroyed in an accident on 28 November that year, resulting in the cancellation of plans to build further prototypes and develop the aircraft to production standards. In fact, the Mirage III-V programme had been under critical review for some time, not only on grounds of escalating costs but also because the programme had slipped badly – originally, it had been expected that the prototype Mirage III-V would fly late in 1963, and that the first squadron would form in 1966, if trials were successful.

Ironically, another Dassault design, the Mirage F, which had been built solely to test the Mirage III-V's armament system and the TF-306 engine that was to have powered the operational version of the VTOL fighter, was found to have enormous potential in its own right as an operational strike fighter. It eventually entered service as the Mirage F-1, and did everything the Mirage III-V was expected to do except take off vertically.

The VJ-101C

In West Germany, the design teams of Bölkow, Heinkel and Messerschmitt had joined forces in 1959 at the suggestion of the German Defence Ministry to develop a Mach 2 VTOL interceptor. The design they adopted involved an aircraft of conventional configuration, but with turbojet engines mounted in swivelling wingtip pods to provide both lift and control in vertical and low-speed flight, together with fuselage-mounted lift engines. A bedstead-type test rig was built and made 126 flights by April 1965, fitted with a single RB.108 lift engine. The consortium, known as the Entwicklungsring Süd Arbeitsgemeinschaft, produced two prototypes of an experimental single-seat VTOL aircraft, the VJ-101C, which were fitted with six RB.145 engines developed jointly by Rolls-Royce and MAN Turbomotoren. Tethered trials of the VJ-101CV-1 began in December 1962, the first free hover being made on 10 April 1963. The aircraft made its first horizontal take-off on 31 August 1963, and its first transition on 20 September that year. During further trials the following spring the VJ-101CX-1 exceeded Mach 1 in level flight on several occasions, proving the viability of the concept; unfortunately, the aircraft crashed after a normal horizontal take-off on 14 September 1964, the pilot escaping thanks to his Martin Baker Mk GA7 'zero-zero' ejection seat.

Hovering trials of the second prototype, the VJ-101CX-2, began in the spring of 1965, and it made its first free flight on 12 June that year. By this time Heinkel had dropped out of the consortium, and the resources of Bölkow and Messerschmitt were being channelled into other programmes, so plans to produce an operational version of the VTOL research aircraft, the VJ-101D, were never implemented.

The VAK 191B

Nevertheless, the two VJ-101Cs had provided a wealth of knowledge about VTOL techniques, and it formed a sound basis for other German companies involved in the field. Foremost among them was the former Focke-Wulf company, which had produced a design study to meet a German Defence Ministry Requirement – VAK 191B – for a subsonic VTOL tactical fighter to replace the Fiat G.91. The initial design study was designated FW 1262, and in 1964 VFW and Fiat agreed to collaborate in development work under a Memorandum of Agreement signed by the German and Italian Defence Ministers. The Italians later dropped out of the programme, but VFW found another partner in Fokker of Holland, and Fiat agreed to carry on as sub-contractor.

Work proceeded with West German Government funding, and the first VAK 191B was rolled out in April 1970. It made its first conventional flight on 10 September 1971, and this was followed by a period of tethered hovering trials. By this time the other two prototypes had also joined the test programme, and on 26 October 1972 one of these made the type's first vertical-to-horizontal transition. During this test the aircraft reached a speed of 444km/h (276mph), and its RB.126 lift jets were shut down and restarted in flight for the first time. At the end of 1972, however, German Government funding of the VAK 191B was terminated, and no further development was undertaken. By this time, RAF Harriers were being deployed to Germany, and their presence more than adequately filled the V/STOL requirement in NATO's front line. Hawker's earlier faith had paid dividends, and the Harrier remained Western Europe's only operational V/STOL combat aircraft.

The Hawker Siddeley P.1154

The story might have been very different, had Hawker Siddeley been allowed to proceed with the development of the Harrier's supersonic derivative, the P.1154, but the P.1154's fortunes had been clouded right from the start. Even though the design was declared the outright winner in the NBMR-3 design contest, thanks in the main to the experience already gained by Hawker Siddeley with the P.1127, its rival, the Mirage III-V, was more of an international project and therefore politically favoured. The crunch came when France declared her intention to pursue a unilateral development course with the Mirage III-V, notwithstanding the greater technical merit of the P.1154. The result was that NATO, faced with little prospect of a truly collaborative VTOL fighter project becoming a reality, withdrew the NBMR-3 requirement altogether.

It was not all the fault of the French. The British Air Staff had shown little interest in the progress of the NBMR-3 contest or the possible development of the P.1154 to fit the European requirement, being preoccupied with Britain's own defence needs. Nevertheless, the P.1154 was a very viable project, and in August 1962 Hawker, at the instigation of the Air and Naval Staffs, submitted draft proposals for a P.1154 variant that would meet the requirements of both services. It was an enormously difficult task, for the requirements differed greatly. They differed, in fact, on fourteen major points, starting with the Royal Navy's insistence on a two-seater as opposed to the RAF's single-seat aircraft.

Nevertheless, Hawker Siddeley worked hard to produce a firm plan. The company had decided to adopt Bristol Siddeley's BS.100/8 engine, provided that a development contract was forthcoming in mid-1963, and was anticipating the first prototype to fly in the summer of 1965, followed by initial service deliveries in 1968. Early in 1963, however, an unexpected complication arose when Rolls-Royce came forward and offered two Spey engines as an alternative to one BS.100. The Naval Staff, who preferred a twin-engined configuration anyway, thought the Rolls-Royce proposal a sound one, especially as the Spey was already available in its civil form and could be ready in a vectored-thrust version far sooner than the BS.100. In the event it was decided to proceed with the latter engine, but the Rolls-Royce representation, sound though it might have been, had served to reinforce growing doubts about the P.1154 programme.

Despite these complications, authorization was given for a development programme costing some £750m. It involved several development aircraft, followed by 700 production machines for the RAF and Fleet Air Arm, and in 1964 Hawker Siddeley embarked on the construction of the first single-seat and two-seat prototypes. There was little likelihood now that the first operational examples would be in service before 1969, and so the Admiralty decided to withdraw from the P.1154 programme altogether and seek the purchase of F-4 Phantoms (fitted with Rolls-Royce Spey engines) from the United States instead.

Hawker Siddeley persevered with the development of the P.1154 for the RAF, and with the design of a V/STOL transport, the HS.681, but in November 1964 the Air Staff was informed by representatives of the newly elected Labour government that there were insufficient funds to support the development of the P.1154, HS.681 and TSR2. Two of the projects would have to go, and so the RAF opted to save TSR2, the aircraft in the most advanced stage of development and on which so many hopes were pinned. Those hopes were forlorn, for TSR2 fell under the axe a few months later.

In retrospect, and with regard to the enormous development potential of the P.1127, the P.1154 was a costly red herring in the mainstream of British VTOL combat aircraft development. It would have proved a complex aircraft, and development problems that were not envisaged at the time might have set back the programme by years.

The Yakovlev Yak-36

Meanwhile, Soviet experiments with VTOL had resulted in an experimental prototype, the Yakovlev Yak-36, dubbed 'Freehand' by NATO. The Yak-36 was powered by two non-afterburning Soyuz Tumanskiy/Khatchaturov R-27-300 turbojet engines of 48.9kN (11,000lb) thrust each, mounted forward of and below the cockpit. They were fitted with louvered nozzles that could be vectored through about 9 degrees and exhausted at the centre of gravity. Air bled from the engines was used for reaction control nozzles at each wingtip fairing, on the tail cone, and at the tip of a 3m (10ft) nose probe. The Yak-36 made its first untethered hover on 9 January 1963. From there, the flight envelope was slowly expanded, with a double transition from vertical take-off to forward flight and back to vertical landing performed on 16 September 1963. The Yak-36 was in effect a technology demonstrator, and led to the development of the Yak-38 (NATO reporting name 'Forger'), an operational strike aircraft that served on the Soviet Navy's *Kiev*-class aircraft carriers.

The Yakovlev Yak-41/Yak-141

The USSR's last venture into the V/STOL field was ambitious, involving the supersonic Yakovlev Yak-41 (NATO reporting name 'Freestyle'). The Yak-41 programme was initiated in 1975, about the same time that the Yak-38 was first being operationally deployed. The supersonic Yak-41 was optimized for air defence with an attack capability as a secondary role. The first conventional flight was made on 9 March 1987 and the first hover on 29 December 1989.

The first official details were not released by the Soviet Union until the 1991 Paris Air Show, by which time the two flying prototypes, now re-designated Yak-141, had accumulated about 210 hours' flying time. A dozen FAI-recognized Class H.III records for V/STOL were set in April 1991, consisting of altitudes and times to altitudes with loads. In flight testing, the Freestyle achieved a maximum speed of Mach 1.7.

Flight testing was originally intended to continue until 1995, but development was stopped in August 1991 due to the shrinking Soviet military budget. Yakovlev funded development from its own resources for a while, in the hopes of attracting a foreign investor. The second flight prototype was destroyed after a hard landing on the aircraft carrier *Admiral Gorshkov* on 5 October 1991. The following year, the surviving prototype was demonstrated at the Farnborough Air Show, but the design bureau was still unable to find a market for the design. The Yak-141 was claimed to be as manoeuvrable as the MiG-29, which is doubtful.

Appendix
Miscellaneous Other Prototypes

The Breguet Br.941. (Breguet)

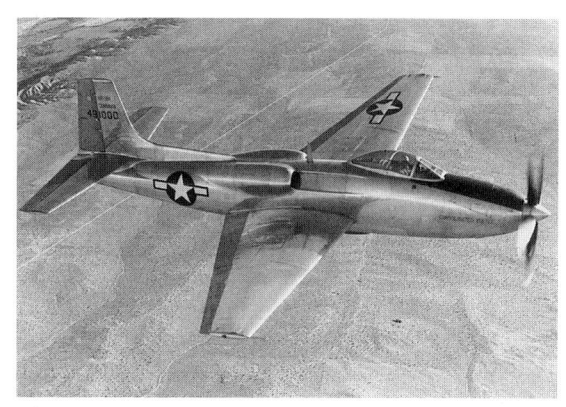

The Convair XP-81. (Convair)

Bell D-188A

The D-188A was a projected Mach 2 V/STOL strike fighter for the US Navy. A mock-up was built in 1959.

Bell X-14

The X-14 was a research aircraft, built in 1956 to investigate jet deflection systems. First transition from the hover to forward flight was made on 24 May 1958.

Breguet Br. 940 Integral

First flown in 1958, France's Breguet 940 was an experimental four-engined STOL aircraft using a combination of large, slow-running propellers and large-area flaps.

Breguet Br.941

First flown on 1 June 1961, the Breguet 941 was a prototype four-engined STOL transport aircraft using a deflected-slipstream technique tested and developed in the Br.940.

Convair XP-81

Flown for the first time on 2 February 1945, the Convair XP-81 prototype long-range escort fighter was the first combat aircraft designed to use a combination of turboprop and turbojet, power being supplied by a GE XT31-GE-3 turboprop and a GE J33-GE-5 turbojet, the latter installed in the rear fuselage and fed via intakes aft of the cockpit. A second prototype was built, but the type as not adopted and an order for thirteen pre-production aircraft was cancelled.

Dassault Mirage G8

In October 1965, Avions Marcel Dassault received a contract to build a variable-geometry fighter known as the Mirage G. This was flown on 18 November 1967, but was destroyed after completing about 400 flying hours. Two prototypes of a smaller, twin-engined VG aircraft, the Mirage G8, were subsequently ordered by the French Government. The first flew on 8 May 1971 and reached Mach 2.03 four days later, powered by two SNECMA Atar 09K-50 engines. The type was not adopted.

The two prototype Dassault Mirage G8s. (Dassault)

Dassault Mirage 4000

First flown in 1979, the Dassault Mirage 4000 was a scaled-up version of the Mirage 2000, and was originally known as the Delta Super Mirage. The project was abandoned. The sole aircraft is in the Paris Air and Space Museum.

Fairey Spearfish

Intended as a Barracuda replacement, the prototype Fairey Spearfish torpedo bomber flew in July 1945 and three more prototypes were built, but an order for forty production aircraft was cancelled.

Federal Aircraft Factory N.20 Arbalete

The Federal Aircraft Factory N.20 Arbalete ('Crossbow'), which flew in November 1951 under the power of four small Turboméca jet engines, was the scale flying model for a futuristic Swiss jet fighter that was never produced.

FFA P-16

The FFA P-16 was designed to meet the needs of the post-war Swiss forces. FFA's Altenrhein-based design team set out to design a transonic replacement for the obsolete, piston-engined D-3802 and C-3604 aircraft then serving in the close-support role. The aircraft was to be a single-seater, able to fly in and out of short strips in narrow, high, mountain valleys; STOL performance, responsiveness at high speeds and low altitudes, high installed power, and first-rate low-speed handling were thus essential. Two prototypes were ordered in 1952, the first flying in April 1955. A third prototype and four pre-series aircraft were ordered later, but the project was cancelled after two of the prototypes were lost in crashes.

Fiat G.82

Developed from the Fiat G.80 and powered by a Rolls-Royce Nene engine, the Fiat G.82 first flew in 1954. It failed to secure a NATO jet trainer order and only five were built.

Fletcher FD-25 Defender

Developed by the US Fletcher Aviation Company and flown in 1953, the FD-25 Defender was a light piston-engined counter-insurgency aircraft. It was not a success, but was developed into the FU-24 agricultural aircraft.

FMA IAe 27 Pulqui

The IAe 27 Pulqui ('Arrow'), which flew in 1947, was Argentina's first jet aircraft, and was the product of a team led by the French designer Emile Dewoitine. A more advanced aircraft, the Pulqui II designed by Kurt Tank, flew in 1950.

FMA IAe 30 Namcu

The IAe 30 Namcu twin-engined fighter first flew in July 1948. It was heavily armed with six 20mm cannon. Only one prototype was built.

FMA IAe 38

Designed in Argentina by Reimar Horten, the IAe 38 was a tailless transport aircraft based on the wartime Ho VIII. It flew in March 1961, but did not enter production.

Handley Page HP.88

First flown in 1951, the Handley Page HP.88 was built to test the crescent-wing configuration that was to be used in the design of the Victor jet bomber.

Hispano HA-300

Originally designed in Spain in the late 1950s by a Spanish-German team led by Professor Willi Messerschmitt, the HA-300 delta-wing fighter project was transferred to the Helwan Aircraft factory in Egypt in 1961. Four prototypes were competed, the first flying at Helwan on 7 March 1964, powered by a Bristol Siddeley Orpheus 703 turbojet. A second prototype, which joined the test programme on 22 July 1965, had the same power plant as the first prototype, but had supersonic intakes and a power control for the rudder. With the Orpheus 703-S-10 turbojet, the HA-300 attained Mach 1.13. The third prototype began taxi trials in November 1969, but the programme was cancelled before this aircraft flew.

Hughes XR-11

Designed specifically for long-range photographic reconnaissance, the Hughes XR-11 (formerly XF-11) twin-engined, twin-boom monoplane flew for the first time on 7 July 1946, but lost a propeller and the flight ended in a crash that nearly cost pilot Howard Hughes his life. A second aircraft flew on 5 April 1947 and subsequently went to Eglin Field, Florida, to be tested, but the US Air Force cancelled the programme in favour of using the much more economical Boeing RB-50 to meet the long-range photo-reconnaissance requirement.

Hunting H.126

First flown in 1963, the Hunting H.126 was a research aircraft, built to test the high-lift qualities of blown flaps. Sixty per cent of the jet exhaust was ducted on to the wing trailing edge.

The Handley Page HP.88.

The Lockheed XV-4A Hummingbird. (Lockheed)

Ikarus Type 451

The Yugoslavian Ikarus Type 451, which flew in 1951, was a twin-engined, prone pilot research monoplane based on the B.5 Pionir, a pre-WWII design.

Ikarus Type 452-M

Powered by two Turboméca Palas turbojets, the Ikarus Type 452-M was a single-seat swept-wing aircraft with twin tail booms supporting a swept tailplane. It flew in 1953.

Lavochkin La-190

The Lavochkin La-190 jet fighter prototype, which flew in 1951, was the first aircraft in the world to feature a zero-track undercarriage, the twin-wheel main unit being positioned directly under the centre fuselage.

Lockheed Constitution

A large four-engined transport, the Lockheed Constitution flew in November 1946. The two prototypes built were allocated to the US Navy as the XR6V-1.

Lockheed XV-4A Hummingbird

The Lockheed XV-4A Hummingbird, first flown in July 1962, was an experimental VTOL aircraft, designed to investigate thrust augmentation systems. Two prototypes were built, one of which crashed.

Lockheed A-12

The Lockheed A-12 was the forerunner of the SR-71, which was actually designated RS-71 (RS for 'Reconnaissance System') to begin with. It was erroneously referred to as the SR-71 by President Lyndon B. Johnson when the secret programme was first unveiled, and officialdom decided that it was easier to re-name the aircraft than inform Johnson that he had made a mistake!

Work on the SR-71 began in 1959, when a team led by Clarence L. Johnson, Lockheed's Vice-President for Advanced Development Projects, embarked on the design of a radical new aircraft to supersede the Lockheed U-2 in the strategic reconnaissance role. Designated A-12, the new machine took shape in conditions of the utmost secrecy in the highly restricted section of the Lockheed Burbank plant, the so-called 'Skunk Works', and seven aircraft had been produced by the summer of 1964, when the project's existence was revealed. By

APPENDIX

The LTV XC-142A. (LTV)

that time, the A-12 had already been extensively tested at Edwards AFB, reaching speeds of over 2,000mph (3,200km/h) at heights of over 70,000ft (21,000m). Early flight tests were aimed at assessing the A-12's suitability as a long-range interceptor, and the experimental interceptor version was shown to the public at Edwards AFB in September 1964, bearing the designation YF-12A.

Two YF-12As were built, but the interceptor project was abandoned. However, work on the strategic reconnaissance variant went ahead and the prototype SR-71A flew for the first time on 22 December 1964.

LTV XC-142A

Designed as a V/STOL military transport for all three US services, the tilt-wing XC-142A was developed jointly by Ling-Temco-Vought, Hiller and Ryan. Five prototypes were built, the first flying on 29 September 1964. During the test programme, the XC-142As carried out successful carrier trials, flew at speeds of between 35–400mph (56–643km/h) and reached heights of up to 25,000ft (7,600m). Despite the XC-142A's promise and versatility, the project was abandoned for economic reasons. The type was powered by four GE T64-GE-1 turboprops.

Martin X-24A

The X-24 series of lifting bodies was designed to investigate flight characteristics in the atmosphere from high-altitude supersonic speeds to landing, and to prove the feasibility of using lifting bodies for return from space. The X-24A made its first powered flight on 19 March 1970.

MiG-MFI

The MiG-MFI multi-role fighter, also known as Project 1.44, was designed as a counter to the Lockheed Martin F-22 Raptor, and a prototype flew in January 2000. There are no production plans.

Morane-Saulnier MS.1500 Epervier

The Morane-Saulnier MS.1500 Epervier ('Sparrowhawk') was a single-turboprop light attack aircraft, first flown in 1958. It was unsuccessful in attracting customers, the two prototypes being used as test beds.

The North American F-107A. (North American Rockwell)

Myasishchev M-55

Code-named 'Mystic' by NATO, this twin-boom straight-wing jet, currently publicized as a high-altitude research aircraft able to carry around 1,500kg (3,300lb) of sensors, is now known to exist in two versions. The first of two prototype aircraft, designated M-17 Stratosfera ('Mystic-A'), first flew in 1988 and was powered by a single Rybinsk RD-36-51V turbojet developed from the Tu-144 SST power plant. The M-55 Geofizika ('Mystic-B'), has two Perm/Soloviev (Aviadvigatel) PS-30-V12 turbojets mounted side-by-side behind a raised cockpit installed in a longer nose, together with a reduced-span wing. The role of the 'Mystic-B' is described as environmental sampling missions or high-altitude research. Production terminated in 1994 after a small number of M-55s had been built.

North American F-107A

The North American F-107 was intended as a tactical fighter-bomber replacement for the F-100. Three prototypes only were built, the first flying in 1956.

Northrop YC-125 Raider

The Northrop YC-125 Raider three-engined transport, first flown in 1949, was intended for

The Northrop YC-125 Raider. (Northrop)

operation from rough airstrips in forward areas. It was abandoned in favour of transport helicopters.

Northrop N-102 Fang

The N-102 Fang was Northrop's submission in an advanced fighter competition of the early 1950s. The competition was won by the F-104 Starfighter.

Northrop M2 F2/3

Another of Northrop's experimental lifting bodies, the M2 F2 made a series of gliding flights in 1966 before flying under rocket power. Damaged in a landing accident, it was rebuilt as the M2 F3.

Northrop YF-17 Cobra

The Northrop YF-17 Cobra was a contender in the 1972 contest to provide a new agile air-superiority day fighter for the USAF. The F-16 was selected in preference after a fly-off, but the YF-17 later formed the basis for the F-18 Hornet selected by the US Navy.

Northrop F-20 Tigershark

Originally known as the F-5G, the F-20 Tigershark was a single-engined development of the F-5, with 80 per cent more engine power, modern avionics and an enlarged wing. It was a capable aircraft but found no customer, because the USAF opted for the F-16. It was also offered to the USN in the 'aggressor' role, but was again rejected in favour of the F-16. Without a home market there was little hope for export orders. Only three examples were built.

Northrop/McDonnell Douglas YF-23A

The Northrop/McDonnell Douglas YF-23A was a contender in the bid for an advanced tactical fighter to replace the F-15. The first of two prototypes flew in August 1990, the second aircraft being powered by General Electric YF120-GE-100 turbofan engines. The YF-23A was designed to be ultra-stealthy and incorporated many of the stealth features of the B-2 bomber; all its planned weaponry was to be housed in an internal bay to reduce the radar signature. The two YF-23s successfully completed their flight test programme, but the Lockheed YF-22 was selected to meet the USAF requirement instead.

Piaggio P.150

The Piaggio P.150, flown in 1952, was an all-metal low-wing radial-engined monoplane designed as a replacement for the T-6 Texan. It was rejected by the Italian Air Force.

Potez 75

The Potez 75, which first flew in 1955, was a fixed-undercarriage ground attack aircraft with twin booms and a pusher propeller. It did not enter production.

The Republic XR-12 Rainbow. (Fairchild Republic)

Republic XR-12 Rainbow

The Republic XR-12 Rainbow was a four-engined reconnaissance aircraft, flown in 1946. Two prototypes of this beautifully streamlined machine were built; six production aircraft were ordered as F-12As, but cancelled.

Republic XF-103

The Republic XF-103 was a high-speed delta-wing interceptor project. It was cancelled in 1957 while in the mock-up phase.

Ryan XV-5A Vertifan

The Ryan XV-5A Vertifan was designed as the forerunner of a two-seat V/STOL battlefield surveillance aircraft. The first of two prototypes flew on 25 May 1964. The aircraft was powered by two General Electric J85-GE-5 turbojets of 2,650lb (11.8kN) thrust, gases from these being diverted to drive large lift fans buried in the wings. The aircraft attained a maximum speed of 550mph (885km/h) at sea level.

Short SB.4 Sherpa

The Short SB.4 Sherpa was a turbojet-powered research aircraft, built to test an 'aeroisoclinic' wing planform and flown in 1953. It was preceded by a glider version, the SB.1.

Short SB.5

The Short SB.5, flown in 1953, was built to carry out low-speed trials of the wing planform intended for the English Electric Lightning supersonic fighter.

The SE.5000 Baroudeaur approaching touchdown with its braking parachute streamed. (Musée de l'Air)

SIPA 200 Minijet

The SIPA 200 Minijet was a single engined, turbojet-powered two-seat training and liaison aircraft. It was distinctive thanks to its twin-boom configuration and short, tubby nacelle housing the engine and cockpit. The S200 made its first flight on 14 January 1952. Early test flights revealed that it was underpowered and that its performance fell short of expectations, and it was unable to compete with contemporary types such as the Fouga Magister. Seven prototypes were built. The SIPA 200 was built at the request of the French government, which was evaluating new aviation concepts as part of the progressive build-up of France's post-war aircraft industry.

SIPA S.1100

First flown in 1958, the SIPA S.1100 was a twin-engined counter-insurgency aircraft, designed for operations in Algeria. The first of two prototypes flew in 1958.

SNCAC NC.211 Cormoran

The first flight of the NC.211 Cormoran four-engined transport in July 1948 ended in tragedy when the aircraft crashed at Villacoublay with the loss of its crew. A second prototype was tested.

SNCASO Delta VX

The SNCASO Delta VX was a very small, delta-wing research aircraft built in 1953 to investigate various methods of control. It was the first aircraft to feature the jet flap principle, where 2 per cent of the Turboméca Marboré's compressor's output was blown through the flaps.

Sud-Est SE.5000 Baroudeur

Like the wartime Messerschmitt Me 163 rocket fighter, the SE.5000 Baroudeur ('Warrior') was designed to be launched from a trolley and land on skids. The first of two prototypes flew on 1 August 1953, powered by a 5,280lb (23.5kN) s.t. Atar 101B turbojet.

Sud-Est SE.116 Voltigeur

The Sud-Est SE.116 Voltigeur was a three-seat, twin-engined counter-insurgency aircraft, first flown in 1958. It did not enter production.

Supermarine Seagull ASR.1

The Seagull ASR.1, optimized for search and rescue duties, was Supermarine's last flying boat design and first flew in July 1948. Two prototypes only were built.

The Sud-Est SE.116 Voltigeur. (Author)

Supermarine Type 559

The Supermarine Type 559 was a mixed-power high-altitude interceptor project, developed in the mid-1950s to Specification F.155T. It was cancelled in 1957.

Supermarine Type 571

The Supermarine Type 571 was a low-level strike/reconnaissance project, designed to meet Operational Requirement GOR.339. The BAC TSR2 was selected in preference.

Tupolev Tu-70

Tupolev's Tu-70 transport, flown in 1946, was derived from the Tu-4 bomber. It retained many military features, such as the glazed nose. The Tu-75, flown in 1950, was a more advanced version, but like the Tu-70 did not enter full production.

Index

Aerfer
  Ariete 131, 132
  Sagittario 131
  Sagittario 1 131
  Sagittario 2 131, 132
Aerocentre
  NC 270 37, 64
  NC 271-01 37
  NC 271-02 37
  NC 1071 64, 104
  NC 1080 64, 104
air bases, American
  Carswell 10
  Davis-Monthan 10
  Edwards 47, 90
  Great Falls 53
  Johns NAS 90
  Muroc 51
  Patuxent River NAS 97
  Wright-Patterson 91
air bases, British
  Boscombe Down 56, 59, 98, 126, 143
  Odiham 60
air bases, French
  Cazaux 119
  Courbevoie 67
  Lyon-Bron 105
  Melun-Villaroche 67, 145
air bases, German
  Leck 44
  Salzburg 44
air bases, Russian
  Kubinka 42
  Podberezhye 77
  Tavrichanka 20
  Toplistan 77
Arado
  Ar 234 36
Armstrong Siddeley
  Snarler 110
  Screamer 110, 113
Arsenal
  VB-10 105, 106
  VG-70 36, 105, 106
  VG-90 64, 104, 105, 106
Atlas IRBM 136, 137
Avro
  Ashton 136
  Blue Steel 137
  Lancaster 9
  Type 707 113
  Type 720 113, 114
  Type 727 129, 133
  Type 730 135, 136
  Vulcan 32, 113
Avro Canada
  CF-100 79, 80
  CF-105 Arrow 80

Bär, Colonel Heinz 44
Beamont, Wg Cdr Roland 126
Bell
  D-188A 149
  X-5 91

X-14 149
XP-59A 44
XP-83 78
Bereznyak, A.Y. 77
Beriev
  Be-R-1 108
  Be-10 108
Blackburn
  A-1 Firecrest 103
  Buccaneer 122
  Firebrand 102, 103
  YA5/YB-1 100, 101, 102
  YA-7 101
  YB-8 101
Blue Streak IRBM 136–138
Boeing
  B-29 9, 10, 20, 77
  B-47 25, 26, 59
  B-52 7, 18, 19
  B-50 10
  EB-29 51
  XF8B-1 86
Booth, Sqn Ldr John 112
Boulton Paul
  P.111 57
  P.120 58
Breguet
  Br.940 Integral 149
  Br.941 149
  Br.960 Vultur 107
  Br.1001 Taon 130, 131
  Br.1050 Alizé 108
  Br.1100 130, 131
Bristol
  Type 182 *Blue Rapier* 35
  Type 188 136
British Aircraft Corporation (BAC)
  BAC 221 119
  Concorde 119
  TSR2 8, 121–127
Brooke-Smith, Tom 143
Brown, Captain Eric 56

Callaghan, James 127
Camm, Sir Sydney 59, 62, 119, 120, 144
Caudron-Renault
  C.714 128
Chance Vought
  F6U-1 Pirate 88
  F7U Cutlass 16, 89
  XF5U-1 87
Coleman, J.F. 'Skeets' 141
Convair
  B-36/GRB-36 10, 11, 15, 48, 51, 52
  F-102 79
  NB-36H 24
  XB-46 26
  XF-92A 4, 46, 47
  XFY-1 140, 141
  XF2Y Sea Dart 92, 93, 94
  XP-81 149
  YB-60 19
Curtiss
  XF15C-1 86, 87

XP-87 Nighthawk 79

Dassault
  Balzac 144
  Etendard VI 130
  MD.550 129
  Mirage I 66, 67
  Mirage II 67
  Mirage III 67,145
  Mirage IIIV 144, 145, 146
  Mirage F.1 146
  Mirage G8 149
  Mirage 4000 150
  Mystère II 66
  Mystère IV 62, 66
  Mystère 22 129
  Ouragan 64, 66
  Super Mystère 62, 66
de Havilland
  Blue Jay/Firestreak AAM 113
  DH.100 Vampire 54
  DH.108 60, 61
  DH.110 82, 83
  Hornet 55
  Red Top AAM 118
  Sea Vixen 83
  Spectre 111
  Sprite 110
de Havilland, Geoffrey Jr. 61
Dellys, Claude 106
Derry, John 61, 82
DFS 346 77
Dornier
  Do 335 44
Douglas
  AD-1 Skyraider 94
  B-19 12
  F4D Skyray 16, 89
  F5D Skylancer 88, 89
  XA2D-1 Skyshark 4, 95
  XB-42 28, 29
  XB-43 28, 30
  XTB2D-1 94, 95

Edwards, Capt Glen W. 14
Elliot, Lt J. 61
English Electric
  Canberra 7, 31, 32, 121, 122
  P.1/Lightning 63, 82, 109, 110
  P-17A/D 122
Entwicklungsring Süd
  VJ-101C 146, 147

Fairey
  F.155T 118, 119
  FD.1 116
  FD.2 117, 118
  Gannet 102
  Spearfish 150
Federal Aircraft factory
  N.20 150
  P.16 150
Fiat
  G.91 133

INDEX

Folland
  Gnat 129
  FO.139 Midge 129
Franchini, Col Giovanni 131
Fraser, Hugh 125

Gallai, Mark 71, 72
Galland, General Adolf 44
Genders, Sqn Ldr G.E.C. 61
General Dynamics
  F-111A 126
Gloster
  CXP-1001 56, 57
  G.42 (E1/44) 56
  Javelin 7, 81, 82
  Meteor 54
  P.376 Thin-Wing Javelin 115
Gotha Go 229 17
Goujon, Charles 67
Green, J.R. 143, 144
Grinchik, Alexei 71
Grumman
  F9F Panther 90
  F9F-6 Cougar 90
  XF10F-1 Jaguar 90
Guignard, Jacques 37
Gunn, A.E. 58

Handley Page
  HP.100 135
  Halifax 9
  Victor 32
Hawker
  P.1005 57
  P.1031 57
  P.1034 57
  P.1035 57
  P.1038 57
  P.1039 57
  P.1040 57, 99, 110
  P.1047 58
  P.1052 58, 59, 60
  P.1067 Hunter 59, 61
  P.1072 110
  P.1081 60
  P.1083 62, 63
  P.1092 119
  P.1121 119, 120
  P.1125 120
  P.1129 120
  P.1150 144
  Sea Hawk 57, 99
  Tempest Mk 2 55
  Tempest Mk 6 55
Hawker Siddeley
  HS681 148
  P.1125 122
  P.1127 144, 147
  P.1129 122
  P.1154 144, 147, 148
Heinkel
  He 162 36, 44
  He 274 37
  He 323 40
Hindustan Aeronautics
  Ajeet 133
Hispano
  HA-300 151
Horten Ho I–Ho VIII 16
  Ho VIIIB *Amerika Bomber* 17

Ho IX 17
Hughes
  XR-11 151
Hunting H.126 151

IAe
  27 Pulqui I 151
  30 Namcu 151
  33 Pulqui II 151
  Type 38 151
Ikarus
  Type 451 152
  Type 452-M 152
Ilyushin
  Il-2/Il-10 43
  Il-20 43
  Il-22 40
  Il-28 40, 41
  Il-30 41
  Il-40 43
  Il-46 41, 42
  Il-54 42
Independent Force, RAF 9

Kaiser-Fleetwings
  XBTK-1 95
Kasmin, P.I. 77
Kennedy, John F 134
Kokkinaki, Konstantin 40
Kokkinaki, Vladimir 40
Kyle, Air Cdre Wallace 62

Lavochkin
  La-15 76
  La-150 75
  La-154 76
  La-156 76
  La-168 76
  La-174 76
  La-174TK 76
  La-190 152
  La-200A 85
  La-200B 84, 85
Leduc
  010 70
  021 69, 70
  022 69, 70
LeMay, Gen Curtis 134
Lippisch, Dr Alexander 46, 47
  DM-1 47
  P.10 46
  P.11 47
  P.12 47
  P.13 47
  P.14 47
Lithgow, Cdr Mike 61
Lockheed
  A-12 152
  Constitution 152
  F-94 Starfire 7, 79
  F-104 Starfighter 115
  P-80 Shooting Star 44, 45
  SR-71A 152, 153
  XF-90 48, 49
  XFV-1 140, 141
  XV-4A Hummingbird 152
Lockspeiser, Sir Ben 56
Ling-Temco-Vought
  XC-142A 153

McDonnell
  F2H Banshee 89
  F3H Demon 89
  F-4 Phantom 7, 89
  F-101 Voodoo 50
  XF-85 50, 51
  XF-88 49, 50
  XFD-1 88
Martin
  P4M Mercator 96
  P5M Marlin 97
  X-24A 153
  XB-48 26, 27
  XB-51 31
  XP6M-1 SeaMaster 97
Messerschmitt
  Me 163 47
  Me 262 36, 37, 74
  Me 263A 72
  P.1101 91
Meyer, Corwin H. 90
Mikoyan & Gurevich
  I-270 72
  I-300 71
  I-320 83, 84
  MiG-9 72, 73, 74
  MiG-15 7
  MiG-17 62
  MiG-19 62
  MiG-MFI 153
  SP-5 85
Miles
  M-52 8, 55, 56
Mitsubishi
  A6M Zero 128
Morane-Saulnier
  MS.1500 Epervier 153
Mountbatten, Lord Louis 125
Muller-Rowland, Sqn Ldr J.S.R. 61
Myasishchev
  DVB-202 21
  M-50 138, 139
  M-52 139
  M-55 Mystic 154
  M-4 22, 23

NATO Basic Military Requirement No. 3 (NBMR 3) 144
Nord
  1402 Gerfaut 67
  1500 Griffon 67
  2200 64
Norstad, Gen Lauris 128
North American
  NA-134 45
  NA-140 45
  B-70 Valkyrie 134, 135
  F-82 Twin Mustang 79
  F-86 Sabre 7, 45, 46, 62
  F-100 Super Sabre 63
  F-107 154
  FJ-1 Fury 45, 88
  FJ-2 Fury 89
  P-51 Mustang 44, 48
  XB-45 27
  YF-93A 49
Northrop, Jack 11
Northrop
  B-2 18
  F-20 Tigershark 155

159

INDEX

F-89 Scorpion 7, 79
F-102 Fang 154
M2/F2 154
N1M 11
N-9M 12
P-61 Black Widow 78
XB-35/YB-35 12, 13
X-4 Bantam 15
YB-49 14
YC-125 Raider 154
YF-17 Cobra 155
YRB-49 14, 15
Northrop/McDonnell Douglas
  YF-23A 155

Perelyot, A.D. 39, 40
Petlyakov
  Pe-8 20
Petter, W.E.W. 129
Piaggio
  P.150 155
Potez
  75 155

Rastel, Daniel 36, 38
Republic
  F-84 Thunderjet 47, 52, 72
  F-84F Thunderstreak 52
  P-47 Thunderbolt 44
  RF-84F Thunderflash 52, 53
  XF-84H 96
  XF-91 47, 48
  XF-103 155
  XR-12 Rainbow 155
Richbourg, Charles E 91, 94
Robin, M. 37
Rockwell
  B-1 8
Rossing, Hans 77
Ryan
  V-13 Vertijet 142
  XFR-1 Fireball 86
  XV-5A Vertifan 155

Sandys, Duncan 114, 137, 138
Saunders-Roe (Saro)
  SR.53 111, 112, 113, 114
  SR.177 (P.177) 111, 114, 115
  SRA1 94
Schoch, Edwin 51
Servanty, Lucien 67
Short
  SA.4 Sperrin 32, 33
  SB-4 Sherpa 155
  SB-5 155
  SC.1 142–144
  Seamew 99, 100
  Stirling 9
SIPA
  200 Minijet 156
Slade, Gp Capt Gordon 117
SNCAC
  NC.211 Cormoran 156
SNCASO
  Delta VX 156

SNECMA C-450 Coleoptère 142, 145
Stefanutti, Sergio 131
Sud-Est
  SE Aquilon (Sea Venom) 104, 107
  SE Durandal 68
  SE116 Voltigeur 156
  SE161 Languedoc 37
  SE 2400 64, 65
  SE 2410 Grognard 65
  SE 2415 Grognard II 65
  SE 2418 65
  SE 5000 Baroudeur 156
Sud-Ouest
  SO 4000 37, 38, 64
  SO 4050 Vautour 38, 65
  SO 6000 Triton 36
  SO 6020 Espadon 64, 65
  SO 8000 Narval 107
  SO 9000 Trident 67, 68
  SO 9059 Trident II 67
Sukhoi
  Su-9 74, 75
  Su-10 40
  Su-15 74, 75, 83
  Su-17 75
  Su-25 43
  T-4 139

Tennant, Sqn Ldr E.A. 129
Trenchard, Major-General Sir Hugh 9
Tupolev
  T-64 20
  Tu-2 39
  Tu-4 20, 21
  Tu-12 39
  Tu-14 41
  Tu-16 23, 41
  Tu-22M 8
  Tu-70 157
  Tu-72 40
  Tu-77 39
  Tu-78 40
  Tu-80 21, 23
  Tu-81 41
  Tu-82 41
  Tu-85 22
  Tu-95 23
  Tu-160 139
Tuttle, AVM Geoffrey 62
Twining, General Nathan F. 42
Twiss, Lt Cdr Peter 117, 118

Units, American
  25th SRS 53
  27th FS 45
  43rd BG 10
  71st FS 45
  71st SRW 53
  82nd SRS 53
  91st SRS 53
  94th FS 45
  407th SFW 53
  412th FG 45
  462nd BW 20G 20
  509th BG 10

  549th SMS 137
  771st BS 20
  VF-51 45
  VF-66 86
  VMF-122 88
  VP-21 96
  VQ-1 96
British
  46 Squadron 81
  49 Squadron 137
  54 Squadron 54
  72 Squadron 54
  87 Squadron 81
  89 Squadron 81
  101 Squadron 32
  141 Squadron 81
  151 Squadron 81
  247 Squadron 54
  504 Squadron 54
  540 Squadron 32
  616 Squadron 54
  813 Squadron 103
  827 Squadron 103

Vereinigte Flugtechnische Werke
  VAK 191B 147
Vickers
  OR.1059 *Blue Boar* 35
  Red Rapier 35
  Type 571 122
  Valiant B.1 27, 33, 34
  Valiant B.2 34
Vickers-Supermarine
  Attacker 98
  Scimitar 99
  Seagull 156
  Swift 61, 63
  Type 505 98
  Type 508 99
  Type 510 58, 61
  Type 525 99
  Type 544 99
  Type 545 63
  Type 559 157
  Type 571 157

Wade, Sqn Ldr T.S. 60
Wallis, Dr Barnes 56
Waterton, Sqn Ldr W.A. 81
Wibault, Michel 144
Wilson, Harold 126

Yakovlev
  Yak-3 71
  Yak-15 71
  Yak-19 72
  Yak-25 72, 85
  Yak-30 73
  Yak-36 148
  Yak-38 148
  Yak-141 148
Yeager, Charles E. ('Chuck') 56

Ziese, Wolfgang 77
Zuckermann, Sir Solly 125